# FINDING
# THE LOST

CONCORDIA
SCHOLARSHIP
*Today*

# FINDING THE LOST

## Cultural Keys to Luke 15

Kenneth E. Bailey

CPH.
SAINT LOUIS

Copyright © 1992 by Concordia Publishing House
3558 S. Jefferson Ave., St. Louis, MO 63118-3968
Manufactured in the United States of America

---

Library of Congress Cataloging-in-Publication Data

Bailey, Kenneth E.
    Finding the lost: cultural keys to Luke 15 / Kenneth E. Bailey.
       p.  cm.—(Concordia scholarship today)
    Includes bibliographical references and index.
    ISBN 0-570-04563-0
    1. Bible. N.T. Luke XV—Criticism, interpretation, etc.  2. Bible. O.T. Psalms XXIII—Criticism, interpretation, etc.  3. Bible. N.T. Luke—Relation to Psalms.  4. Bible. O.T. Psalms—Relation to Luke.  5. Sociology, Biblical.  I. Title.  II. Series.
BS2595.2.B33   1992
226.4'06—dc20                                91-44904

---

4   5   6   7   8   9   10      01   00   99

*To Dale K. Milligan*
*with inexpressible gratitude*
*for all the grace*
*of all the years*

# Contents

Foreword      7

Preface      9

Abbreviations      13

Introduction      15

1. The Good Shepherd and the Lost Sheep (Luke 15:1–7)      54

2. The Good Woman and the Lost Coin (Luke 15:8–10)      93

3. The Good Father and His Two Lost Sons
   Part 1: The Younger Son (Luke 15:11–24)      109

4. The Good Father and His Two Lost Sons
   Part 2: The Older Son (Luke 15:25–32)      163

5. Luke 15 and Psalm 23: A Vision Expanded      194

Bibliography      213

Index of Authors      223

Index of Biblical References      225

Index of Old Testament Apocrypha and Pseudepigrapha      229

Index of Rabbinic References      230

Index of Middle Eastern Christian Sources      232

# Foreword

The Concordia Scholarship Today series explores current issues from a theological point of view and asks how the household of faith may meet the challenges to self-understanding that come from the surrounding culture. The hope is that we "may be able to comprehend [more fully] with all the saints what is the [extent of] the love of Christ" toward all His creatures (Eph. 3:18-19).

Like all volumes in the CST series, *Finding the Lost: Cultural Keys to Luke 15* offers insights at the level of theory that ultimately relate to current concerns. The assumption is that a broadened and deepened understanding of the Scriptures and of the Christian faith will clarify and enrich our analysis of issues that beset us and in so doing help us "comprehend the love of Christ." The intended meaning as well as the implications and applications of the parables of the prodigal son, the lost coin, and the lost sheep, the subject of this volume, have been standard fare in New Testament studies.

The CST series encourages Christians to think theologically about all matters of life. Exploration of an issue must grow out of reliable probing and research of the Scriptures and every other related, legitimate field of study. That may not always yield theological applications which differ markedly from the past. The greater value of such study lies in the learning process and in the assurance that the issue has been properly addressed.

Kenneth E. Bailey has immersed himself for many years in studying the languages, religions, and cultures of the Middle East as he served the church professionally. His present book, as well as his previous ones, demonstrate how meaningful the Biblical text becomes when a broad background of study and analysis is permitted to illuminate the text. The encumbrances of Western cultural reflection may be only grudgingly discarded. But Western readers will gain an array of new insights from this volume and will be fascinated by the author's nuances of interpretation that would be otherwise overlooked. Readers will be amazed at what has passed by them in previous probings of these parables in Luke's gospel. They will be immensely enriched by the author's findings and colorful exposition.

A glance at the list of abbreviations provides a hint of the thoroughness of the author's scholarly exploration. Those resources together with the bibliography offer a good basis for those who wish to pursue further study.

*Finding the Lost* does not claim to provide final interpretations, nor can any research ever be definitive for what is not empirically demonstrable or verifiable. But the author's thorough understanding and his rich conceptual treatment of the parables yield unique insights and make fascinating reading. At the same time his research indirectly undergirds and reinforces the foundations of our faith, satisfies our personal needs, and nourishes and contributes to an inner consistency for him and for us that is intellectually honest and defensible. He exudes a genuiness of faith and of person that brings a breath of fresh air to Biblical study.

Your comments and opinions on this volume and others is invited.

*The Publisher*

# Preface

This study is an attempt to describe a "love affair." The love affair is between the writer and the text of Luke 15 and has extended for over 30 years in Egypt, Lebanon, Jerusalem, and Cyprus. No one can adequately describe a love affair. I will do my best.

The love affair began in the late '50s in Jerusalem where I heard Bishop Kenneth Cragg lecture on the Arabic language debates that took place in the Middle East between Christians and Muslims during the Middle Ages. I knew of those debates and of their polemical character. But Bishop Cragg explained to us that the parable of the prodigal son featured prominently in the confrontations. Muslim scholars noted that the prodigal left home and then returned to it with no assistance. As traditionally interpreted, the parable has no cross, no suffering, no incarnation, and no mediator.

As a young listener to the bishop's lectures I went into shock. This parable is the most comprehensive statement from Jesus about how people are reconciled to God! Are all hints of the atonement missing from it? Was Jesus a good Muslim, and did St. Paul make a Christian out of him? As regards this parable, what could be said about the mind of Jesus on the question of the atonement? Did these questions have answers?

Bishop Craig thoughtfully noted that the "agony of rejected love" is suffered by the father all through the story. The father's willingness to endure that agony makes possible the prodigal's return home at the end of the story. Thus, noted the bishop, hints of the cross are reflected in the pain of the father's heart. This was very helpful, but I sensed that there was more.

I turned initially to the commentators of the past and present. Many of them failed even to take note of the problem. Some who saw the point admitted the difficulty, shrugged their exegetical shoulders, and pressed on. After all, they wrote, the parable is not a compendium of theology! Others observed that this parable stands in the center of the "travel narrative" (Luke 9:51–19:48). This central section of Luke opens with the affirmation that Jesus "set his face resolutely towards Jerusalem" (NEB). Thus the cross is "in, around, and under" the entire 10 chapters. It is not specifically noted in Luke 15, the argument goes, but the long shadow of the cross is cast over the entire travel narrative. This was helpful. As a Christian it made sense to me. But the old sheikh of the medieval debates would not have been satisfied. Neither was I. Thus the love affair was launched.

For more than three decades the present writer has lectured on the New Testament in the Arabic language across the Middle East. This has been primarily from Syria to the Sudan. Traditional story-tellers share a common culture with their listeners. Penetrating to the value judgments and assumptions of that culture is a critical key for interpreting stories in any age and from any culture. The same is true with regard to the stories of Jesus. As we will note below, the findings of this contextual search have been a critical key to unlock the secrets of the parables. But the recording of my findings have been piecemeal.

In 1973 I was privileged to record the first stages of my quest, thanks to Concordia Publishing House (Bailey, *Cross*). A second stage was recorded in briefer and more technical fashion in 1976 (Bailey, *Poet,* 142–206). A recent article (1990) marked a third try (Bailey, *Psalm*). What then justifies a fourth attempt to capture the meaning of this inexhaustible Biblical treasure?

Recently I have found myself to be like a person who for 30 years enjoys the beauty of a garden walled with plastered stone. Then in the fading light of a particular evening the person's eye is suddenly caught by what appears to be a faint blue line in the plastered wall. The patron of the garden turns aside to examine the line and to his amazement finds it to be in the shape of an arch. Digging feverishly through the plaster, a sealed doorway appears. With intense excitement he breaks through the doorway to discover a long abandoned room, and in the room a chest—of gold!

Having for three decades made Luke 15 the centerpiece of my understanding of Jesus and the New Testament, and having tried to read everything of note—East and West—that has been written in the past and present on this chapter, I thought I had done my homework on all the important aspects of the three parables that the chapter contains. Then recently, by accident, the "blue line"

10

appeared. This was the discovery of the fact that Luke 15 can be seen as an expansion of Psalm 23.

All of the above has left me with an awareness that only piece-meal sections of the material assembled on this chapter have thus far appeared in print. I am profoundly grateful to the editors of Concordia Publishing House for the opportunity to do my best to put it all together and to attempt a full presentation of what has been given to me, as I have earnestly sought, in the light of Middle Eastern culture, to understand this great chapter.

The 20th-century literature on the parables of Jesus is enormous (Kissinger, 231–415; Scott, 431–52). Recently the continued flow of that literature seems to increase rather than diminish. Across the years my debt to C. H. Dodd, J. Jeremias, T. W. Manson, and many others has been immeasurable. Yet in this study, notes and refer-ences are few. This slim volume is not intended to be a full review of current scholarly opinion in the West. Rather I have tried to add new data to the insights and knowledge already shared in the Chris-tian world with regard to this great trilogy. For this reason alone, extensive references have been omitted.

Inexpressible thanks is due to all others, past and present, who have assisted me with my love affair. Early Christian scholars in the Arabic and Syriac Christian traditions are at the top of the list. The authors, compilers, transcribers, and translators of the Mishnah, the early Midrashim, and the two Talmuds are not far behind them. In addition to modern Western scholarship, countless numbers of stu-dents, friends and participants in seminars (East and West) have challenged and encouraged me to try again and again to search out meaning. To all of them I am deeply grateful.

All sources are fully noted in the bibliography. Following the method of the New Century Bible, references appear in the text. The notes are reserved for additional information or discussion that is secondary to the main argument and may not be of interest to all readers. With regard to the English translations cited, the Greek NT has always been open before me; yet there is heavy reliance on both the NRSV and the RSV. The centuries of Syriac and Arabic versions have significantly influenced my choice of words in critical places.

Modern post-Enlightenment historical science demands "objec-

11

tivity." With regard to this expectation and the study of the Bible, Lesslie Newbigin has written,

> This "objectivity" involves the absence of prior commitment to the truth of the text, but the presence of a prior commitment to the validity of the scientific method (p. viii).

With Newbigin the present writer finds himself committed in both directions. The goal of this study is to discover as precisely as possible the original intent of Jesus of Nazareth as he created the parables recorded in Luke 15. At the same time, I am a Christian believer and am writing "from faith to faith" in the hope that readers of this brief work will find their faith strengthened and deepened by seeing Jesus as a theologian, even as my faith has been so strengthened.

Soli Deo Gloria!

Kenneth E. Bailey

Easter 1991
Jerusalem and Cyprus

# General Abbreviations

(See also the bibliography.)

| | |
|---|---|
| Ar. | Arabic |
| Arc. Gr.-Ar. | archaic Greek-to-Arabic version |
| BAGD | W. Bauer, W. F. Arndt, F. W. Gingrich, and F. W. Danker, *A Greek-English Lexicon of the New Testament and Other Early Christian Literature* |
| b. | *ben* (son of) |
| BT | Babylonian Talmud |
| Cop. | Coptic |
| *IDB* | *The Interpreter's Dictionary of the Bible* |
| JT | Jerusalem (Palestinian) Talmud |
| M | Mishnah |
| *NTS* | *New Testament Studies* |
| R. | Rabbi |
| Si. Gr.-Ar. | Mt. Sinai Greek-to-Arabic version |
| Sir. | Sirach |
| *TDNT* | *Theological Dictionary of the New Testament* |
| Vat. | Vatican |
| *ZNW* | *Zeitschrift für die neu testamentliche Wissenschaft* |

# Tractates Quoted

(Mishnah, Babylonian Talmud, Jerusalem Talmud)

| | | | |
|---|---|---|---|
| Ab. | 'Aboth (Pirke 'Aboth) | Meg. | Megilla |
| B.B. | Baba Bathra | M.Kat. | Mo'ed Katan |
| B.K. | Baba Kamma | Pe'a | Pe'a |
| B.M. | Baba Metsi'a | Pes. | Pesahim |
| Bek. | Bekoroth | Sanh. | Sanhedrin |
| Ber. | Berakoth | Shab. | Shabbath |
| Dem. | Demai | Sof. | Soferim |
| Erub. | 'Erubin | Sot. | Sota |
| Hag. | Hagiga | Sukk. | Sukka |
| Kel. | Kelim | Taan. | Ta'anith |
| Ket. | Ketuboth | Toh. | Toharoth |
| Kidd. | Kiddushin | | |

# Introduction

Every student of the New Testament gradually develops a series of lenses through which he/she examines the text. For the serious student these lenses are conscious and reflected. Thus it seems appropriate to expose the reader to the answers to some of the major methodological questions that I have hammered out across decades of study of the NT in a Middle Eastern context. The reader will then be fully informed regarding the various lenses brought into focus for this study. If the reader prefers a different set of lenses, it will then, hopefully, be easier to sift the insights here set forward in that the vantage point of the author is exposed.

## 1. Jesus as Metaphorical Theologian

Our first lens views Jesus as a theologian and not merely as an ethical example for the Christian life. At least since the fifth century B.C., and the great days of classical Greece, the Western mind has done its serious thinking in concepts. In most forms of discourse, we from the West begin with an idea and then occasionally *illustrate* that idea with a simile, metaphor, or parable. The conceptual language is primary and the metaphor or parable is secondary. The first is critical, the second is optional. If the listener/reader is intelligent enough, the speaker/writer may dispense with illustrations. For indeed, the story is presented only to clarify the meaning of the concept. If people are able to catch that meaning without using up time with illustrations, so much the better. The illustration is useful for simplification, the Western mind thinks. It aids memory. It assists in adding emotional coloration and in catching and holding attention. But through all of this, the pictorial remains a secondary form of speech. The concept continues as the primary form of theological language. A theological discourse is created by attaching one concept to another by means of logic. Philosophy then provides an overall structure for the material. This has been the primary Greco-

15

Roman form of theological discourse and thereby the dominant Western form. It has been in use for centuries.

In the early years of the Christian era, Platonism was the dominant philosophy. Theology was then done in Platonic terms. Aristotelian philosophy dominated the Middle Ages, and St. Thomas did his theologizing in an Aristotelian, philosophical framework. The same patterns prevailed through scholasticism, rationalism, Hegelianism, and existentialism, and now process philosophy has given birth to process theology. We can but offer gratitude and pay tribute to the diligent men and women who have struggled with the dominant philosophical systems of the day and who have across the centuries used the structures of those systems as pathways of the mind along which the Gospel might travel. But there is another way to "do theology."

Middle Eastern creators of meaning do not offer a concept and then illustrate (or choose not to illustrate) with a metaphor or parable. For them the equation is reversed. Rather than

*concept* + *illustration*
the Middle Easterner offers
*parable* + *conceptual interpretation.*

The Middle Eastern mind creates meaning by the use of simile, metaphor, proverb, parable, and dramatic action. The person involved is not *illustrating* a concept but is rather creating meaning by reference to something concrete. The primary language is that of the metaphor/parable and the secondary language is the conceptual interpretation of the metaphor that in Biblical literature is often given with it. To assure the reader that the present writer still remembers his Western roots, having set forth the *concept,* an *illustration* is now perhaps appropriate.

The above can be illustrated by noting Johannine literature which affirms that the believer is "born of God" (1 John 4:7; 5:1; John 3:5). Thus female imagery is used to enrich the reader's understanding of God. God gives birth to the believer. The author creates meaning by use of a powerful metaphor. Particularly in 1 John 4:7 the metaphor is then surrounded with conceptual language that sets the direction of any interpretation. Starting with the interpretation in the text, exegetes for centuries have struggled to

16

adequately conceptualize the meaning created by the metaphor. Quickly two realities become evident.

First, conceptualization/interpretation of the metaphor is not a strange aberration imposed on the Biblical metaphor by a non-Middle Eastern mind. Existentialists have decried *any* form of conceptualization of metaphor (Via, 2–107). But Biblical authors themselves often encase their metaphors in conceptualizations which focus the reader's interpretive reflection. Dozens of cases of this phenomenon are on display in Isaiah alone. One example is Is. 55:8–9, which is structured as follows:

| | |
|---|---|
| For my *thoughts* are not your *thoughts,* | THOUGHTS |
| nor are your *ways* my *ways,* says the LORD. | WAYS |
| For as the heavens are higher than the earth, | parable |
| so are my *ways* higher than your *ways* | WAYS |
| and my *thoughts* than your *thoughts.* | THOUGHTS |

This deceptively simple stanza of prophetic speech has metaphorical language at its center. Around that center there are two semantic envelopes. The inner envelope has to do with contrasting the *ways* of God to those of his people. The outer concentrates similarly on their *thoughts.* The reader is not left with a metaphor which is like a floating balloon that drifts freely with the wind of the interpreter. Rather a specific conceptual framework encases the metaphor. A second example of this same structure is in the well-known text of Is. 53:7–8a:

| | |
|---|---|
| He was *oppressed,* and he was *afflicted,* | INJUSTICE |
| yet he did *not open* his *mouth*; | SILENCE |
| like a *lamb* that is led to the *slaughter,* | parable |
| and like a *sheep* that before its *shearers* is silent, | parable |
| so he did *not open* his *mouth.* | SILENCE |
| By a *perversion* of *justice* he was taken away. | INJUSTICE |

Again, the parable appears in the center and is *encased* with concepts that direct any reflection on the parable's meaning. The meaning is created by *metaphor.* At the same time the metaphor, as it were, "cries out" for conceptual interpretation which appears in the text as a frame set around the metaphor. Thus concepts appear *with* the parable in Biblical literature and are not strangers to it (cf. also Is. 5:1–7).

Second, clearly the metaphorical language is the *primary* language which creates the meaning set forth in the discourse. The metaphor says *more* than the conceptual frame. The conceptual interpretive language is important yet secondary. The reader of Is. 53:7–8 knows that the lamb is unjustly treated and that it is silent. Thoughtful contemplation on this "parable of the lamb before its killer and shearer" has for centuries taken readers into great depths of meaning that reach far beyond the interpretation that encases the parable. Again, an illustration may be appropriate.

Beethoven's Ninth Symhony rises to its climax in the final movement. In that movement the instruments try again and again to carry the freight of the meaning the composer intends. The strings strain and strain and are unable to succeed. Finally resolution appears as the symphony breaks into human voices with language in the great "Ode to Joy." In like manner Isaiah begins with conceptual language and then breaks into metaphor as a form of language with a higher potential for the creation of meaning. The Biblical author then often returns to the conceptualizations to form what we have chosen to call an "encased parable," such as appears in the texts set forth above. So metaphor and concept appear together in the Biblical tradition, but the metaphor is primary.

Furthermore, the concepts that surround the Biblical metaphors (as can be seen in the above texts) catch only a part of the meaning of the metaphor. Yes, the servant of God is unjustly treated. Yes, he is silent. But the picture of the lamb standing mute before the butcher or shearer creates far more meaning than the concepts which surround it. In the book *Speaking in Parables,* Sallie McFague TeSelle discusses the parable of the prodigal son. She writes,

> One could paraphrase this parable in the theological assertion "God's love knows no bounds," but to do that would be to miss what the parable can do for our insight into such love. For what *counts* here is not extricating an abstract concept but precisely the opposite, delving into the details of the story itself, letting the metaphor do its job of revealing the new setting for ordinary life. It is the play of the radical images that does the job (p. 15).

Put in another way, we could note a person who buys an orange, takes it home and squeezes the juice into a glass for breakfast. The methodology of squeezing the orange assists the person in putting the content of the orange into a form that is easily accessible to the purchaser. Well and good. But the full orange (before squeezing) is a greater reality than the small glass of juice, however appropriate the squeezing of the orange may be. Even so, Biblical metaphors can be "squeezed" and concepts extracted. To do so is not a violation of the metaphor. It is a useful exercise of great antiquity. As noted, the Biblical author often does so himself. But the end result is less, not more, than the metaphor. The condensation of the meaning of the metaphor into concept catches a part, but not all, of the metaphor. The metaphor speaks to us on a deeper level. Perhaps this is because the metaphor is a reflection of our own constitution. We are body and mind/spirit, held together in a mysterious "solution" that none can understand. Even so, the metaphor combines a concrete base in the physical world that can be seen and touched and felt with an unseen spiritual reality. Thus the metaphor speaks to the whole person in a way that concept does not. No list of concepts can fully catch the meaning of the metaphor "born of God."

George Orwell of *Animal Farm* fame gives a different kind of insight into this same reality. In an essay on the English language Orwell first quotes Eccl. 9:11 from the King James Bible which reads:

> I returned, and saw under the sun, that the race is not to the swift, nor the battle to the strong, neither yet bread to the wise, nor yet riches to men of understanding, nor yet favor to men of skill; but time and chance happeneth to them all.

Orwell then translates this verse into what he calls "modern English." His efforts could also be called "translation into concept." The result is as follows:

> Objective consideration of contemporary phenomena compels the conclusion that success or failure in competitive activities exhibits no tendency to be commensurate with innate capacity, but that a considerable element of the unpredictable must invariably be taken into account (pp. 133–34).

If Western theologians had written the Bible it might have read like George Orwell. They didn't. Rather Middle Eastern metaphorical theologians wrote the Bible.

Abraham Rihbany, a native of 19th-century Lebanon, understood himself to be "one of the Master's fellow countrymen" (p. vi; the Turkish province of Syria then included what is now the Holy Land,

Lebanon, and Syria). This Arabic-speaking Christian offers a NT parallel to Orwell's example. Rihbany writes,

> It is ... because the Syrian loves to speak in pictures, and to subordinate literal accuracy to the total impression of an utterance, that he makes such extensive use of figurative language. Instead of saying to the Pharisees, "Your pretensions to virtue and good birth far exceed your actual practice of virtue," John the Baptist cried: "O generation of vipers, who hath warned you to flee from the wrath to come? Bring forth, therefore, fruits meet for repentance: and think not to say within yourselves, We have Abraham to [sic] our father: for I say unto you that God is able *of these stones to raise up children unto Abraham*" (pp. 117–18).

Rihbany's conceptual summary of John the Baptist's speech is precise, rational, and devoid of feeling. John's actual speech is charged with strong emotion. Rihbany is again helpful as he explains to a Western reader the Middle Eastern "manner of speech." He notes,

> A Syrian's chief purpose in a conversation is to convey an impression by whatever suitable means, and not to deliver his message in scientifically accurate terms. He expects to be judged not by what he *says,* but by what he *means* ... he piles up his metaphors and superlatives, reinforced by a theatrical display of gestures and facial expressions, in order to make the hearer *feel* his meaning. ... [His] speech is always "illustrated." He speaks as it were in pictures (p. 115).

Rihbany here admirably describes John the Baptist noted above. Not to be overlooked is the point that the Biblical speaker/writer wants to communicate not only how he/she *thinks* but also how he/she *feels.* Whereas in Western communication emotion is often considered a hindrance to the communication of truth, indeed a perverter of truth, the Middle Easterner feels truth is *not served* unless the full emotional component of that truth is also communicated. Thus discerning how people in a parable *feel,* as the parable evolves, is critical to an understanding of the meaning that is being created by the parable. What difference then does all of this make for our understanding of Jesus as a metaphorical theologian? Exposure of my own pilgrimage may at this point be meaningful.

The present writer earned degrees in philosophy and then systematic theology before turning to graduate work in New Testament.

Thus in my younger days I was in full accord with the Latin phrase *Theologia parabolica non est theologia argumentative* (Scharlemann, 30). I uncritically assumed that my own Western Greco-Roman mental processes were the only natural valid human way of creating meaning. A lifetime of ministry among Arabic-speaking Christians has led me to see otherwise. Here in the Middle East, from the beggar to the king, the *primary* method of creating meaning is the creative use of metaphor and story, as Rihbany has noted. As I gradually began to reorient myself to "metaphorical theology" and its methodology, I discovered a deep unexamined assumption in my own tradition about the mind of Jesus.

I discovered that I had been unconsciously trained to admire everything about Jesus except his intellectual astuteness. Jesus was for me the Christ of the creed. He was perfect man, perfect God, and Savior of the world. His earthly life presented the perfect example of love. Paul was the theologian and Jesus was the supreme ethical example of that theology. Starting with Pauline theology the believer can appropriately move from theology (Paul) to ethics (Jesus) and thereby discover from Jesus how to live the Christian life (so I thought).

Indeed, in the Apostles' Creed we confessed our faith by saying,

> ... conceived by the Holy Spirit,
> born of the virgin Mary,
> suffered under Pontius Pilate,
> was crucified, ...

All of the teachings of Jesus, indeed everything he ever said and all that he ever did, with the one exception of his cross, is reduced in the creed to one comma. We knew that Paul was well educated. Certainly Paul was a theologian. Jesus, however, was a village boy who grew up and told childlike stories. These stories offer marvelous patterns of life for all ages, but—serious theology? Hardly! Such were the unexamined assumptions of my Western theological tradition. But this equation of *Paul = serious theologian; Jesus = storyteller/example of love* I was obliged to reexamine in the light of the style of doing theology that I gradually discovered among the Christians of the Arab world.

My quest slowly focused on the searching out of "the water down the other side of the mountain." The sayings of Jesus can be likened to water that comes out of a spring at the very top of a mountain. The water has come down our Western side of the mountain. As noted, in two thousand years it has made its way through all of our Western philosophical systems from Platonism to process philosophy, and it presents itself at the bottom to the thirsty pilgrim. But that same water also flowed down the other side of the mountain from Aramaic-speaking Christianity into Syriac Christianity and then into Arabic-speaking Christianity. So how does the water taste on the other side of the mountain? The primary task of my life has been an attempt to find out.

One of the significant discoveries for me from that "other side of the mountain" has been the very fact of the metaphorical thinker in Middle Eastern society who can be observed functioning on all levels of society. This then led to a reevaluation of the life and teachings of Jesus. It obliged me to rethink deeply held attitudes toward Jesus as a teacher and to see him as a serious theologian. The result has been a slow discovery of the fact that his intellectual acumen is no less significant than the matchless quality of his ethics. This shift was for me of the deepest significance. For if Jesus is an uneducated young man who tells stories primarily for children and simple fisher folk, then one set of perceptions apply as we examine his teachings. But if he is the first *mind* of the NT (Paul being the second), and if Jesus' teachings are to be considered as serious theology, offered primarily to intellectuals, then a quite different set of assumptions and perceptions come into play for the interpreter. This brief study is an attempt to take Jesus seriously as the major theologian of the New Testament and to follow his theological thinking as that thinking is set forth in the trilogy of stories in Luke 15, which is to be examined in the light of Middle Eastern culture.

To accomplish the above, some often overlooked aspects of first-century Palestinian Judaism need clarification.

## 2. Jesus within First-Century Judaism

Curiously, both Islam and popular Christianity have seen fit to honor their founders and to try to heighten the miraculous nature of their respective revelations by claiming that they were uneducated. Islam insists that Muhammad was *al-nabi al-'ummi* (the illiterate prophet). This affirmation is for Islam critical proof of the inspiration of the

Qur'an. If the messenger was an illiterate man, then the case for the divine nature of the message, which comes in a lofty rhetorical style, is in their view greatly strengthened. In much the same vein, popular Christianity across the centuries has taken the evidence for Jesus being a carpenter (Mark 6:3) as an indication of his (uneducated) "blue collar" identity. The marvel of who he was and what he said is thus seen as all the more amazing. But Christian perceptions at this point are imprecise.

Jesus was indeed a *tektōn* which is probably better understood as a carpenter/builder rather than a cabinetmaker. Middle Eastern peasants have very little wooden furniture in their homes. But everyone has a house with doors, windows, and roof beams, all constructed of wood. Furthermore, a significant number of gospel parables exhibit builders' imagery, but the cabinetmaker never appears. In any case, he was a worker with his hands, a craftsman. However, the Western image of blue collar is misleading.

In both the East and the West today the popular image of blue collar worker is that of a *nonintellectual*. But in the rabbinic tradition, the rabbi was *expected* to have an earthy, practical profession working with his hands. Pirke 'Aboth (Sayings of the Fathers) is an important early Jewish document. This remarkable work is a collection of the sayings of the early rabbis from around 300 B.C. to the time of Judah the Patriarch, the editor of the Mishnah in ca. A.D. 200 (Danby, 446, n.1). 'Aboth 2:2 reads as follows:

> Rabban Gamaliel the son of R. Judah the Patriarch said: Excellent is study of the Law together with worldly occupation, for toil in them both puts sin out of mind. But all study of the Law without [worldly] labor comes to naught at the last and brings sin in its train (Danby, 447).

The phrase that occurs again and again through the Mishnah and the Babylonian Talmud is that no one shall "reap material benefit from the crown." The "crown" referred to the Torah. The person of faith is expected to learn the Torah and, if given opportunity, to teach it. But the teacher shall not receive wages for his teaching. No material benefit from "the crown" was allowed. This prohibition is attributed to the great Hillel who lived one generation before Jesus. Again quoting from 'Aboth,

> Make them [the words of the Law] not a crown wherewith to

23

magnify thyself or a spade wherewith to dig. And thus used Hillel to say: He that makes worldly use of the crown shall perish. Thus thou mayest learn that he that makes profit out of the words of the Law removes his life from the world (4:5; Danby, 453).

This principle, that a religious teacher may not receive any material benefit from religious things, is the background of an illuminating story in the Babylonian Talmud about Johanan ben Zakkai. This venerated scholar was contemporary with Jesus and was the key figure in restarting the rabbinic schools after the disaster of the fall of Jerusalem in A.D. 70. But before that event, while teaching in Jerusalem, he occasionally took his students to sit in the shade of the temple for his lectures. Tractate Pesahim of the Babylonian Talmud states,

> It was related of R. Johanan b. Zakkai that he was sitting in the shadow of the Temple and teaching all day. Now here it was impossible [not to lecture], and he intended [to benefit from the shade], and is it permitted? But Raba said: The Temple was different, because it was made for its inside (p. 26a).

The incident recalled must date from the 50s or early 60s of the first century. This learned scholar appeared to the rabbis to be receiving material benefit from "the crown." He was enjoying the shade of the temple and it was not by accident: He went there *intending* to reap that benefit. The discussion concludes that the temple was constructed for the purpose of what happened *inside* its walls, not outside. Thus, by implication, the outside shade created by those walls was of a nonreligious nature and therefore Johanan ben Zakkai had *not* "reaped benefit from the crown" by sitting in its shade. The story indicates the strictness with which the principle of "no benefit from the crown" was applied. The religious professional was *expected* to support himself by having a craft. Thus the fact of Jesus being a carpenter and Paul being a tentmaker (Acts 18:3) was the rule for a first-century Jewish religious professional, not the exception. If Paul had remained in Jerusalem as a rabbinic scholar he would *still* have supported himself as a tentmaker. Thus the image of Jesus as the carpenter/scholar is not an exceptional picture. Was he not called "Rabbi"?

The title *Rabbi* was just beginning to come into common use early in the first century.[1] It is applied unreservedly to Jesus. Obviously his contemporaries saw him as a religious teacher of merit who deserved this title. Indeed, in the NT period (before the fall of Jerusalem) formal rabbinic training was not a critical matter for a religious professional. One could be a priest and even become the high priest without such training. After the fall of Jerusalem and the formation of the rabbinic schools around Jabneh in Palestine, and more particularly in the second century, such a title it seems was more formalized and applied specifically to official graduates of recognized schools. But in the time of Jesus, this address was more fluid and could be applied generally to anyone recognized as a religious authority.

At the same time there were opportunities available across the countryside in first century Galilee and Judea to learn the tradition. These were the local religious clubs called the *haberim* (associates).

The *haberim* were societies of scrupulous Jews who pledged themselves to the study and strict observance of the law. Special emphasis was given to the Sabbath, the rules of ceremonial purity, and tithing. Regarding these societies, George Foot Moore writes,

> Those who assumed these engagements called themselves "associates" (haberim), and it is not improbable that the name "Pharisee" was originally applied to them as men who separated themselves from uncleanness (*People,* 440; also *Judaism,* II, 73).

To join such a society one needed only take a pledge in the presence of three members (BT Bek., 30b). What then of those who were not members?

The *haberim* lived in an apparent perpetual state of hostility with the *'am ha-'arets* (the people of the land). These latter where those who (in the eyes of the former) did not keep the law in a precise fashion. Intense hostility between these two groups is reflected all through the tradition. The *'am ha-'arets* were consistently seen by the *haberim* as impious slackers in religious matters. Any contact with them was defiling for the *haber* (associate). The Babylonian Talmud records the depth of this hostility:

> Our Rabbis taught: Let a man always sell all he has and marry the daughter of a scholar. . . . but let him not marry the daughter of an *'am ha-arez,* because they are detestable and their wives are vermin, and of their daughters it is said, *Cursed be he that lieth with any manner of beast. . . .*

> R. Eleazar said: An *'am ha-arez,* it is permitted to stab him [even] on the Day of Atonement which falls on the Sabbath. . . .
>
> R. Eleazar said: One must not join company with an *'am ha-arez* on the road (Pes., 49b).

But not only did the associates despise the people of the land, but similar feelings were exhibited on the other side. The same passage continues,

> It was taught, R. Akiba said: When I was an *'am ha-arez* I said: I would that I had a scholar [before me], and I would maul him like an ass. . . .
>
> Greater is the hatred wherewith the *'amme ha-arez* hate the scholar than the hatred wherewith the heathens hate Israel, and their wives [hate even] more than they (Pes., 49b).

The above passages are not exceptional. We hasten to add that they reflect typical Middle Eastern hyperbole and that they exhibit the "anticlericalism" that can be found in any religious system, along with the counter disregard on the part of certain types of religious professionals for the "unwashed." Again we must ask, What does this have to do with Jesus?

The remarkable account of Jesus in the temple at age 12 (Luke 2:40–52) is the only canonical window into the "silent years" from the birth stories until the opening of his public ministry. Raymond Brown accepts it as a pre-Lucan account (*Birth,* 480) and calls it a "biographical apophthegm" (p. 483).[2] Generally, discussion of this text focuses on the self-awareness of Jesus or on the Lucan affirmation of Jesus as Son of God. However, the passage itself appears to have a different emphasis. The story as a whole exhibits the inverted structure shown in figure 1.

The story opens with five brief scenes. The movement of the story then comes to its climax in the center. The remainder of the account reflects a repetition (in some fashion) of the first five themes, only the order is reversed. As noted, in such inverted rhetorical structures the climax is usually placed in the center. The climactic center often relates to the beginning and to the end of the pericope (as occurs here). So here a reference to *wisdom* opens and closes the story. In the center the reader is told first that Jesus is a *student* (5). Just past the center in such rhetorical structures

26

## Figure 1
## Jesus in the Temple (Luke 2:40–52)

1. The child grows, is wise, has God's favor (v. 40)
   2. The family goes up (vv. 41–42)
      3. Jesus stays in Jerusalem (vv. 43–44a)
         4. Parents seek and find (vv. 44b–46a)
            5. Jesus: among the teachers
               *listening*
               *asking questions* (v. 46b)
            6. Jesus: heard by all
               displaying *understanding*
               *answering* questions (v. 47)
         7. Parents seek and find (v. 48)
      8. Jesus in his father's house (vv. 49–50)
   9. The family goes down (v. 51)
10. Jesus increases in wisdom and stature, has the favor of God and man (v. 52)

there is often a critical turning point, or point of special emphasis.[3] This feature also appears when suddenly and dramatically in stanza 6 Jesus has become a teacher. The student who is *asking questions* (5) is suddenly doing the *teaching*. All are "amazed at his understanding and *his answers*" (6). In this manner the theme of *wisdom* is affirmed at the beginning and at the end and comes to its critical expression in the center. Thus the rhetorical structure of the material affirms the wisdom, understanding, and answers of Jesus as the central focus of the passage. So the inevitable question becomes, What does this text assume about the intervening years from this scene until Luke 4:1, when at age 30 the public ministry of Jesus begins?

If there is even a shred of history in the Luke 2:40–52 account, and if Luke is using pre-Lucan Jewish Christian sources, then the first-century Jewish reader would naturally assume that Jesus remains in the village, labors at his carpenter's bench, and continues asking questions and giving answers. He becomes a part of the *haberim*. At age 30 he has had 18 years of almost daily discussion with the brightest minds in the village about Moses and the prophets and what it is that God is expecting of them in their day. As his public ministry opens, the people instinctively recognize the speech of a master of the tradition and thus naturally call him Rabbi. He accepts the title because of its appropriateness. His ability to hold his own in debate is evidenced all through the gospels. Such skills are only gradually acquired by anyone. No supernatural gifts are ever assumed by the text as sources for these debating skills. Thus we are left with the picture of a very bright young man who joins the *haberim* (the associates), and after he has spent nearly two decades in serious study, reflection, and debate on the sacred tradition of the past, he is finally ready for his "manifestation to Israel." The theologian is ready to take on his fellow theologians in public and he proceeds to do so.

## 3. The Cultural Problem and Sources for Its Solution

We have observed Jesus as a metaphorical theologian and seen him as a participant in the intellectual life of his society. A further "lens" that is critical for an understanding of any metaphorical theologian is the need for a clear perception of the culture of which he was a part. If theology is composed with philosophy as its base, then training in that philosophy is all that one needs to pursue that theology. But if theology is created by simile, metaphor, parable, and dramatic action, then the culture of the theologian and his/her people is a critical key for unlocking the theological intent of the metaphorical language.

The present writer has already discussed this topic at some length, and repetition is unnecessary (*Poet,* 27–37). The problem is clear. To be properly interpreted, any story must be seen from within the culture of the storyteller and his/her audience. If we ignore the problem we substitute our own culture for that of the speaker/author. Having struggled for more than a generation with this problem in both the East and the West, it is my perception that for us as Westerners the cultural distance "over" to the Middle East is greater than the distance "back" to the first century. The cultural gulf between the West and the East is deeper and wider than the gulf between the first century (in the Middle East) and the contemporary conservative Middle Eastern village. Rihbany writes, "[the Middle Easterner's] faithful repetition of the past has left no gulf between him and his remote ancestors" (p. 83). Very briefly, the only answer I have managed to bring to this critical problem is to try to see the Biblical stories through the world of traditional Middle Eastern village society and with their perceptions (rather than our own), to search out pre-NT literature (the OT and inter-testament literature) and early Middle Eastern Christian literature along with the extensive literature of the Jewish oral law.

The inclusion of post-NT Christian and Jewish literature in our list of sources raises a critical methodological consideration. Obviously, if we are looking at the development of *ideas,* then naturally the stream of history does not run backwards. Literature from after the NT period is not a major source in trying to understand the development of NT theological ideas. Granted, "trajectories" of thought can be traced. Where and how an arrow lands can tell the careful observer something of its flight. In like manner, an idea may appear for the first time in a third-century Jewish or early Christian document, but may have had a significant, unrecorded flight in earlier centuries. Yet for ideas we look primarily for "background," not "foreground." When the interpreter seeks to understand an idea she/he generally seeks what led to the formation of the idea, rather than what it produced. But does this apply to culture?

When trying to determine the *cultural* presuppositions of a story in a traditional conservative society, the researcher must examine literature as close to the historical period of the story as is available. The custom of wrapping babies at birth appears in the birth story of Jesus (Luke 2:7). The only other time this custom is recorded in Scripture is in Ezek. 16:4. The same custom prevails today among Palestinian peasants. The Ezekiel reference is appropriately seen as important background for the Lucan account, even though the book of Ezekiel is more than 500 years older than the gospel of Luke. One could argue, 500 years is a long time. Culture changes. Surely such a long passage of time makes the Ezekiel text worthless as background to Luke 2:7. However, Middle Eastern cultural patterns have millennia behind them and are extremely slow to evolve. If this is the case for 500 years *before* the NT period, what about 500 years *after* that same period? Surely the answer is the same. Thus, for example, Ps. 23:5 (dated ca. 1000 B.C.) talks of the anointing of the head with oil. Luke 7:46 discusses the same cultural practice. What then of a text from the Mishnah (A.D. 200) or the Babylonian Talmud (ca. A.D. 400)? The latter two texts are 800 and 600 years closer to the NT than the psalm! If we are discussing the history of the development of *ideas,* much of the Jewish oral law is too late to help us. But if we are looking for a *culture* other than our own as a place to stand as we view the metaphors and stories of the NT, they can prove invaluable.

The exegete is not an acultural being who comes without feelings, attitudes, and assumptions about the basic realities of life. Even after all options are considered, one is inevitably obliged to respond to the text by saying, "It is only reasonable to assume ..." The "reason" we refer to is naturally our method of reasoning, which is in turn conditioned by our own cultural background. Was it Archimedes who said, "Give me a lever, a fulcrum, and a place to stand [outside of the world], and I will move the world"? However he had no place to stand and so his claim (a theoretical possibility) could never be tested. Even so the interpreter. Stories invoke feelings, reflect attitudes, make value judgments, expose assumptions, and create expectations. All of these are culturally conditioned. No interpreter can avoid having a culturally conditioned place to stand. The only question is, whose culture will be a starting point for us?

The extensive literature of the Jewish oral law includes the Mishnah, the Talmud of Babylon, the Talmud of Jerusalem, the Tosephta, and the Sifras of Genesis and of Leviticus. Important also are the translations of the Old Testament into Aramaic (the Targumim). Depending on which edition one examines, this material is well over 70 volumes. It was committed to writing between the years (ca.) A.D. 200–400. The Babylonian Talmud alone is more than two and a half million words. Only in our day is this vast literature in its entirety being published in English. The Babylonian Talmud discusses an endless array of different aspects of Middle Eastern Jewish social and religious life. Thus it is invaluable as a source for the study of early Jewish culture.

Jacob Neusner, the highly respected contemporary American Jewish scholar, has appropriately warned against a "parallelomania" that finds parallels between Jewish and Christian sources under every text. Neusner also has harsh words for anachronism. He writes,

> Many New Testament scholars are still guilty of massive and sustained anachronism in their use of Rabbinic sources. Time and again we find them quoting texts from the 3rd, 4th or 5th centuries A.D., or even later, to illustrate Jewish teaching in the 1st century. It must surely be a basic assumption in the historical study of any religion that religions change and develop through time. . . . caution demands that we regard it as a priori unlikely that the Judaism of Hillel in the 1st century A.D. was identical to the Judaism of Hoshaiah in the 3rd (*Paul,* 422).

Neusner also discusses other important aspects of this same problem, such as the lack of published critical texts, the dating of those texts and the literary analysis yet to be done on them. I take Neusner's point. His words of caution and reprimand are important.

However two things may be worth saying. The first is to note the reflections of the distinguished Israeli New Testament scholar of Jerusalem David Flusser. In his collected essays on the NT, Flusser writes,

> Later rabbinic parallels to New Testament passages provide great help for the elucidation of the New Testament. . . . [E]ven if the rabbinic sources are later, they still preserve evidence of an earlier stage which gave birth to the New Testament concepts and motifs. . . . Even if individual sages can be described as innovators, they still based their achievements upon the oral material which they received from their predecessors. "Every scribe . . . is like a householder who brings out from his storehouse both the new and the old" (Matt. 13:52). Thus the specific character of rabbinic literature not only permits us, but even obligates us to include post-Christian rabbinic sources as an inseparable part of the investigation of the Jewish roots of Christianity (pp. XIII–XIV).

Thus Neusner's remarks must be balanced by Flusser's confidence in the value of the rabbinic sources. In addition, the distinguished Harvard authority on Judaism, George Foot Moore, discusses the relationship between the gospels and the teachings of the rabbis and notes,

> It is this relation between the Gospels and the teaching of the rabbis, whether tacitly assumed or criticized and controverted,

which makes them the important source they are for a knowledge of the Judaism of their time, and on the other hand makes the rabbinical sources the important instrument they are for the understanding of the Gospels (*Judaism,* I, 132).

The extensive use of these same rabbinic sources made by Jeremias throughout his works is also worthy of note.

Then second, as a life-long observer of change in the Middle East, some of it dramatic and rapid, a number of observations can be made. Change in our Middle Eastern world can be categorized into at least five types:

1. *Economic* change: Such change can take place almost overnight, as in the case of war or famine. One winter with no rain, and the economy of an entire area is dramatically changed.

2. *Political* change: This can literally happen overnight and can require radical adjustments on the part of an entire region.

3. *Conceptual* change: People's ideas develop. New theological perceptions appear. This aspect of change appears to be Neusner's main concern which Flusser feels he has met.

4. *Legal* change: New laws are enacted or old laws refined by the community to regulate its life.

5. *Cultural* mores are the slowest to change. This is our concern. To interpret the parables of Jesus, the interpreter (consciously or unconsciously) will inevitably make decisions about attitudes toward women, men, the family, the family structure, family loyalties and their requirements, children, architectural styles, agricultural methods, leaders, scholars, religious authorities, trades, craftsmen, servants, eating habits, money, loyalty to community, styles of humor, story-telling, methods of communication, use of metaphor, forms of argumentation, forms of reconciliation, attitudes towards time, towards governmental authority, what shocks and at what level, reactions to social situations, reasons for anger, attitudes toward animals, emotional and cultural reactions to various colors, dress, sexual codes, the nature of personal and community honor and its importance, and many, many other things.

It is impossible to communicate in writing the utter frustration I have endured as I have, across the years, read the works of very able Western scholars who time and time again have read into the text of the NT their own Western attitudes toward the above topics, with little or no apparent awareness that their own feelings and attitudes on these topics are not universals. A cat will act like a cat in Baghdad, Berlin, or Boston. But people do not respond to the issues of life in the same way, irrespective of their cultural heritage, language and historical experience.

The NT itself often does not give us enough scope to answer the cultural questions that the text requires us to answer. Yes, we do discover by a simple reading of the NT that Pharisees and sinners do not like each other. But no NT texts describe *the depth of feelings* on the topic such as are on display in folio 49 from Pesahim in the Babylonian Talmud quoted above. Once this latter material comes into focus, the parable of the Pharisee and the publican (Luke 18:9–14) and the story of the woman in the house of Simon the Pharisee (Luke 7:36–50) emerge with bright colors rather than shades of gray.

Another way to state our problem is to observe that roughly every 500 years there has been a major split in the Christian church. These are as follows:

1. The *Semitic* churches and the rest of the church separate—A.D. 451.
2. The *Latin* and *Greek* churches break fellowship—A.D. 1054.
3. *Latin* Christianity is divided—A.D. 1517.
4. ???—ca. A.D. 2000

Our concern is the first of these divisions. After A.D. 451 the Semitic churches of the Middle East were no longer in fellowship with the rest of Christianity. Thus from that year onward the churches of the Greek and Latin world interpreted Scripture without any *Semitic* voice joining the discussion. Anti-Jewish attitudes precluded (for the most part) use of their sources. Indeed, in the Middle Ages those sources were often burned when discovered. Thus the Greek and Latin churches became culturally cut off from those sources (Jewish and Christian) that could have preserved cultural awarenesses critical for interpretation. One cannot interpret Luke 15 without discussing the concept of personal honor. But what is the nature of personal honor that is presupposed in the parables under consideration? Shall we use a modern 20th-century Western understanding of personal honor if Ephraem the Syrian (d. 378) and the Mishnah (ca. A.D. 200) give us another view? Surely not. Thus the early literature of the Semitic churches and the oral torah of early Judaism will be seen as important documents, along with the OT and the intertestamental literature, as the best sources available for rediscovering the culture that informs the parables before us. These sources can perhaps best save us from unconsciously reading our own cultural perceptions into the text.

The documents of the oral torah are known. What sources do the Semitic churches have that are significant for NT exegesis?

## 4. The Middle Eastern Ancient Christian Biblical Tradition

As judged by the volume of extant early Christian literature, the first great Christian language is Latin, the second is Greek, and the third is Arabic. Georg Graf's catalog of Arabic Christian literature (from its first appearance through the 19th century) fills five volumes. What then were the sources of this extensive literature?

Historically, Arabic speaking Christians fall into two broad classifications. First are those early Christians whose mother tongue was always Arabic. Second are those Christians whose first language was historically Aramaic, Syriac, Coptic, or Greek, who after the Muslim conquest gradually became Arabic speaking and who, in the process, recorded and translated their spiritual heritage into Arabic.

With regard to the first, the origins of the early Arabic-speaking Christian communities are only in our day being systematically researched. Spencer Trimingham's recent work, *Christianity Among the Arabs in Pre-Islamic Times* is a significant advance. Irfan Shahid's volume, *Byzantium and the Arabs in the Fourth Century,* opens a new world to the reader (cf. also L. E. Browne). Christian Arab bishops from the Arabian Gulf attended early Christian councils (Browne, 9–13). I have personally visited the recently discovered remains of an ancient Christian church in the eastern province of Saudi Arabia. Trimingham documents the existence of extensive Christian communities known to have existed among the Arabs centuries before the rise of Islam. The famous massacre of Arab Christians by Jewish rulers in Najran (Yemen) took place in A.D. 523 (cf. Shahid, *Martyrs*). Entire Arab tribes were Christian before the sixth century (Browne, 10). These Christians inevitably had their liturgies in Arabic, which necessitated Arabic language lectionaries if not full gospels. As Voobus has written concerning the pre-Islamic Arabic Christian communities of the Middle East,

> Christian missions and missionaries hardly took their task so light-heartedly as to leave their converts without any sacred litera-ture. . . . And if they neglected to furnish the newly won Christians with any literature, it is hard to understand that during the course of time this need did not arise at all among the converts themselves (*Arabic,* 275).

Voobus argues that not only was there such literature but that in regard to the NT,

> early Christian Arabic literature reveals that an archaic Arabic trans-lation of the Gospels existed which was made from the Old Syriac type (*Arabic,* 280).

This archaic Syriac-to-Arabic translation of the gospels may be preserved in the famous Vatican Arabic 13, which is sprinkled with key terms which carry Syriac meanings. Unfortunately the gospel of Luke is missing from that manuscript. However there exists an ar-chaic Greek-to-Arabic version. It's origin is unknown but there is evidence that Christians of Jerusalem, the monasteries of the Judean Desert, and St. Catherine's monastery at Mt. Sinai were among the earliest to Arabize their sacred literature (Guidi, 25). The Coptic church was also involved in this Arabization process. However an archaic Coptic-to-Arabic version has yet to be established.

The second classification of Arab Christians, as noted, is that of Greek, Syriac, and Coptic Christians who gradually became Arabic speaking. By the eighth to the ninth centuries the scholars (and increasing numbers of the faithful) in each of these communities were fully competent in Arabic. Syriac and Coptic continued in use as Arabic was acquired. All the while Arabic gradually gained in significance as an important Christian language. The Greek Ortho-dox of the Middle East Arabized their life and literature at an early stage. Gradually Arabic became the "receiver language" of the sacred literature and tradition of all three of these communities. The NT texts are one portion of this vast collection of material.

For this brief study we will be looking at two aspects of this great exegetical heritage. The first is the three Syriac translations of the NT and four representative translations of the Bible into Arabic.

The second is the noting of two Syriac-Arabic Christian interpreters of the gospels.

First then, the Syriac and early Arabic versions. What is their significance? It is simply this: to translate is to interpret. A careful examination of a translation yields significant insight into the translator's understanding of the text translated. The three Syriac versions of the NT, along with the early Arabic versions, are together important witnesses regarding how Semitic Christians living in the Semitic Middle East understood material originating in a Semitic cultural world.

The history of the Arabic NT is the longest and perhaps the richest of any of the versions. The early centuries produced a variety of Latin translations, but with the Vulgate of St. Jerome that translation activity stopped (the NT was finished in A.D. 383). The Armenians produced one translation in the fifth century. With some early revision it is still in use. The Syriac community produced the Old Syriac (second century), the Peshitta (fourth century), and the Harclean (early seventh century). The Coptic Sahidic and Bohairic versions were also fixed by the sixth century. Thus when Thomas of Harclea put down his pen after completing his Harclean Syriac NT in about A.D. 614, the task of biblical translation was set aside for nearly a thousand years to be taken up by Martin Luther with his famous German Bible (A.D. 1522–34).

The translators stopped translating in all languages but one— Arabic! All during that 900-year period an amazing number of translations into Arabic from Greek, Syriac, Coptic, and Latin were produced (cf. Guidi, 5–33).

This garden of delights has barely been entered. For two decades I have been privileged to work with more than 50 translations of the NT into Arabic. Most of these are unpublished manuscripts. What little work has been done on these texts is usually carried out by people interested in NT textual problems and questions relating to exemplars (i.e., was Arabic NT manuscript "X" translated from a Greek or Old Syriac exemplar?). Such questions are interesting and important. For example, the phrase "fashion out of me a craftsman," which the prodigal in the far country anticipates saying to his father (v. 19; my translation), is then omitted when the prodigal delivers his speech at the edge of the village (v. 21). Some Greek manuscripts added this phrase to verse 21 and thereby lost one of the critical turning points of the entire parable. Of all the Arabic versions studied only Sinai Arabic 72 has this textual error. The question of the Greek exemplars of these versions has not been studied with care and fresh light on textual problems may yet emerge from such research. But these questions are beyond the focus of this study. Rather I am interested in how the text was *understood* by the translator and the community that produced the translator and used the translation. Thus the more freedom of expression the translator exhibits the more the textual critic is *frustrated* and the more I am *delighted* in that, as this happens, the text becomes a mini-commentary.

As mentioned, seven Semitic versions will be seen as sources for the interpretive insights of the Semitic churches. The Old Syriac, Peshitta, and the Harclean versions have been ably described and need no explanation (cf. Voobus, *Syriac*). The four Arabic versions chosen are as follows:

1. The archaic Greek-to-Arabic version (cited as Arc. Gr.-Ar.). This translation appears in the following manuscripts: Berlin Staatsbibliothek Orientel Oct. 1108; Vaticana Borgiana Arabica 95; Sinai Arabic 54; Sinai Ar. 72 (dated A.D. 897); Sinai Ar. 74; Sinai Ar. 97 (dated A.D. 1125).

2. The Mt. Sinai Greek-to-Arabic translation (cited as Si. Gr.-Ar.). This translation is found in Vaticana Borgiana Arabica 71; Sinai Ar. 69; 82; 84; 90; 91; 94; 95; 96; 103; 104; 106; 110. Many of these texts are complete and dated. The colophons of many indicate that they were copied at St. Catherine's monastery. The earliest is 106 (A.D. 1056) and the latest 91 (A.D. 1289).

3. The Ibn al-'Assal critical edition of the four gospels (cited as Ibn al-'Assal). Preserved in British Museum Oriental 3382; Oxford Bodleian Hunt 118; Oxford Bodleian Arch Seld 68; Coptic Patriarchal Library, Cairo, Ibn al-'Assal gospels; Vatican Ar. 610.

4. The Arabic Diatessaron. Tatian's second-century Diatessaron was translated in the early 11th century into Arabic by Ibn al-Tayyib of Baghdad. Our purpose is not to establish the text of the Diatessaron but to glean the interpretive insights of Ibn al-Tayyib. (His commentary on the gospels will also be examined with care.) This translation of the Diatessaron is likewise thoughtful. The text was published in a critical edition in 1935 by Fr. A. S. Marmardji.

I have examined with care the 34 oldest Arabic manuscripts of the four gospels preserved at the St. Catherine's monastery at Mt. Sinai. Some of the Arabic gospels in the Vatican Library, the Berlin Staatsbibliothek, the National Library of Paris, the British Museum, and the Bodleian Library of Oxford that I have also used have previously been studied by Guidi, Peters, Baumstark, Voobus, and others. To my knowledge the Mt. Sinai Arabic NT texts have not previously been examined for exegetical purposes by any NT specialist.

The reasons for the selection of the above four Arabic translations as sources for this study are as follows:

1. For some time now Vaticana Borgiana Arabica 95 and Berlin 1108 have been recognized as copies of a single, very early translation from Greek into Arabic (cf. Levin). My own work with the Mt. Sinai Arabic gospels has uncovered four more manuscripts of this same translation. Of these six manuscripts Sinai Ar. 72, Sinai Ar. 97, and Berlin 1108 have colophons with dates. Sinai Ar. 72 was copied in A.D. 897 and Sinai Ar. 97 in A.D. 1125. The Berlin manuscript colophon gives a date of "438 *hilaliyyah.*" *Hilal* is the Arabic word for the moon. So literally the text reads, "in the year 428 of the moon calender." Some have thought this to be another way of saying *hijriyyah,* i.e., the "year of the emigration" (A.D. 622), which would make A.D. 1036 the date for the completion of this manuscript. But the script of this copy of the translation would indicate it to be much earlier.[4]

The conclusion of the matter (for our purposes) is that this archaic version was translated directly from Greek into Arabic in the ninth century or before and thus reflects early Semitic Christian understandings of the text. Where relevant, I will note its witness to the meaning of Luke 15.

2. The "Today's Arabic Version" for the 11th century that first appeared at Mt. Sinai in A.D. 1056 (Sinai Ar. 106) is thoughtful and authentically reflects a Middle Eastern understanding of the text. I have called it the "Mt. Sinai Greek-to-Arabic" version (Si. Gr.-Ar.) because of the 250-year unbroken loyalty to this translation evidenced by the scribes of Mt. Sinai. Insights from its witness to the meaning the parables under consideration will also be observed.

3. The remarkable work of Hibat 'Allah Ibn al-'Assal, mentioned above, will also be noted. Serious textual criticism of the NT did not begin with Richard Simon and his *Critical History of the Text*

*of the New Testament* (A.D. 1689; cf. Kummel, 40–50). Rather, Ibn al-'Assal, a brilliant Coptic Orthodox scholar, was hard at work on the textual problem in A.D. 1252 (cf. Bailey, *'Assal*). His critical edition of the four gospels is preserved intact in British Museum Oriental 3382. (Sadly, his notes gradually disappear in subsequent copies of his translation.) Those notes are a gold mine of how the text was understood by Coptic, Greek, and Syriac Christians in the centuries prior to his time. Where relevant his translation and notes will be discussed.

4. The significance of the Diatessaron as an early Eastern Christian document is well known and needs no comment. In its Arabic dress an additional layer of Semitic cultural perception is available through a careful reading of the text.

In addition to the above, the three earliest printed versions of the Arabic NT have also been consulted. These three maintain their own Eastern distinctives. The manuscript exemplars behind the printed texts are considerably earlier than the printed editions. Later Western Arabic Bibles were "cleaned up" from their Eastern exegetical nuances and brought into line either with the Vulgate or the Greek text. Such editing is commendable but yet the Eastern "flavor" and interpretive detail was lost in the process. The three printed versions listed in the bibliography predate this editorial process.

Constance Padwick discusses numerous early Arabic NT texts and observes thoughtfully,

> All these mediaeval Arabic codices are precious for the light they throw on the inner life of those parts of Christ's church that were living in comparative isolation, whether through formal secession or by reason of the surrounding Islam (p. 135).

Perhaps Padwick's comment should be extended one step further. Not only does this literature shed light on the "inner life" of Middle Eastern Christians in the ninth and tenth centuries of our era and before, but in addition this material is an authentic witness to the early exegetical tradition of Semitic-speaking and Semitic-thinking Christians of the Middle East. As such they are invaluable resources for our quest to understand and rightly interpret the Middle Eastern cultural nuances of the parables of Jesus. They are a place to stand as we attempt to escape the tyranny of our own cultural perceptions which constantly influence our understanding of the text.

No uncritical romanticism regarding these versions is intended. At times they are not helpful. For example, the Old Syriac describes the prodigal's lifestyle in the far country by saying, "there he scattered his property in foods which are not fitting, because he was living wastefully with harlots" (Burkitt, 353). The extra verbiage agrees with the colorful imagination of the older brother at the end of the story (v. 30) but violates one of the powerful tensions of the story as it appears in the Greek text. Thus the task has been to use these Syriac and Arabic versions selectively and to attempt to find where Eastern cultural perceptions from different sources come together to illuminate the text of the parables.

But not only did Syriac/Coptic/Arabic Christianity make and preserve translations, they also produced commentators. After Ephraem the Syrian, the two great almost unknown exegetical giants of the Middle East are Ibn al-Tayyib and Ibn al-Salibi. The full name of the first is 'Abu al-Faraj 'Abdallah Ibn al-Tayyib al-Mashriqi (d. 1043). This famous Syriac Christian of Iraq was "Philosoph, Arzt, Monch und Priester in einer Person" (Graf, II, 160). As a Biblical scholar he translated the Syriac Peshitta and the Diatessaron into Arabic. He also completed a full commentary on the gospels. This commentary had wide influence across the Middle East beyond his own Syriac church, particularly among the Copts of Egypt. In 1908 it was edited (and revised) by a Coptic Orthodox scholar, Yusif Manqariyus. The result is a combination of the perceptions of Ibn al-Tayyib and the Coptic exegetical tradition. The great drawback to this edition is that the Biblical text printed in the two volumes is a 19th-century Arabic version translated in Lebanon rather than Ibn al-Tayyib's own translation. I have occasionally noted his original translation (and his orginal comments) preserved in Paris Oriental 85 and 86. Ibn al-Tayyib was a part of his own allegorizing age. Yet time and again his authentic cultural perceptions appear and are extremely useful.

The second is Diyunisiyus Ya'qub Ibn al-Salibi. Ibn al-Salibi (d. 1171) completed commentaries on the entire Bible. His work on the gospels was translated from Syriac into Arabic in the 18th century and then published in Arabic in two volumes in 1914. Ibn al-Salibi affirms that he is looking at the text for "literal, allegorical and spiritual" interpretation (vol. I, introduction, page "tha"). It is the first that interests us for he consciously explains the parable as a Middle Eastern story before he starts his curious allegorizing. For our cultural quest his work is also significant.

The introduction to Ibn al-Salibi's commentary lists his sources. They include Ephraem the Syrian, Ya'qub al-Sarrugi, Filiksinus al-Manbaji, Sawirus al-'Antaqi, Watha al-Takriti, Ya'qub al-Rihawi, 'Andarawus al-Urushalimi, Zur'a al-Nasibini, Danial al-Suluhi, Yu'annus al-Dari and many others. The ravages of centuries of persecution have destroyed the works of most of these scholars. Ephraem the Syrian alone is known to us. I mention these unknown names only to expose the fact that Ibn al-Tayyib and Ibn al-Salibi are only two out of a great company of Middle Eastern Semitic Christian commentators on the NT whose works are early, unknown, and for the most part lost. Ibn al-Tayyib and Ibn al-Salibi are the tip of an iceberg and representatives of the iceberg itself. Where relevant they will be noted.

Champollion unlocked Egyptian hieroglyphics by studying Coptic. He rightly surmised that Coptic must be the inheritor of the ancient Egyptian language. Even so, these Semitic churches in the Middle East were and are the inheritors of the apostolic tradition in a unique way. This is true in many aspects of Christian faith and life. Our interest is the interpretation of the parables of Jesus.

The quotes and references to the Arabic versions and the commentaries noted above are all "my translation." It seems pedantic to be constantly repeating this phrase. Any translation errors are my responsibility alone.

## 5. Luke and His Sources

A full discussion of the synoptic problem is beyond the scope of this brief study. The various views set forth in the modern period are known and need no repetition. We would but expose another "lens" used for the interpretation set forth below.

In a recent essay Joseph Fitzmyer argues tellingly for the historicity of the we-sections of the book of Acts. He concludes,

> I have preferred ... that they are drawn from a diarylike record
> that the author of Acts once kept and give evidence that he was
> for a time a companion of Paul—not an inseparable companion,

as Irenaeus would have us believe, but a sometime companion of the Apostle (*Aspects,* 22).

Fitzmyer estimated that Paul arrived in Jerusalem on his last recorded visit (Acts 21:1–15) the spring of A.D. 58. Luke was with him. One of the we-sections begins in Acts 21:1 and continues to verse 18 with, "The next day Paul went with *us* to James; and all the elders were present." After verse 18 the first person plurals suddenly disappear, only to reappear two years later at 27:1 with, "When it was decided that *we* were to sail for Italy ..." (cf. Jewett, 40–44). Thus if we follow Fitzmyer in affirming the historicity of the we-sections of Acts, then it is likely that Luke is in Palestine for approximately two years (A.D. 58–60) but is evidently not at Paul's side during most of that time. This occurs before the disruption of the Jewish-Roman war of 66–72. The *'anawim* (the poor) of Jerusalem, i.e. the Jewish Christian community, is resident in the Holy Land. Luke is in touch with them.

Indeed, Luke specifically tells the readers of his gospel that he had access to documents. He also claims that he is describing "events that have been fulfilled among us" which were "handed on to us by those who from the beginning were eyewitnesses and servants [Greek: *hupēretai;* RSV: ministers] of the word" (Luke 1:2). The single definite article which governs the two words (*eyewitnesses* and *ministers*) strengthens the strong probability that those two words refer to a single group of people. Blass-Debruner[5] and Robertson[6] explain this particular grammatical construction as indicating that the two words refer to the same people. Kittel writes,

Ministers of the Word does not mean those who repeat sayings—Tannaites—but eye-witnesses who recount what has taken place (Lk. 1:2 ...) (*TDNT,* IV, 124).

Obviously Kittel understands the two classifications to refer in Luke 1:2 to the same people. Stendahl argues cogently that the ministers of the word were indeed eyewitnesses, but that the eyewitnesses then took on the special responsibility of teaching the new tradition (p. 32). Fitzmyer translates the full phrase, "the original eyewitnesses who became ministers of the word."[7] Marshall notes succinctly, "The syntax demands that the eyewitnesses and servants are one group of people" (p. 42). Who then were these people?

The synagogue of the first century had a salaried official called a *hazzan*. He was responsible for running the synagogue. He officiated at worship, taught in the synagogue school, administered punishment if such was decreed by the elders, and more important for our purposes, was responsible for the scrolls. As Plummer notes, "It was among the duties of the *chazzan* to take the Scriptures from the ark and put them away again" (p. 123). Safrai notes that in the first century the Scriptures were "brought in when required from an adjoining room and brought back there afterwards" (*JPFC*, II, 909). Stendahl tells us that the Greek term *hupēretē* (minister) "is consistently used for *hazzan*" (p. 32). So in the *synagogue* the *hazzan* was a keeper of the scrolls. He is seen functioning in this capacity in Luke 4:20 and is called *hupēretē*. What then of early Christians?

The earliest Christian churches, it appears, borrowed the title from the synagogue. They also had the office of *hazzan/hupēretē*. But of what is the Christian a *hazzan?* Here in Luke 1:2 he is not called an "*hazzan* of the synagogue" but rather "*hazzan* of the word," and to qualify for this office he must be an eyewitness of the historical Jesus. If the Jerusalem Jewish Christian community required the *hupēretē* (minister) of the word to be an eyewitness, then obviously they created a special form of ministry that they knew would disappear after one generation. The same categories functioned for the selection of a new apostle to replace Judas (cf. Acts 1:21–22). During this first generation period in the life of the church, what "word" is referred to? Is it not possible that this Christian *hazzan* is also a "keeper of the scrolls" in the sense that he, as an eyewitness, is a guardian of the authenticity of the oral tradition?[8]

As eyewitnesses the *hupēretai* mentioned in Luke 1:2 would have had a special place in the new community. They could authenticate or fail to authenticate any recitation of the tradition from/about Jesus. He/she was an eyewitness! Thus the church created a special ministry in its earliest days—that of the "*hazzan* of the word." The word is the oral (and partially written) stories from and about Jesus of Nazareth. Special people who must be eyewitnesses are given the critical task of being the keepers of this precious tradition. It is a tradition that is passed on, as Luke specifically indicates with his use of the phrase "delivered to us" (Luke 1:2 RSV).[9] When Luke arrived in Jerusalem about 57/58 he inevitably found a wealth of information about Jesus. It is our conviction that the special sources he mentions were people specifically designated by the church of Jerusalem and given the title of "*ḥazzan* of the word." Luke was an educated man. With the extended imprisonment of Paul, he suddenly had a great deal of time on his hands. He was a believer in Jesus of Nazareth, and in Jerusalem he suddenly had access to Jewish Christians who had seen, looked upon, and touched Jesus himself. Is it not natural to assume that he used this time to gather the data which at some later date he put together in "an orderly account" (Luke 1:3)?

To summarize, Luke had available to him authentic data recalled by eyewitnesses who may have been given the specific task of preserving the Jesus tradition. Thus, as indicated, it is most likely that during the two years Luke is in the Holy Land he "does his field research." It is not my purpose here to solve the synoptic problem. The position I am trying to enunciate does not rest on any one of the classical theories. Anyone who has done research on any extended topic knows full well that the time of the gathering of the data and the time of the completion of a document incorporating that data is not necessarily the same. It is my conviction that in Jerusalem in the late 50s of the first century, Luke gathered authentic data regarding Jesus of Nazareth from documents and from Jewish Christian eyewitnesses.

Furthermore, the contemporary discussions of the role of the eyewitnesses in Luke's gospel focus on the nature of their contribution to his sources. This is naturally important. But there is another aspect of the role of the eyewitnesses that is generally overlooked. By the way he has worded his introduction, Luke has placed on himself a special burden. He does this by specifically mentioning the eyewitnesses who have entrusted him with their data. He thus makes himself publicly responsible to be faithful to that trust. Anyone who has accepted to "give an interview" to a reporter or publishing writer knows something of the expected fidelity that such an acceptance assumes. When Luke completes his gospel there are "judges" waiting in the wings who will read *very carefully* what he has written and nod with approval or shake their heads in dismay. No ventriloquist act will be possible. No free Lucan composition can be easily attributed to Jesus of Nazareth without triggering the rejection mechanism of those who shared their oral and written treasures with him. Editorial freedom was not only allowed but expected, as can be seen in the Targums and deduced from synoptic comparisons. Luke can easily reflect his own theological interests by his selection of material. But if Luke's living sources judge his gospel merely "Lucan" and not also profoundly "Dominical," there will be no second copy of his work produced by Christians. In short, we are dealing in Luke 15 with early authenticated material that as a part of Luke's gospel has passed the critical test of approval by those very Jewish Christian eyewitnesses who trusted Luke with their identity-forming knowledge of Jesus of Nazareth.[10] Luke may be the translator of the material from Aramaic/Hebrew into Greek. Or he may have edited Greek material using his own word choices. This would account for the appearance of some of his often used words, constructions, and phrases. But the three parables of Luke 15 can best be attributed to Jesus of Nazareth. I find the setting in 15:1–3 to be authentic.[11]

## 6. The Hebrew Pause Sentence and Rhetorical Analysis

In an earlier work the present author attempted a preliminary review of various types of rhetorical structures that appear in the Old and New Testaments (*Poet*, 44–75). More recently the very helpful work of James L. Kugel entitled *The Idea of Biblical Poetry: Parallelism and Its History* has appeared. Kugel argues that "Hebrew parallelism" is better named "the Hebrew pause sentence" and that it is not specifically a feature of *poetry* but rather a major characteristic of *all* types of Hebrew Biblical writing (pp. 1–58). The ancient author is saying, "This is true (pause), and this is true too! (longer pause)." The second line can be related to the first in a wide variety of ways. Starting with Kugel's analysis, the interpreter is set free to trace the extensive use of this Hebrew pause sentence, irrespective of whether or not the material dealt with falls into Western categories of prose or poetry. Namely, it is appropriate to subject parables to rhetorical analysis.

My own study of these matters has led me to conclude that in the parables of Jesus we are indeed dealing with parallelisms but that sometimes these are parallelisms of single lines and sometimes of whole stanzas in a larger structure. The three basic ways that the two halves of the parallel interrelate in Biblical literature I prefer to call straight line sequence parallelism, step parallelism, and inverted parallelism. A single example of each of these types may be helpful.

---

## Figure 2
## Straight Line Sequence Parallelism (Luke 21:23–24)

| | |
|---|---|
| 1. Woe to those who are *pregnant* | PREGNANT |
| and to those who are *nursing infants* in those days! | NURSING |
| 2. For there will be great *distress* on the *earth* | DISTRESS |
| and *wrath* against this *people;* | WRATH |
| 3. they will *fall* by the edge of the *sword* | FALL BY SWORD |
| and be *taken away* as *captives* among all nations; | TAKEN CAPTIVE |
| 4. and Jerusalem will be trampled on by the *Gentiles,* | GENTILES |
| until the times of the *Gentiles* are fulfilled. | GENTILES |

---

## Figure 3
## Step Parallelism (Luke 11:9–10)

So I say to you,

| | |
|---|---|
| 1. *Ask,* and it will be given you; | ASK |
| 2.     *search,* and you will find; | SEARCH |
| 3.         *knock,* and the door will be opened for you. | KNOCK |
| 1. For everyone who *asks* receives, | ASK |
| 2.     and everyone who *searches* finds, | SEARCH |
| 3.         and for everyone who *knocks,* the door will be opened. | KNOCK |

---

Straight line sequence parallelism is shown in figure 2. The NRSV and other major modern translations format this material as prose. This is appropriate. However, it exhibits a series of *precise* Hebrew parallelisms (as can be seen by noting the summary words to the right of the text in fig. 2). The parallel lines are side by side in each case and the pairs of ideas together form a progression, a straight line sequence.

Figure 3 shows step parallelism. Jesus could have presented the six lines found in Luke 11:9-10 as shown in figure 4. However, rather than straight line sequence parallelism (fig. 4), 11:9–10 presents the reader with step parallelism (fig. 3). Thus in these two verses Jesus deliberately chose the step parallelism style from among the literary styles available to him from the writing prophets.

---

## Figure 4

| | |
|---|---|
| 1. *Ask,* and it will be given you, | ASK |
| 1. for everyone who *asks* receives. | ASK |
| 2. *Search,* and you will find, | SEARCH |
| 2. for everyone who *searches* finds. | SEARCH |
| 3. *Knock,* and the door will be opened for you, | KNOCK |
| 3. for to everyone who *knocks,* the door will be opened. | KNOCK |

---

Inverted parallelism is shown in figure 5. Again pairs of ideas appear in the text. Jesus is again composing by using the Hebrew pause sentence. As above, Jesus could have structured this little six line composition as shown in figure 6.

This latter formatting is clearly artistically inferior to what appears in the gospel. But it was certainly an option for the poet. Jesus deliberately *chose* to compose six lines and structure them into three Hebrew pause sentences. But rather than a straight line sequence, he presented the first three lines and then reversed the order for the second three. This created an *enclusio* (a return at the end of

## Figure 5
## Inverted Parallelism (Luke 16:13)

| | |
|---|---|
| 1.  No slave can serve *two masters;* | TWO MASTERS |
| 2.     for a slave will either *hate* the one | HATE |
| 3.        and *love* the other, | LOVE |
| 3.        or be *devoted* to the one | LOVE |
| 2.     and *despise* the other. | HATE |
| 1.  You cannot serve *God* and *wealth.* | TWO MASTERS |

## Figure 6

| | |
|---|---|
| 1.  No slave can serve *two masters;* | TWO MASTERS |
| 1.  nor can you serve *God* and *wealth.* | TWO MASTERS |
| 2.  The slave will *hate* the one master | HATE |
| 2.  and *despise* him | HATE |
| 3.  and *love* the other | LOVE |
| 3.  and be *devoted* to him. | LOVE |

a stanza to its beginning). It also created an opportunity for a clear climax—the *middle*. The *love* for the one master is given special emphasis by its central position. As noted, this is a common feature of inverted parallelism.[12]

In summary, with Kugel we have noted that the Hebrew pause sentence is a prominent feature of Hebrew writing in general and have observed three different ways these pause sentences are put together in Luke's gospel. None of the texts examined is formatted in the NRSV as poetry even though they exhibit tightly constructed Hebrew pause sentences. Thus Hebrew parallelisms do appear in material our Western sensitivities identify as prose. We conclude that it is thereby appropriate to look for the use of these classical Hebrew stylistics in the parables. They will surface in our study of Luke 15.

## 7. The Parable, Then and Now

Any story that is told to a particular audience at a particular time speaks uniquely to that original audience. Anyone who would seek significance and meaning from that same story for another people living in another time must find a way to bridge the gap of the centuries. This is why interpretation is necessary. For Jesus' original audience the parable was like a political cartoon—the full weight of its message was clear to any perceptive listener who shared the language, religion, history, and culture of the speaker. But what of the reader who comes to that same story two thousand years later? The cultural gap between our world and his prevents full participation without interpretation. Granted, any family that has had a "prodigal son" can identify with important parts of Luke 15:11–32. But even that identification can cloud rather that clarify Jesus' original purpose. What the original speaker intended to say to the original listeners remains the center of our quest. But modern Western culture and mentality diverge significantly from that of the Middle East, ancient or modern. Thus we must do our best to see what the story meant to them before we can find what it can mean to us. But if we "stand at the back" of Jesus' original audience and examine with great care what he was saying to them, we gradually find that he is speaking to the Pharisees and also to the human predicament of which we are a part. The parable goes beyond ideas, but ideas (concepts) are a means of unlocking its secrets. To return to our "parable of the orange," if one needs to squeeze an orange to make its content available to the guest, then surely the enterprise is legitimate. As noted, the prophets encased their parables in concepts.

Early in the 20th century, exegetes were struggling to escape from the irresponsible allegorizing of the past. One of their chosen tools for this enterprise was the theory that each parable had only *one* point. For a generation and more there has been a growing consensus that the parables of Jesus usually embody more than a single theme. A parable of Jesus is not a logical argument that proceeds systematically to a single conclusion. Rather, each parable is like a great diamond that sheds light in a variety of directions. At the same time a white diamond cannot legitimately be examined through a blue lens and declared to be blue in color. The interpreter should not impose modern Western (or Eastern) ideas onto the parables. Rather *the* question for the interpreter becomes—what are the various aspects of truth that *Jesus* is creating for his first-century Jewish audience? I have described this elsewhere at length and called it the "theological cluster." The image I intend is that of a cluster of grapes that forms a unit with its own integrity (and often beauty) and is yet made up of a number of grapes (*Poet*, 37–43). Even so, a number of theological themes are often set forth in a single parable.

Some sensivitity to multiple themes in a single parable is surely inevitable. In the parable of the prodigal son are we to discover only the theme of repentance or sonship or the nature of sin or grace or fatherhood? All of these themes are present and only as they are seen together is the meaning of any one discernible in its fullness. Another way to understand the multiple themes in a parable is to note that they often have four levels. The first is the entertaining story. "Children of all ages" quickly catch this aspect of the parable. A second level is that of ethics. The parable sets forth ethical patterns to be imitated or avoided. The third is theology. The parable usually contains a revelation of the secrets of the kingdom of God. Finally, the parable *may* (?) exhibit Christology. Jesus may be saying something about himself. It is surely inappropriate for any interpreter to decide ahead of time that Christology is necessarily present or absent. Each parable needs to speak for itself. If Christology is present, it should be noted. If it is absent, it should not be superimposed onto the text. Most well-known storytellers in history do reveal a great deal of themselves in the process of telling their stories. Jesus should not a priori be categorized as an exception. In this study we will search out all four levels in the parables of Luke 15.

With the above "lenses" in focus we would proceed to the text.

## Notes

1. *Enc. Jud.*, vol. 13, 1446. The title appears as a designation for a teacher by his students as early as 110 B.C. with Joshua ben Perahiah (M Ab. 1:6; E. Lohse,

# INTRODUCTION

*TDNT,* VI, 962). Dalman observes that the title was "the usual form of address with which the learned were greeted" (p. 331).

2. Fitzmyer (*Luke,* I, 436) accepts Brown's designation. Marshall argues cogently for its historicity (*Luke,* 125–26). Special features that support such a view include the fact that there is no attempt to harmonize the account with the virgin birth. Mary's amazement is puzzling in the light of the Magnificat and the Song of Simeon. The account closes with a reference to Jesus "increasing in wisdom." No miraculous features appear. Marshall concludes, "In itself the story is a natural one, and does not include any supernatural features which might lead to sceptical estimates of its historicity" (*Luke,* 126).

3. All three of these features were imperfectly noted by N. W. Lund. He discusses what he calls "the laws of chiastic structures" (pp. 40–41). Lund gives seven such so-called laws. The first three he defines as follows:

   (1) The center is always the turning point. . . . (2) The law of the shift at the centre (*sic*). . . . (3) Identical ideas are often distributed in such a fashion that they occur in the extremes and at the centre (*sic*) of their respective system, and nowhere else in the system" (ibid.).

   Lund's work is flawed by his failure to work within the framework of the Hebrew pause sentence. He also failed to observe the grouping of the material into stanzas, and tried to bring very large blocks of material into a single "system." Yet he broke new ground.

   In comment on Lund's above formulations it must be said that his first and second "laws" say the same thing in different words. More precisely stated, the first general principle of inverted parallelism is that the *climax* of the pericope is almost always in the center. There is often a "shift at center" but more often this shift occurs just past the center. But to call this and other rhetorical devices "laws" is inaccurate. Biblical authors do not seem to have been bound by laws but rather followed literary conventions that they were free to break. In regard to his third point, the feature he describes is often found as in the case of the passage under study.

4. The Berlin Arabic manuscript 1108 may (?) represent a pre-Islamic translation. No clear case can yet be made. The date is listed as "438 *hilaliyyah,*" which may refer to an Arabic Christian calender dating from A.D. March 22, 106 (cf. Dahdal). However the Bryn Mawr College Psalter also has a *hilaliyyah* date that appears to be related to the Islamic calender. The problem is that Berlin 1108 is written in an archaic script that could date it as early as the eighth century.

   My tentative conclusion is that this Greek-Arabic version survives in a dated ninth-century copy (Sinai Arabic 72, [897 A.D.]). The translation may well be considerably older.

5. Blass notes, "The article is (naturally) omitted with the second of two phrases in apposition connected by *kai.*" He gives the example of Titus 2:13, "the great God and Savior of us" (my translation). There is only one article which governs both nouns. The "God" is not a different person from the "Savior" (Blass-Debrunner, 144–45).

6. Robertson notes that when there is a special emphasis on different aspects of one person or thing that then a number of articles appear. For example, Rev. 1:17 reads, "the first and the last and the living." The same person is meant

by all three, but there is a special emphasis placed on each aspect of that person by the use of multiple articles. Robertson continues, "Outside of special cases like these only one article is found when several epithets are applied to the same person." He also notes that "sometimes groups more or less distinct are treated as one for the purpose in hand, and hence use only one article." Luke 15:9 has a case of this where the text reads, "the friends and neighbors." There is only one definite article because, even though the friends and neighbors are not necessarily the same people, they are treated as a group (Robertson, 785–89).

7. Fitzmyer, *Luke*, II, 294. Fitzmyer lists Stendahl as opposing his view, but Fitzmyer has apparently misread Stendahl. Stendahl in fact agrees that the ministers of the word were eyewitnesses, but that the latter took on an additional task. Stendahl writes, "the *huperetei tou lougou* (ministers of the word) in Lk. I 2 are the instructors and the term is not *only* [emphasis ours] synonymous with the term for eye-witnesses" (Stendahl, 33). Stendahl then specifically observes that his view clashes with Dibelius. Dibelius is the one who reduces the "ministers of the word" to preachers and affirms that the two groups must have been different because not all preachers in the early church were eyewitnesses. The question turns on the exact nature of the *huperetai tou lougou*. Were they merely first-century preachers? The best evidence, as we observe above, does not support such a judgment (cf. Dibelius, 12).

8. Cf. Bailey, *Informal*. This essay is the result of 30 years of reflection and study on the question of how oral tradition functions in the traditional Middle Eastern village. The case argued is that there is in Middle Eastern village culture an *informal* yet *controlled* form of tradition transmission. It is our suggestion that these Jewish Christian *hupēretai* functioned as a critical element in the controls.

9. The full rabbinic phrase for the formal passing on of the tradition used the two phrases "received from" and "delivered to" (*qibbel min* and *masar li*). M 'Aboth 1:1 opens with, "Moses received the Law from Sinai and committed it to Joshua" (Danby, 446). In its Greek dress this full expression appears in 1 Cor. 11:23 and 15:3. The appearance of one of these key phrases in Luke 1:1–4 strengthens its Jewish and Jewish-Christian framework of tradition transmission.

10. My essay on the nature of the oral tradition behind the synoptic gospels discusses at length both the freedom for individual expression and the controls that assure authenticity in Middle Eastern informal controlled oral tradition. Such freedom, within limits, provides a framework within which to understand both the unity and diversity exhibited in the synoptic gospels (cf. Bailey, *Informal*, 34–54).

11. Regarding Luke 15:11–32 Fitzmyer writes, "Commentators such as A. Julicher, R. Bultmann, J. M. Creed and many others see no decisive reason not to ascribe the parable as a whole to Stage I of the gospel tradition" (*Luke*, II, 1085).

12. In 1820 John Jebb observed inversion of lines in Biblical literature and called it introverted parallelism (p. 53). We have slightly revised this term to inverted parallelism. The more common designation is *chiasmus* or *chiasm*. Chiasmus is a Greek rhetorical term that refers to two lines in which the themes of the first are reversed in the second, thus forming an X (the Greek letter *chi*). Thus the verse

The sabbath was made for humankind,
and not humankind for the sabbath (Mark 2:27)

is a true chiasmus (in modern usage often shortened to *chaism*). It seems to me more precise to preserve the word *chiasm* for this meaning. Furthermore, the designation *inverted parallelism* ties this rhetorical device to the Hebrew pause sentences of Biblical literature within which it finds its Biblical cultural home.

# Chapter 1

# The Good Shepherd
# and the Lost Sheep
## Luke 15:1–7

Before turning to the text, the setting in Luke 15 needs examination.

In its simplest form the gospel of Luke can be understood to fall into three sections. These are as follows:

1. The prolog, infancy narratives, and Galilean ministry (1:1–9:50)
2. The "travel narrative" (9:51–19:48)
3. The passion and resurrection (20:1–24:53)

Luke 15:1–32 is near the center of the so-called "travel narrative." Thus this special section of Luke's gospel must be briefly examined.

The 10-chapter collection at the center of Luke's gospel concentrates on the teachings of Jesus. Its opening verse reads, "As the time approached when he was to be taken up to heaven, he set his face resolutely towards Jerusalem" (9:51 NEB). Thus already in 9:51 Jesus is on his way to Jerusalem and the long shadow of the cross falls over the entire narrative, for at its end the passion begins.

As indicated, the synoptic problem is beyond the scope of this study. However, these 10 chapters can be seen as a special section regardless of what solution to the synoptic problem is adopted. The material itself is "special" in that it does not appear in Mark. Any diagram of synoptic relationships quickly shows that Mark and Luke have nearly the same outline except that almost all of Luke 9:51–19:48 is missing from Mark (cf. Barr). More than 20 parables of Jesus appear in this section. Many of them, (like Luke 15:1–32) appear *only* in this travel narrative. Thereby a brief glance at the way this material is composed is appropriate.

Many recent scholars have found this narrative without any order (cf. Fitzmyer, *Luke,* I, 825; Bailey, *Poet,* 79, n. 1). Yet the idea that

Luke has composed/edited the material around the "journey theme" persists. This I find problematic. Jesus starts *resolutely* for Jerusalem in 9:51. By 10:38–39 he has arrived in Bethany at the edge of Jerusalem and the goal of his journey (?) is reached. But then strangely, in 13:22 he is still on his way (?) and there are towns and villages yet to traverse before he reaches the Holy City. More complications appear in 13:31 where he is warned about Herod's plot to kill him; thus presumably he is back in Herod's territory in Galilee or Perea. In 17:11 he is "between Samaria and Galilee." Finally, as it were, he "comes out of the woods" in 19:1 in Jericho and for the second time proceeds to Jerusalem. Fitzmyer reaffirms the traditional "travel motif" point of view but holds that "Luke's knowledge of Palestinian geography is not what it should be" (*Luke,* I, 824). This is hardly adequate for an intelligent man (Luke) who has visited the Holy Land. Where Bethany is and where Samaria and Galilee are in relation to Jerusalem is rather basic! Luke claims contact with eyewitnesses. Any one of them or any other Palestinian Jewish Christian or apostle (including Paul) could have given him this information in 30 seconds. Ellis comments succinctly on Conzelmann's defense of the "travel motif" and notes, "Conzelmann . . . must assume Luke's ignorance of the very geographical elements that the Evangelist supposedly is concerned to stress" (p. 147).

Luke *is* an intelligent man. This *is* a special section of his gospel. Luke must have had *some* reason for the order which presents itself to us in this section. As noted above, the material does not follow a geographical progression across the countryside from Galilee to Jerusalem. What then might that order be?

It is my conviction that the entire section has a precise outline that is fashioned after models unfamiliar to us. My suggestion, published some years ago in an imprecise form (*Poet,* 79–85), is that the material is organized around nine topics that start with reference to "saving events in Jerusalem" and end with that same subject. This makes a total of 10 sections. The list then repeats, only it does so backwards and thus ends with the same topic of "saving events in Jerusalem." The 19 sections thus exhibit inverted parallelism (chiasm).

Some of the parallels are unmistakable. There are two sections on prayer (11:1–13 and 18:1–14). Why are these not assembled in one place in the text? Two people ask the question, "What must I do to inherit eternal life?" These two passages are eight chapters apart (10:25 and 18:18). There are two laments over Jerusalem, one in the center and one at the end (13:34–35 and 19:41–44). The first includes and the second follows the invocation "Blessed is he/the king who comes in the name of the Lord" (RSV). All of this apparent lack of order turns into a precise outline when the inverted parallelism of the 19 stanzas is identified.

Because of this threefold emphasis on Jerusalem (at the beginning, the center, and the end), the connection with the Holy City is clear and strong. The outline is too long to make it likely that it is an oral collection. *Who* compiled it and *when* will remain a topic for speculation unless new manuscripts are discovered. Currently we have only theories. It is my own conviction that it is pre-Lucan and that it is composed in Jerusalem by the Jewish Christian church of that city. Most likely it is a compilation brought together before A.D. 58 (at the time of Luke's visit to Jerusalem) by one of those many who had "undertaken to compile a narrative" referred to in Luke 1:1 (RSV). The compiler(s), like Luke, had access to the "eyewitnesses and ministers of the word" (1:2 RSV) discussed above. Because of this unmistakable emphasis on Jerusalem, I prefer to call this section "the Jerusalem document." This special section is a prominent part of the tradition and its discernible order is significant for interpretation.

Furthermore, Luke 9:51–19:48 is early. The material preserves the bulk of the parables, as noted. Time and again, when the same material appears in Matthew or in Mark and Matthew, the Lucan account is shorter, crisper, and with fewer descriptive details. The Hebrew words for weights and measures that appear in 16:5–7 are not translated from Hebrew into Greek but rather the Hebrew words appear, written with Greek letters. In this section of Luke the word for Jerusalem appears 10 times spelled *Ierousalēm,* which is close to the Hebrew spelling, and only twice in the the less Hebraic form *Hierosolyma.* The woman's lost coin is called a *drachma* which was replaced by the *denarius* during the rule of Nero (A.D. 54–68, cf. Fitzmyer, II, 1081). The older word *drachma* appears in the NT only in our parable. Jesus' sharp debates with his opponents maintain their cutting edge in Luke.[1] The parable of the great banquet is far more elaborate in Matthew than in Luke.[2] The Hebrew pause sentences (Hebrew parallelisms) in this central section of Luke are clear and bold. Thus, there are significant reasons to conclude that this material was committed to writing, probably in Jerusalem, at an early stage in the process of the compilaton of the gospels.

In the past 20 years, I have simplified the above mentioned outline, but I still find its basic form valid. I originally argued that 90 percent of the material fits the outline (*Poet,* 80–83). A full 95 percent is perhaps more accurate. For our purposes in this study, it is the central section of this Jerusalem document that concerns us. This appears as shown in figure 7.

The compiler of the material has set out *the call to Israel* (8), and followed it with a discussion of *the nature of the kingdom* (9). The entire Jerusalem document then climaxes in the middle with a second discussion of *saving events* in *Jerusalem* (the first being at the beginning of the entire document; Bailey, *Poet,* 80). This climactic center includes significant references to the death of Jesus (10). The document continues with a parallel to 9 as it presents a second description of *the nature of the kingdom* (9'). In stanza 8' (14:12–15:32) the call of the kingdom to Israel is expanded to the call of the kingdom to Israel *and to the outcasts.*"[3] The order is significant in that the compiler of the document notes first the clear and uncompromising call of Jesus to *Israel* (8). Then the reader is told of the widening of the grace of the Gospel to include the outcasts (8').[4] What conclusions can be drawn from the above?

These five sections have three themes important for our topic. The first appears in the climactic center with the focus on the saving events in Jerusalem. Thus the significance of the suffering of Jesus is critically emphasized. The second theme is placed like a semantic envelope around 10 and focuses on "love and not law" (9 and 9'). The third theme in 8 and 8' tells the reader that there is a special call of the kingdom for *Israel* and for the *outcasts of Israel.* All three of these topics will appear in the chapter under study. The compiler of the Jerusalem document has put his/her material together with a sophisticated sense of theological balance and interrelatedness.

With this in mind we turn to an examination of the opening verses of our chapter.

## The Introduction (Luke 15:1–3)

The text is as follows:

Now all the tax collectors and sinners were coming near to listen

## Figure 7

8. *The Call of the Kingdom to Israel* (13:1–9)

   a. Repent or perish—Pilate and the Galileans (vv. 1–5)

   b. Produce or perish—the unfruitful fig tree (vv. 6–9)

9. *The Nature of the Kingdom* (13:10–21)

   a. Love and not law—the healing on the Sabbath
     • A woman (vv. 10–14)
     • What about your ox or ass? No reply (vv. 15–17)

   b. Humility—the kingdom is like mustard and leaven (vv. 18–20)

    10. *Jerusalem: Eschatological Events* (13:22–35)
     • Salvation, judgment, fulfillment, death, the day, blessed is he who comes

9'. *The Nature of the Kingdom* (14:1–11)

   a. Love and not law—a healing on the Sabbath
     • A man (vv. 1–4)
     • What about your ass or ox? No reply (vv. 5–6)

   b. Humility—"Those who humble themselves will be exalted" (vv. 7–11)

8'. *The Call of the Kingdom to Israel and to the Outcasts* (14:12–15:32)

   a. The great banquet (14:12–24)
     • The cost of discipleship (vv. 25–35)

   b. The lost sheep, coin, and sons (15:1–32)

(Cf. *Poet*, 80–82)

---

to him. And the Pharisees and the scribes were grumbling and saying, "This fellow welcomes sinners and eats with them."

So he told them this parable:

The word *all* is a typical case of Middle Eastern hyperbole. It simply means "many" (Plummer, 367).

The already noted possibility that the Pharisees were related to the *haberim* is further strengthened by the fact that early Arabic versions translate the word "Pharisee" with *al-'ahbar* (the Arabic plural of *habr*). One such version is the work of Ibn al-'Assal who often puts *al-'ahbar* in the text and *Phariseen* in the apparatus. (The word *'ahbar* consistently appears as a translation for the word *Pharisees* all through Vatican Arabic 13 and Vatican Coptic 10.)

The hostility that existed between the *haberim* (the religious "associates") and the *'am ha-'arets* (the people of the land) has been discussed. The Mekhilta on Ex. 18:1 has what Samuel Lachs calls "an old Rabbinic rule" which states, "Let not a man associate with the wicked, not even to bring him nigh to the law" (p. 306). Meals were a particular problem.

Jacob Neusner reflects thoughtfully on the critical nature of meals for the Pharisee. He observes that the community at Qumran lived in isolation from the common folk of the countryside. But not so the Pharisees. The Pharisee lived in the village among the *'am ha-'arets*. Neusner writes:

> Pharisaic table-fellowship took place in the same circumstances as all non-ritual table fellowship: common folk ate everyday meals in an everyday way, among ordinary neighbors who were not members of the sect, and who engaged in workaday pursuits like everyone else. This fact made the actual purity-rules and food-restrictions all the more important, for they alone set the Pharisee apart from the people among whom he constantly lived (*Law,* 340).

Following Neusner, it is easy to see why meals were so critical for the Pharisees. They had decided that it was possible to keep the law in a precise manner and still live among the *'am ha-'arets*. To do this they had to be very careful about the food laws and the demands of ceremonial purity. That is, they had to be strict about *what* they ate and with *whom.*

Danby notes that these were the very issues that distinguished the *haberim* from the *'am ha-'arets*. He writes that *people of the land* is

> the name given to those Jews who were ignorant of the Law and who failed to observe the rules of cleanness and uncleanness and were not scrupulous in setting apart Tithes from the produce. . . .

Those Jews who, on the contrary, undertook to be faithful in observing the requirements of the Law are known as 'Associates'
(*haberim*) (p. 793).

The food laws were an important part of the rules of cleanness
and uncleanness mentioned above. Eating was related to tithing.
One could not eat untithed food. Regarding this same topic of food
laws the Babylonian Talmud lists six things that are "unbecoming
for a scholar." One of them is, "he should not recline (for a meal)
in the company of the *'am ha-'arets*" (Ber., 43b; my translation). For
some rabbis the concern about purity in regard to food and meals
was so exacting that two acquaintances were not allowed to sit on
opposite sides of the dining room in a boarding house if one was
eating cheese and the other meat. The reason being that because
they knew each other, their minds could "mix" in the middle of
the dining room and thus milk and meat would be mixed, which
was against the law. If they did not know each other then it was
permitted (BT Shab., 13a). But it was more than merely a matter of
food.

The concern on the part of the *haber* to avoid any conduct with
the *'am ha-'arets* was profound. The Mishnah records, "For Pharisees, the clothes of an *Am-haaretz* count as suffering *midras*-un-
cleanness [uncleanness from contact]" (Hag. 2:7; Danby, 214). This
is further clarified in Mishnah Demai which affirms,

> He that undertakes to be an Associate [*haber*] may not sell to an
> *Am-haaretz* ... ; and he may not be the guest of an *Am-haaretz*
> nor may he receive him as a guest in his own raiment (2:3; Danby,
> 22).

Letting one of the *'am ha-'arets* into the house for any reason
was a serious matter. The Mishnah records,

> If the wife of an Associate [*haber*] left the wife of an *Am-haaretz*
> grinding flour within her house and she ceased from the grinding,
> the house becomes unclean; if she did not cease from the grinding,
> only that part of the house is unclean which she could touch by
> stretching out her hand. If there were two of them the house
> becomes unclean in either case, since the one can go about and
> touch while the other grinds (Toh. 7:4; Danby, 726).

Granted, even though the Mishnah was compiled at an early
date (A.D. 200), this specific legislation may not have been in force

at the time of Jesus, but it reflects cultural attitudes that were certainly to be found in his day.

On the other hand, for Jesus the matter of table fellowship was also critical. Jeremias notes,

> The inclusion of sinners in the community of salvation, achieved in table-fellowship, is the most meaningful expression of the message of the redeeming love of God (*Theology,* 115).

Ibn al-Tayyib, 800 years earlier, observed,

> The Pharisees blamed the Christ for his invitation to sinners and his acceptance of them. But [in these three parables] he made clear to them that these very acts for which they blamed him were the very purposes for which he came into the world. Thus that for which they blamed him, which they considered shameful acts, Christ considered a great honor (*Tafsir,* II, 262).

Thus the issue of table fellowship was critical for each party.

But worst of all, from the Pharisees' point of view, was the fact that Jesus not only ate with *sinners* (read: *'am ha-'arets;* cf. Rengstorf, *TDNT,* I, 323, 328), *tax collectors* were also at his table. Tax collectors were religiously defiled by contact with Gentiles. But there was more.

Only one who has been privileged to be a part of a community living under military occupation can fully understand the feelings of such a community toward the "collaborator." French collaborators at the time of the Nazi occupation were bitterly resented and after the war killed or imprisoned. In South Africa collaborators have been burned to death with rubber tires and gasoline. In Jerusalem during the winter of 1990, Israel Shahak of Jerusalem, a Warsaw ghetto survivor, told of the butchering of Jewish collaborators (by Jews) before the fall of the ghetto. Palestinians on the West Bank, during their uprising (1987–), have also executed collaborators. All of this is a tragic and yet understandable response of an oppressed people in their community reaction to those who are cooperating with their oppressors. In like manner, during the ministry of Jesus the land was ruled by hated Roman conquerers. Thus the Pharasaic objection to Jesus' table fellowship with tax-collectors was both religious and political.

The conclusion of the matter is that for both Jesus and for the Pharisees, table fellowship (or lack of it) was a critical symbol of identity. It is little wonder that a confrontation on the issue occurred. The Pharisees and scribes appear with an accusation against Jesus: this man eats with tax collectors and sinners. As Jeremias notes, "The parable was addressed to men who were like the elder brother, men who were offended at the Gospel" (*Parables,* 131). How is Jesus to respond?

Initially, the style of Jesus' response must be noted. He did *not* reply with something of the following:

> Gentlemen, I see that you are upset over my welcome of sinners into table fellowship. This is perfectly reasonable, and I can sympathize with the way you feel. Ostracization of such types is critical for ceremonial purity. But please understand that for me such invitations are the exception, not the rule. Furthermore, I insist on welcoming only *repentant* sinners, and they are always "cleaned up" before I let them in. I do not do this often, and it is always in private away from the eyes of other *'am ha-'arets* so as to prevent misunderstandings. You will recall, I am sure, that the God of our tradition is a God of mercy as well as a God of judgment and we are merely trying to reflect that mercy in our dealings with these unfortunate types.

Jesus replies with a set of stories rather than with a conceptually argued defense. Put into conceptual language we can summarize his reply as follows:

> Gentlemen, you accuse me of reclining to eat with the *'am ha-'arets* and with tax collectors! Your information is *correct.* This is exactly what I do. And not only do I *let them in*—I go out into the streets and shower them with affection, *urging* them to come in and eat with me!

The story of Zacchaeus gives eloquent testimony that the above was the lifestyle of Jesus. What Jesus does in the story of Zacchaeus, the father does in Luke 15:20–24. Each eats with a sinner. Thus, here in these opening verses there is a *strong* suggestion that Christology is built into the chapter as it now stands. This can be seen as follows:

a. The Pharisees come complaining:
   "This *fellow* welcomes *sinners* and *eats* with *them!*"
b. Jesus replies with a story (vv. 11–32) in which
   a certain *man* welcomed a *sinner* and *ate* with *him!*

In the parable of the prodigal son, the father does *exactly* what the audience is accusing Jesus of having done. The father *welcomes* a *sinner* (the prodigal) and *eats* with *him*. Luke 15:2 and 15:20–24 confront the reader. Reflection on the meaning of the second in the light of the first is unavoidable. It is my conclusion that the text itself obliges the interpreter to raise the Christological question and to ask if and in what sense Jesus is telling stories about himself.

The singular "parable" in verse 3 is followed by three parables. As the text now stands this singular affirms the three parables to be a unity. That unity can be observed on many levels as we will see. This brings us to the first story.

## The Parable of the Lost Sheep (15:4–7)

The text of this parable is printed in modern Bibles as prose. According to our literary tastes this judgment is correct. Yet, the material exhibits a sophisticated set of parallelisms. These can be seen in figure 8.

The rhetorical structure of the passage is clear and strong (Bailey, *Poet,* 144). Three themes appear in the opening lines. These are (1) you; (2) one; (3) ninety-nine. These same three themes (in the same order) reappear in the Dominical interpretation at the end (cf. 4, 5, 6). Thus the opening stanzas and closing stanzas exhibit *step parallelism.*

The center is composed of seven brief stanzas. The themes of (A) *lost,* (B) *find,* and (C) *rejoice* are presented and then repeated backwards at the end in C', B', and A'. The rhetorical climax of the entire passage is in the center in D with the theme of restoration to the house and the calling of the community for a party. This center section uses *inverted parallelism* and the three major divisions of the passage are A-B-A as we have noted. Thus the entire parable (with interpretation) forms an artistic whole.

The literary models here followed can be traced to the writing prophets and are authentic to the Jewish milieu of the first century.

In addition, there is an Aramaic word play in the text. The Aramaic word for one is *had* and Aramaic for joy is *hedwah.* The story begins with *had* (2), climaxes with *hedwah* (C, C') and then in the Dominical interpretation (4, 5, 6) there is *hedwah* over the *had* (Black, 194).

The parable is authentic in every detail to the Middle Eastern

## Figure 8
## The Lost Sheep (Luke 15:4–7)

1. *Which one* of *you,*                YOU
   having a hundred sheep
2. and losing *one* (*had*) of them,    ONE
3. does not leave the *ninety-nine*    NINETY-NINE
   in the wilderness
      A. and go after the one that is *lost*    LOST
         B. until he *finds* it?    FIND
           And when he has *found* it,
            C. he lays it on his shoulders    REJOICE
              [*rejoicing*] (*hedwah*).
              D. And when he comes *home,*    RESTORE
              he calls together
              his *friends* and *neighbors,*
           C'. saying to them,    REJOICE
             "*Rejoice* (*hedwah*) with me,
        B'. for I have *found* my sheep    FIND
      A'. that was *lost.*"    LOST
4. Just so, I tell *you,* there will be    YOU
   more *joy* (*hedwah*) in heaven
5. over *one* (*had*) sinner who repents    ONE
6. than over *ninety-nine* righteous    NINETY-NINE
   persons who need no repentance.

(Bailey, *Poet,* 144)

shepherd world as I have experienced it in Lebanon, Syria, and Israel/Palestine over the past 25 years (cf. Bailey, *Poet,* 151–53). At the same time, a number of details are striking.

First, Jesus addresses the Pharisees and scribes as if they were shepherds. The text does not mention a mixed audience that could have included shepherds, and there is no need to artificially imagine them. In any case the reader is told specifically "So he told *them* [Pharisees and scribes] this parable: . . ." Shepherds, in the oral law, were a proscribed trade. These trades were listed by the rabbis as being those professions that no law-abiding Jew should teach to his son because in the judgment of the rabbis it was impossible to keep the law and practice such trades. Two such lists appear in the Mishnah (Kidd. 4:14; Ket. 7:10) and three in the Babylonian Talmud (Kidd., 82a; Sanh., 25b; Sof., 41a2). Of these five lists, three of them record "herdsman."

The puzzle is that the shepherd is a symbol for God in the OT (Psalm 23) and for the leaders of Israel (Ezekiel 34). Those leaders were remembered as shepherds and were honored (BT Sukk., 52b). But the down-to-earth experience of the people by NT times was that herdsmen drove their sheep intentionally onto other people's lands and were not to be trusted (cf. Jeremias, *Jerusalem,* 313–15, 310–11). Thus to address Pharisees as if they were shepherds would be considered by the Pharisees as aggressive and offensive. There must have been a *very* good reason for Jesus to have done so.

No doubt Jesus addressed the Pharisees in this manner partially as a rejection of their "apartheid" society with its clean and unclean professions and people. But the reasons for the language of the text may reach yet deeper. The very structure of life and language in the Middle East requires that people do *not* blame themselves. No one says, "I lost my sheep." The appropriate idiom is "the sheep went from me." I did not "miss the train" but rather "the train left me." I did not "break the dish," what happened was "the dish fell from my hand." (Knowledgeable friends tell me the same linguistic tradition and cultural attitude holds sway in both Spain and South America.) This traditional form of discourse appears in Matt. 18:12 which reads, "if . . . one of them has gone astray," putting the blame on the sheep.

So who is to blame in the first two parables? Four verses are worth examining. These are verses 4, 6, 8, and 9. In each parable the storyteller makes a statement and in each the central figure makes a speech to his/her friends. This can be seen as follows:

V. 4—Losing one of them        (shepherd *blamed* by
                                       storyteller)

| | |
|---|---|
| V. 6—I have found my sheep that was lost | (shepherd *does not blame self* in public) |
| V. 8—If she loses one of them | (woman *blamed* by storyteller) |
| V. 9—I have found the coin that I had lost | (woman *does blame self* in public) |

The cultural fine-tuning of the text is very interesting. The storyteller clearly affirms that each is to blame. But the shepherd announced in public at his party that *he found* the sheep, but did not publically accept blame for having *lost* it. The woman is braver and more open. The storyteller blames the woman. She has lost her coin. But unlike the shepherd who protects his "image" at his party, she admits to her friends that she is responsible for having caused the problem in the first place. What then happens to this fine-tuning?

The impact of this question was minor on the Greek manuscripts. A few changed the word "lost" in verse 4 into a subjunctive (B*, D). But this strong Middle Eastern linguistic tradition of not blaming self had a powerful infuence on the Syriac and Arabic translations from the second century onward. Already in the Old Syriac the phrase "losing one of them" (v. 4) becomes "if one of them be lost," and the shepherd is declared innocent (Burkitt, 351). The woman is blamed in the Old Syriac with "and she lost one of them" (v. 8). But even the woman is not asked to admit fault at her party. So before her friends she says, "I have found my drachma that *was lost*" rather than "that *I had lost.*" The Peshitta Syriac is identical on these points with the Old Syriac. Only the literal Harclean is faithful to the nuances of the original Greek.

The Arabic versions from the ninth to the nineteenth centuries have an *almost* universal tendency to turn all three occasions of blame (one against the shepherd and two against the woman) into passives. The one exception I have discovered is the archaic Greek-to-Arabic version. Even Ibn al-Tayyib's commentary exonerates the shepherd from all blame. This thousand-year flight from the "bad shepherd" with which the story opens is certainly cultural; it may also be theological. These translators saw Jesus in the first parable and so did not want to present him as a bad shepherd who lost his sheep. They did not find any Christology in the story of the good woman and so she could be blamed by the storyteller. But even she is allowed to "save face" with her friends at her party. Thus the original of Luke 15:4c has a jarring ring to it when read in a Semitic language in a Middle Eastern cultural context. The language is bold and deliberate! The text clearly affirms "*losing* one of them, . . ." The *shepherd* is *blamed* for the loss of the sheep. The account in Luke opens with a picture of a *bad* shepherd who loses his sheep! It is a "Bo Peep" story. What is the purpose of this criticism?

Jesus intends an "eyeball to eyeball" confrontation with his accusers. He is saying to them,

> You are the shepherds of Israel. You have lost your sheep. I pay the price to go after them and bring them back and now you come complaining to me because I have compensated for your mistakes! This is outrageous!

Yet, even though the shepherd is blamed, the sheep are not assumed innocent. When one has had the privilege of watching herds move through the rugged open grazing lands on the West Bank this is clear. It is the nature of sheep to wander off and/or lag behind. Jesus' audience, whatever their walk in life, know this and there is no specific need to mention it. Sheep nibble and nibble, moving from one tuft of grass to another with no awareness of their surroundings. By contrast a cat eats with a constant heightened awareness of its environment. Not so a sheep. If the flock is not guided by an alert shepherd there will be a sheep lost every hour or so all day long. The shepherd knows this, and it is his specific responsibility to constantly keep individual animals moving with the herd. Thus when a sheep is lost the *shepherd* is at fault, and the lost *sheep* is *not* innocent. Without this assumption the lost sheep could hardly have provided a symbol for repentance.

At the same time, in Luke 15:4 the bad shepherd quickly becomes a good shepherd who pays a high price to find the sheep and carry it home over the rugged hills. Thus, the symbol of the shepherd is used twice in rapid succession, first for a bad shepherd who loses his sheep, and then for a good shepherd who goes after it. This remarkable phenomenon is important for two reasons. First, the daring parabolic device (which appears here) of using a single character in the story in two different ways will reappear in the third story. Second, the "good shepherd" together with the "bad shepherd" have already appeared twice in the OT tradition. Brief reflection on this "intertextuality" seems appropriate.

67

Themes that appear in Luke 15:4–7 are prominent in three OT texts. This can be seen as follows:

| **Psalm 23** | **Jer. 23:1–8** | **Ezek. 34:1–24** | **Luke 15:4–7** |
|---|---|---|---|
| 1. ——— | Bad shepherd | Bad shepherd | Bad shepherd |
| 2. Lost sheep | Lost sheep | Lost sheep | Lost sheep |
| 3. Good shepherd | Good shepherd | Good shepherd | Good shepherd |
| 4. Repentance/ restoration (*shub*) | Repentance/ restoration (*shub*) | Repentance/ restoration (*shub*) | Repentance/ restoration (*metanoia*) |
| 5. ——— | ——— | Good/bad sheep | Good/bad sheep? |
| 6. Return to *God* | Return to *land* | Return to *land* and to *God* | Return to *God* |
| 7. Story ends in the house | ——— | ——— | Story ends in the house |

The repetition of common themes through the four texts makes it clear that later authors were retelling an old story and selecting, shaping, and expanding material for the new situation each faced. A full examination of the movement through these four texts is beyond the scope of our study. Yet we would note briefly the flow of key ideas.

Psalm 23 and its relationship to the whole of Luke 15 will be examined with care in chapter 5. Yet some specifics need to come to our attention here. Psalm 23 clearly has a good shepherd. But it also has a *lost sheep* and the language of *repentance/restoration*.

Ps. 23:3 is traditionally translated "he restores my soul." Popularly understood this phrase means, "I felt depressed, the Lord restored my soul. I am no longer depressed." However the Hebrew text reads *naphshi yeshobeb*. The word *nephesh* is a freighted word that runs throughout Semitic languages and means breath and life/soul, but it is also the common word for *self* (cf. Lev. 11:44; Ps. 131:2; Is. 5:14; 46:2; etc.). The second word (*yeshobeb*) is an intensive form of *shub*, the great Hebrew word for repentance. Thus Ps. 23:3a can be translated "he brings me back" or "he causes me to repent."

The intensive form (Polel) of this verb is rare in the OT. It occurs in Is. 49:5 where the suffering servant *brings* Jacob *back* to *God*. The same intensive form appears in Ezek. 39:27 which reads,

When I have *brought* them *back* from the peoples . . .
and through them have vindicated my holiness.

Finally Jer. 50:19 also has the Polel form and reads, "I will *return* Israel to his pasture, and he shall feed on Carmel and in Bashan" (my translation). Jeremiah, like the psalmist, attached the intensive form of *shub* to shepherd images. As noted, the Polel form of this verb is used in one OT text to refer to the idea of returning to *God* and in another to the theme of returning to the *land*. Thus, "he brings me back" is a strong possibility for an understanding of Ps. 23:3a. Yet the verb *is* the verb "to repent," and thus "he causes me to *repent*" is clearly implied if not intended.

The next phrase in the psalm is "He leads me in the paths of righteousness" (RSV). Again, the natural question is this: What paths was the psalmist wandering in before he was so led? The assumption of the text appears to be the paths of unrighteousness. Thus, hidden in Ps. 23:3 under the Elizabethan English of the King James Version ("he restores my soul"), is the story of a lost sheep and a good shepherd who brings him back/causes him to repent and leads him in the paths of righteousness.

In summary, Psalm 23 has a good shepherd (no bad shepherd) and a lost sheep. The direction of repentance and of that sheep's return is to the *shepherd* (God). The psalm is written at a time when the nation is secure in the land, and thus naturally a return to it is not on the psalmist's agenda. The psalm ends with the psalmist in the *house*.

Jer. 23:1–8 introduces a bad shepherd–good shepherd contrast. The bad shepherds are called to account. Then God himself is seen acting as the good shepherd. He says, "I myself will gather the remnant of my flock, . . . and I will bring them back [*hashoboti;* from *shub*] to their fold." New shepherds will then be appointed, and "I will raise up for David a righteous Branch, and he shall reign as king." Finally, the people will be reestablished in the land (v. 8). Thus Jeremiah keeps the same basic list of themes but introduces important changes. The bad shepherd appears, and the return is not to *God* but to the *land*. David's Branch also appears. There is no house.

Ezek. 34:1–24 endorses Jeremiah's expansion of Psalm 23 and adds a great deal of detail to each theme. The bad shepherds are more severely criticized. Particular emphasis is laid by Ezekiel on God the good shepherd (vv. 11, 15). Ezekiel also introduces David as the new good shepherd who will (as it were) "take over" from God the good shepherd. A form of the great word *shub* (return/ repent) appears where God says, "I will *bring back* the strayed" (v. 16). The failed leadership of the community appears twice. They are the bad *shepherds* who are sharply criticized at the beginning of the chapter. Then at the end of the account, "the house of Israel" is called "the sheep of my pasture" (vv. 30–31). The failed leadership is naturally a part of Israel and thus a part of the *flock*. Finally, the return (as in Jeremiah) is also to the *land*. A return to God is also affirmed in that God also says, "I will be their God" (v. 24), but the theme of national restoration is more prominent.

As noted, Jeremiah introduces the new theme of the bad shepherd. Ezekiel then adds the good sheep–bad sheep picture. The sheep for Ezekiel are not all innocent (vv. 17–19).

If any one or all of these three texts in any way stand behind the theological intent of Luke 15:4–7, the Christology in the latter text is bold and unmistakable. A fuller discussion of the possible Christology of the parable will be reserved for the end of our study.

Luke 15:4–7 advances this long, noble exegetical history. (1) Jesus opens (as in Jeremiah and Ezekiel) with a bad shepherd. (2) The lost sheep theme is prominent. (3) The picture of a good shepherd who goes after the lost sheep then immediately appears. (4) The Greek word *metanoia* (repent) carries the meaning of the Hebrew verb *shub*. Both "brings me back" and "causes me to repent" are clearly affirmed in the parable. Repentance is more prominent than in the early texts. (5) The good sheep–bad sheep theme is preserved in a subtle form, for the ninety-nine are last heard of in the wilderness as we will observe. (6) Of critical significance is the fact that Jesus clearly returns to the original picture of Psalm 23 and affirms a return to *God* and (7) to God's house. The themes of return to the land and national restoration that feature so prominently in Jeremiah and Ezekiel are set aside and the theology of Psalm 23 is reaffirmed. Jesus "de-Zionizes" the tradition. Finally, like in Ezekiel, the failed leadership is initially symbolized by the bad shepherd who loses his sheep (as we will note). Then at the end of the parable, that same leadership reappears as a part of the flock.

It is my conviction that Jesus uses some of the images of Jeremiah

## Figure 9

| Psalm 23 | Luke 15 |
|---|---|
| The good shepherd and a lost sheep (vv. 1–4) | The good shepherd and a lost sheep (vv. 4–7) |
| | The good woman and a lost coin (vv. 8–10) |
| A noble host and a costly banquet (vv. 5–6) | A noble host and a costly banquet (vv. 11–32) |

and Ezekiel but has deliberately chosen Psalm 23 as a focus for the creation of the parable of the lost sheep *and* as a structure for the trilogy of three parables that appear in Luke 15.

What then of the psalm and the rest of Luke 15? As noted, this question will be examined in chapter 5. However a brief overall comparison between the two texts may be helpful and is shown in figure 9.

Here we would note that each text opens with a good shepherd and a lost sheep. This brings us to an examination of the details of the parable itself.

1. "*Which one* of *you,*                              YOU
   having a hundred sheep

2. and losing *one* (*had*) of them,              ONE

3. does not leave the *ninety-nine*            NINETY-NINE
   in the wilderness

We have noted that in stanzas 1 and 2 above, the listening Pharisees (the shepherds of Israel) are challenged by Jesus to see that they have lost their sheep and that they are responsible. In stanza 3, the bad shepherd has turned the corner to becoming the good shepherd. He prepares to go after the one that is lost.

However this is not his only alternative. In the Mishnah tractate Baba Metsiʿa, there is a discussion of the responsibilities of the shepherd in the case of a lost sheep. If the incident of losing the sheep is an "unavoidable accident," the shepherd is not responsible. If attacked by one wolf or two dogs, he should be able to manage and any loss is his fault. But if each of two dogs attacks from a different side of the flock, then the shepherd is not held responsible. The attack of a brigand is an unavoidable accident. The assault of a lion, bear, leopard, panther, or serpent are likewise unavoidable accidents. If the shepherd leads the flock to a "place of wild animals or brigands," then accidents are not counted as unavoidable. It is the shepherd's fault if he leads the flock to the top of a crag. If a sheep dies a natural death, the loss is judged unavoidable, but not so if it dies from cruel treatment (7:8–9; Danby, 360). This Mishnaic legislation may have been formalized in the late first or second centuries. But such legislation often spells out the details of common practice. Natural human failings lead people to start looking for excuses. Any shepherd careless enough to lose his sheep could well start to concoct a story that would prove his innocence or run away perhaps out of fear (cf. John 10:12). Obviously there are ordinarily no witnesses to these things other than the shepherd. With a hundred sheep there is usually an assistant. Yet that assistant will naturally support the shepherd in any story he chooses to tell. Thus is it not *every* shepherd who chooses to search for his sheep.

The Pharisees in the audience no doubt had excuses as to why they were not responsible for the lost of their society. Not so the shepherd of the parable. With no hint of an inner struggle, the shepherd is presumed to have said to himself, "I am responsible. My duty is clear. I will find my sheep."

The ninety-nine are left in the wilderness. This is a point at which there is inevitable tension between the theological purpose of the parable and the story line in the real world of Jesus and his audience. As a Palestinian story, no shepherd would leave ninety-nine sheep alone in the wilderness without some provision for them. As noted, ordinarily a herd of a hundred sheep has two shepherds. In the case of a lost sheep, one would proceed to look for the missing animal and the other would return in due time to the village with the rest of the flock. Or if there is only one man, he will quickly lead his flock across the hill or valley to another shepherd herding nearby, leave his sheep under the neighbor's care and strike out to seek the lost sheep. However none of these details are mentioned. We are convinced that their omission is deliberate. The ninety-nine are left dangling in the wilderness. The story gives no further information about them. Thus, how can the village rejoice over them if they have not yet returned? This subtle theme is there for any perceptive listener/reader to catch.

Its subtleness disappears in the third parable. The guests at the banquet cannot rejoice at the coming home of the older son as long as he is still in the courtyard shouting at his father and refusing to come in! Thus, in this trilogy of parables, Jesus is like Paul in his letter to the Galatians. Paul opens with a gentle "lapel touch" as he writes, "I am astonished that you are so quickly deserting him who called you" (1:6 RSV). But by the time he warms to his topic he is thundering, "O foolish Galatians! Who has bewitched you, before whose eyes Jesus Christ was publicly portrayed as crucified?" (3:1). In each case a gentle hint evolves into a bold statement.

The wilderness theme also provides a subtle tie between the first and third stories in this trilogy. In the parable of the prodigal son, each son, at a critical point in the story, is discovered in the field. Each needs, in the deepest sense, to be brought home. The only one who truly arrives home is the one returned by the costly love of the father as we will observe. The older son, even while standing in the courtyard of the house is yet, in terms of his relationships, in a distant place. In like manner here, both the *one* and the *ninety-nine* are in the wilderness. The one we know is carried home by the shepherd. The fate of the others remains a mystery. So the ninety-nine fade as the story moves on to concentrate on the one that is lost.

---

A. and go after the one that is *lost*    LOST
  B. until he *finds* it? And when he has    FIND
    *found* it,

    C. he lays it on his shoulders [*re-*        REJOICE
        *joicing*] (*hedwah*).

      D. And when he comes *home,*      RESTORE
         he calls together his *friends*
         and *neighbors,*

   C'. saying to them, *"Rejoice*       REJOICE
      (*hedwah*) with me,

  B'. for I have *found* my sheep      FIND

A'. that was *lost."*          LOST

---

The above structure is deliberate with clear rhetorical features. The long speech to the friends and neighbors is consciously constructed so that its themes parallel the first three lines, as can be seen above. The parables of Jesus are brief and natural. The expected cry in this case would be, "I found it!" (which in Semitic languages is a single word). The carefully crafted long speech is deliberate and creates a climax for the stanza. This climax appears in the center and tells of restoration to community. With these literary features in mind the text itself needs examinaton.

The image of the good shepherd is now spelled out. The open pasture lands of Israel/Palestine are rugged. Each rock could have a sheep quivering behind it. Again, with the briefest of strokes an entire picture is painted. The reader is merely told the shepherd goes until he finds it. My shepherd friends of Lebanon and Palestine tell me that a sheep once lost is terrified. It sits down, usually in as sheltered a place as is immediately available and starts shaking and bleating. When found it is in such a state of nervous collapse that it cannot stand or be made to stand. It cannot walk or be led, nor will it respond to the shepherd's well-known call. If it is to be restored to the fold the shepherd must carry it on his two shoulders. The animal can weigh up to 70 pounds. As noted, the country is rugged. It is a mark of the strength, courage, and character of the shepherd that he rejoices when he finds it.

I have named the shepherd's costly rescue "the burden of restoration" (cf. *Cross,* 22–23). Ibn al-Tayyib notes,

74

The lost sheep was exhausted in the Golan Heights, and the shepherd did not beat him but carried him. And in like manner, Christ sought and constantly seeks to return the sinner to holiness and to rescue him from destruction (*Tafsir*, II, 262).

In this action of the shepherd we are convinced that Jesus is setting forth a part of the meaning of his own suffering. Is it possible then that the doctrine of the atonement originates in the parables? Hengel's discussion of the atonement traces the origins of the doctrine to the Upper Room. He writes,

It was not primarily their [the disciples'] own theological reflections, but above all the interpretive sayings of Jesus at the Last Supper which showed them how to understand his death properly (p. 73).

Hengel's study is most helpful. Yet if the mind of Jesus was clear as to the meaning of his death when he approached the Upper Room, we are obliged to ask, Are there any hints from Jesus regarding the significance of his sufferings *before* the Upper Room? I am convinced that in this parable Jesus is specifically addressing that very topic. The shepherd *pays a price* to carry the sheep back to the village. If it is not found and carried back, it will die (cf. Jeremias, *Parables,* 134). The sacrificial action of the shepherd *alone* saves the life of the sheep. This theme of the price paid for salvation is deeply imbedded in each of the three stories under consideration. The understanding of the atonement here set forth may be as significant as is found anywhere in the NT.

In the early centuries the Christian churches of the Middle East seem to have understood this. For them the cross itself was (apparently) too horrifying a symbol for use in worship. The cross as a method of execution was outlawed by Constantine in the fourth century (cf. "Cross," *CBTEL,* II, 588). Before that time early Christian feelings about the use of a cross in worship might be comparable to the feelings of French Christians if someone were to hang a guillotine in the front of the church. A comparison for modern Americans might be the display of an electric chair as a focus for worship. As long as such instruments are in use by the state they are too closely attached to raw brutality for effective use in worship. It seems that early Eastern Christians often chose an alternative to the cross as a symbol of the atonement. The good shepherd carrying

75

a large sheep home over its shoulders was an image that enjoyed widespread use.

There is a magnificent life-size marble statue of just such a good shepherd in the Graeco-Roman Museum in Alexandria, Egypt. A fresco of the same figure appears in the house church at Dura-Europos on the Euphrates, which dates from 232. A third statue (third century A.D.) of the same type is on display at the Rockefeller Museum in Jerusalem. All three of these early representations of the good shepherd share an important, often overlooked feature. In each case the sheep is as large or larger than the shepherd. The Dura-Europos painting has the sheep clearly heavier than the shepherd (cf. *IDB,* supplementary volume, plate XXXVII [between pages 454 and 455]). The statue in Jerusalem presents an enormous sheep that appears to be twice the size of the *smiling* young shepherd. The Alexandrian statue has the two of roughly the same weight. Normally a full grown sheep weighs 50–70 pounds and the shepherd more than twice that much. The creators of these pieces of early Christian art lived in a world of shepherds and sheep. They knew full well the relative sizes of each. Thus we are obliged to conclude that the disproportionate size of the sheep in each case is deliberate and that the artist's intentionality was evident to the viewers of the art. Surely the high price the shepherd must pay to carry such an extraordinary weight is the impression the artist intends to leave with the viewer.

In John, the good shepherd "lays down his life for the sheep" (John 10:11) but does so *fighting wolves,* not carrying the sheep. Matthew has the lost sheep parable, but the sheep is *not* brought home. The shepherd finds the sheep and rejoices over it. There is no record of moving the sheep (Matt. 18:12–14). It is only in Luke that the carrying of the sheep home to the village is mentioned. Thus these artists have picked the good shepherd of Luke 15:4–7 as their model. Is it not possible to suggest that this art, scattered from Egypt to Mesopotamia, is a pictorial representation of the interpretation of the cross which the Eastern Christian community saw in the redeeming actions of the good shepherd in Luke 15:4–7?

By contrast, when the good shepherd (with a lost sheep) appears in the art of the Latin West, the sheep is small and the shepherd large. A good example from the third century is on display in the Lateran Museum in Rome (Finegan, plate 167). The texts from Is.

40:11 and 49:22 are not helpful. The first image is not of a lost sheep but of an exhausted newborn who is too small and weak to keep up with the traveling flock and needs to be carried. The second is of people carrying children.

A further question must be asked which is, Why does the shepherd go after the lost sheep? The answer that the Christian tradition has almost universally given across the centuries is this: He seeks the lost sheep because he loves it. No doubt he does. But on the story level the shepherd is herding these sheep for his benefit, not for theirs. Granted, no parable "stands on all four legs" and some aspect of any metaphor/parable does not fit the intent of the storyteller. Yet we are convinced that meaning has "spilled" into this parable from the good shepherd songs in John 10:1–18. In these latter texts the reader is specifically told that the hireling "cares nothing for the sheep" (v. 13 RSV). The good shepherd by contrast "lays down his life for the sheep" (v. 11). By implication he does so because he *does* care for the sheep. Aside from this one hint there is no indication even in John 10 as to why the shepherd lays down his life for the sheep.

In like manner, the parable under consideration in Luke 15 offers only the slightest hint as to motive. The shepherd is specifically held responsible for the lost sheep. After all, he *is* the shepherd and he has *lost* the sheep. The implication is should not *he* go after it? Other than this, no reasons for the shepherd's actions are indicated. But what of Psalm 23?

If the good shepherd of Psalm 23 is in any way related to the good shepherd of Luke 15, then the former text must be examined. In Psalm 23, popular piety may assume that the good shepherd brings the psalmist back/causes him to repent because he loves him. The text offers another motive. God "brings me back" (v. 3a; my translation) and "leads me in the paths of righteousness" (v. 3b RSV), "for *his* [own] name's sake" (v. 3c).

The OT offers two primary reasons why God acts in history to save. He does so because of his love for his people. He saves "for *their* sake." This is the message of Jeremiah and Hosea (cf. Hos. 11:1–4; Jer. 3:12; 4:19–22; 8:18–22; 13:17; 14:17; 31:20). But Ezekiel and Isaiah tell another story. Ezekiel records the word of the Lord as follows:

77

> Therefore say to the house of Israel, Thus says the Lord GOD: It
> is *not for your sake,* O house of Israel, that I am about to act, but
> *for the sake of my holy name,* which you have profaned among
> the nations to which you came. I will sanctify [make holy] my great
> name . . . and the nations shall know that I am the LORD . . . when
> through you I display my holiness before their eyes (36:22–23).

Verses 32–36 then reaffirm that God is *not* acting for their sake but
rather that the nations will know the power of God to restore.

Isaiah 40–55 echoes the same theme. In these latter chapters
again and again it is the *Holy One* who will reach out to *save* (cf.
Is 41:14; 43:3; 43:14; 47:4; 49:7).

Then in a carefully structured set of parallelisms love and holiness are brought together in Is. 43:1–7, which climaxes in the center
with verses 3–4. Its structure is shown in figure 10.

---

## Figure 10
## Isaiah 43:3–4

1. For I am the LORD your God,
   the *Holy One* of Israel, your *Savior.*

2.     I give Egypt as *your ransom,*
       Ethiopia and Seba in *exchange* for you.

3. Because you are *precious* in my sight,
   and *honored,* and I *love you,*

4.     I give people in *return* for *you,*
       nations in *exchange* for your life.

---

The parallels between 2 and 4 are clear and strong. 1 and 3 also
correspond closely. Thus the passage tells the reader:

> Because God is *holy*—he will *ransom/exchange* you (1, 2).
> Because God is *love*—he will *ransom/exchange* you (3, 4).

Thus the prophets tell the people that God is *love* and out of
his compassion he will save for *their* sake (Jeremiah, Hosea). God

is also *holy* and out of concern for *his holy name* he will save for his sake (Isaiah 40–55, Ezekiel).

The idea of the holiness of God is one of the great themes of the Bible. Jacob observes,

> Holiness is not one divine quality among others, even the chiefest, for it expresses what is characteristic of God and corresponds precisely to his deity ... to the fullness of power and life (p. 86).

In Isaiah, Eichrodt finds holiness expresses "the marvel of his [God's] mode of being" (p. 281). This holiness is in turn profoundly related to honor and glory (Bietenhard, *TDNT,* V, 258). These are the ideas in focus in the Ezekiel passage quoted above. God, affirms Ezekiel, will not save *for your sake,* but he will certainly act in history to save *for his sake.* Thus God promises that he will save to "vindicate the holiness of my great name" (36:23 RSV). The name of God, the holiness of God, the greatness of God are here all bound up with the honor and glory of God. The nations are mocking God because his people are in exile. God will not endure this forever, affirms the prophet. He will act to protect his *holiness* (that is, his *honor* and *glory*).

In Ps. 23:3 it is this latter aspect of the nature of God that is affirmed. The psalmist declares that God my shepherd will come after me and "bring me back" and lead me in the paths of righteousness "for his [own] name's sake." When the shepherd loses a sheep in the wilderness, he goes after it. He does so, not only, and not even primarily because of the sheep itself. Rather he says to himself,

> I never lost a sheep! My *father* never lost a sheep! My *grandfather* never lost a sheep! Let it not be said in the village that I am lazy and afraid. I know who I am and what I must do! If a *good* shepherd loses a sheep, he goes after it until he finds it. *I will find my sheep!*

This is specifically what happens in Psalm 23. Middle Eastern Christians have no difficulty with this concept of God. Westerners, I find, are sometimes troubled. It sounds like self-interest, and thereby ignoble as a motive for God. However in the West we perhaps express some of the same concerns using other words. We raise our children to have a good self-image. Our social scientists tell us that antisocial behavior and lack of motivation grow out of a low self-image. The oppressed everywhere cry out for their personal dignity and worth to be recognized and respected.

The prison literature of the 20th century speaks of the same reality. Shining through the pages of Solzhenitsyn, Ginzburg, Ratushinskaya, and Cheng is the clear message that there is an inner core to the human person that is of supreme value.[5] Namely an inner awareness of worth. In the brutal prisons of this century, that self-worth has been under relentless attack. Those prisoners who surrendered their own sense of worth under the battering of their tormentors lost everything and usually died. This personal sense of worth is known to all people and is identified as good. The prophets affirmed that God also had an integrity that must not be violated. For Ezekiel, Isaiah, and the psalmist, God acts to save "for his name's sake!"

As noted, Ps. 23:3c clearly affirms a motive for the shepherd's actions. Thus, if Psalm 23 stands behind Luke 15 then the same motive applies at least to the shepherd and to the woman, if not to the father. Initially we can observe that the question is not one of replacing love with holiness/honor. For as Is. 43:3–4 brings love and holiness together, even so these same two themes join in the sayings of Jesus. The Lord's Prayer is a primary example. In that prayer the believer is first guided to pray "Our Father." Jeremias has argued convincingly that behind this language is the Aramaic *Abba* which means "daddy" (*Theology*, 60–68). Thus "Our Father" invokes a God of love. The prayer continues, "May thy name be made holy." The verb is a "divine passive." God is here called on to demonstrate his own holiness by his saving action (Jeremias, *Prayer*, 21–23). God is called on to save because he is holy.

A similar combination of love and holiness/honor is surely present in Luke 15 irrespective of its connection to Psalm 23. The weight of the language of the text of Luke 15:4–7 leans in the direction of *holiness/honor* as a motive for action in the case of the shepherd and his lost sheep. The woman in the parable of the lost coin (as we will note) is probably motivated both out of love for the coin and out of concern for her own integrity. The motive of the father in the third story is declared in the text. He is moved by compassion. The second motive may also be present, but the theme of *love* is closer to the surface of the text. Yet surely both themes are also present in each half of the third parable.

So here, the shepherd, no doubt does *love* his sheep. The long search for the lost animal can hardly be empty of that emotion. At the same time, his integrity as a shepherd is critical to him. He has standards he will not violate. He *will* maintain his own sense of worth at any cost. This concern is further reinforced by the shepherd's actions when he returns to the village.

The shepherd calls in his friends. If his motive for saving the lost sheep was strictly that of love, he would spend the evening petting, feeding, and grooming the lost sheep like a man who had just found a lost, much-beloved dog. But the shepherd has preserved the honor of his respectable name. This honor is community related. The community has not witnessed his saving efforts. Thus he calls them in that they might know of and remember the kind of shepherd he is. "Rejoice with me" (indeed, "share my joy"). But also "because *I have found* my sheep" ("hear and remember the story of how *I* saved the sheep!"). Growing out of our cultural presuppositions we in the West have emphasized the first and generally ignored the second. The fact of calling the party is indicaton of his joy *at the preservation of his integrity.* He saved the sheep for "his name's sake!" His party is egocentric. He says, "Rejoice with *me* for *I* have found *my* sheep." The party is in his *honor!*

Middle Eastern custom requires that all guests be served some food and/or drink. The rabbis said, "There is no joyous celebrating without eating and drinking" (BT M.Kat., 9a). This point is often overlooked. The third story closes with a banquet. In miniature form the first two stories likewise close with festive occasions where eating and drinking is assumed. The return of the lost sheep is an occasion for joy, not only for the shepherd, but also for the *community.* The Pharisees have made it into an occasion for complaints.

There is an intriguing possibility regarding this sharp contrast between the reaction of the "friends and neighbors" in the parable who rejoice with the shepherd and the scribes and Pharisees who are offended at Jesus doing the same thing in real life. This is to be found in the fact that the very words "friends and neighbors" (v. 6) overlap remarkably with the word *haberim* that designated the "companions/associates" who banded together to observe the law. Just as the "sinners" of 15:1 can be a translation for the *'am ha-'arets* so here "friends and neighbors" can at least indirectly refer to the *haberim* of the Pharisees.

As an Aramaic (and Syriac) word, *haber* carries the meanings of "friend, neighbor, and associate" (cf. Jastrow, I, 421–22; J. P. Smith, 125). If this meaning is intentional in the mind of Jesus then Jesus is making a very pointed reference. He is saying,

> The shepherd who finds his sheep deliberately calls his friends/ associates in to celebrate *with* him. You are the "friends/associates" of this community. Like them you should rejoice when I bring in a lost tax collector.

To my knowledge the Western exegetical tradition has missed this possibility. Not so the Eastern tradition.

An early Arabic version of the gospel of Luke (Vat. Ar. 18), copied in A.D. 993, translates Luke 15:6b as

> wa da'a al-sadiq wa al-*habirat* al-aqribin (and he called his friend[s] and neighborhood companions/associates).

The striking feature of this Arabic translation is that the very word *habr* appears in the text. As an Arabic word, *habr* does not mean friend/associate. As an Aramaic/Syriac word it does. However the three Syriac versions of the NT (second to seventh centuries) do not use this word in Luke 15:6 even though it was available in the language. Thus the translator of Vatican Arabic 18 did not borrow the word from a Syriac NT. He deliberately chose this word as appropriate for the intent of the text. His reasons are unknown. Did he know of the *haberim* of Middle Eastern rabbinic Judaism? Or did he simply use this Christian Arabic word available to him from Syriac? We cannot tell. In any case the Greek of 15:6b, "tous *philous* kai tous *geitonas,*" and the Aramaic word *haberim* are almost identical in their meaning. Thus, as suggested, the "associates" come to Jesus complaining about his welcome of the lost "people of the land." Jesus then tells a story where the "associates" of the shepherd *rejoice* with the shepherd when *he* finds a lost sheep and brings it home from the wilderness!

In any case, our parable does not picture private feelings of happiness, but a community celebration in honor of a good shepherd who has upheld the honor of his noble profession. Rather than complain, the friends/neighbors/associates rejoice with the shepherd at the success of his costly saving venture.

Remarkably similar tensions appear in Luke 19:1–10 with the story of Zacchaeus, a lost soul found by Jesus. Jesus pays a price to find Zacchaeus and then enters the tax collector's house. At the evening meal (banquet?) Zacchaeus *stands* to speak. He has been reclining at a meal, and he now stands to offer a formal reply in response to the events of the day. The parallels between this account of Zacchaeus and the parable of the lost sheep can be seen as follows:

| Luke 15:1–7 | Luke 19:1–10 |
| --- | --- |
| Pharisees are angry (because Jesus eats with tax collectors) | A crowd is angry (because Jesus enters the house of a tax collector) |
| A lost sheep | Zacchaeus |
| A good shepherd | Jesus |
| A costly search | In public, Jesus chooses the village "collaborator" as his host for the night and enters the collaborator's house |
| A sheep is found | Zacchaeus accepts the offer of love |
| A banquet | Zacchaeus stands at the banquet to respond |

There are some differences. Yet the remarkable list of similarities indicate that what Jesus sets forth in a parable in 15:4–7 is indeed a description of his ministry among the outcasts.

The Christology of the parable is unmistakable. Jesus is under attack for having welcomed and eaten with tax collectors and sinners. Rather than defending his actions, he boldly affirms that he not only welcomes sinners but searches the wilderness in order to find such and at great cost brings them home. There is no mistaking the fact that Jesus is talking about himself. Donahue writes, "Readers are to see in the parable an allusion to God's action made present in the ministry of Jesus to the marginal" (p. 149). What then does Jesus mean by casting himself in this role?

A full answer to the Christological question is only possible after all three parables are studied. The full list of points of contact between Luke 15 and Psalm 23 will also need examination (cf. chap. 5). Yet some initial observations are perhaps worthwhile. At least this much can here be said. In the light of Ezek. 34:1–16 alone, it is possible to affirm with confidence that Jesus (at least) sees himself as the one through whom God is acting to fulfill the promises of the above text. Ezek. 34:15–16 reads,

> I myself will be the shepherd of my sheep . . . says the Lord GOD.
> I will seek the lost, and I will bring back the strayed.

The Pharisees criticize Jesus for finding the lost of Israel. When Jesus replies by creating the parable of the good shepherd, the biblically literate pharisaic audience would almost inevitably have made a connection in their minds (at least) between the words of Jesus and the Ezekiel shepherd parable quoted above. They could hardly escape seeing themselves as the shepherds under criticism and Jesus as claiming to be the agent of God fulfilling the promise of the above text. Thus in the deceptively simple parable of the lost sheep, Jesus in some indefinable sense is proclaiming himself as the presence of God among his people, seeking the lost sheep of the community.

This brings us to a consideration of the concluding Dominical comment.

---

4. Just so, I tell *you,* there will be more          YOU
   *joy* (*hedwah*) in heaven
5. over *one* (*had*) sinner who repents          ONE
6. than over *ninety-nine* righteous per-          NINETY-NINE
   sons who need no repentance.

---

The parable of the vineyard in Is. 5:1–6 is followed in verse 7 by an interpretation and application of the parable. Thus there is prophetic precedent for creating a parable and then attaching interpretation to it. Jesus' meaning is clear. Ibn al-Tayyib notes,

> This means that Jesus is saying, "If the angels are able to rejoice
> at repentant sinners, why are you scribes and Pharisees not able
> to rejoice at their repentance?" (*Tafsir,* II, 266).

The "joy in heaven" is a circumlocution to avoid attributing emotion to God. To do so was not acceptable in rabbinic theological circles (cf. Jeremias, *Parables,* 135).

This Dominical reflection on the parable specifically identifies *repentance* as the central theme. If numbers 4–6 above were not in the text, few listeners (or readers) ancient or modern would have discovered repentance at the center of the parable. If asked, "What is the story all about?" one might answer that the parable discusses

1. the bad shepherd who loses his sheep;
2. the good shepherd who goes after it;
3. the price the shepherd pays both to find and to restore the lost sheep;
4. the rejoicing in community at the restoration.

All of these themes are in the story. But where is the repentance? Who repents? The story tells of a lost sheep found and restored by the costly efforts of the shepherd. The modern reader's familiarity with the text obscures the startling nature of the Dominical conclusion. Indeed, Jesus here *redefines* repentance. All great theologians and philosophers define their terms. Western thinkers formulate their definitions in carefully worded abstractions. But the metaphorical theologian defines his/her terms in story form. The definition is clear and precise. It is more unforgettable than any concept. Yet a conceptual formulation may clarify what Jesus has done. For Jesus, repentance means *acceptance of being found.* Granted, the lost sheep is an animal. It is shaking and bleating in terror and is delighted to be found. But one can talk in only limited terms of the sheep's "acceptance" of the offered rescue. In the second story the coin found is inanimate. It is in the third story that all the actors are people and the full nature of the *acceptance* of being found can be spelled out. Yet this theme is unmistakably introduced in the first story.

Jesus' redefinition of repentance needs to be seen in the light of the understanding of repentance that was held by his audience. The Hebrew word for repentance is the great word *shub* already noted in Ps. 23:3. Its primary meaning is "to return." A great deal of theological energy is expended in the OT on this topic. However, often the return envisaged is a return to the land, to Jerusalem, to Zion, and to the temple. One of the striking features of Isaiah 40–55 is the emphasis on the return *to God.*

Those privileged to live among a refugee people, longing to go home, can fully appreciate the anguish such people feel over their lost homeland. Refugees naturally see themselves as the oppressed, and rightly so. The very oppression which they suffer naturally and understandably colors their theological outlook. Their *oppressors* need to return to *God,* but they, the oppressed, need only to return to their political and geographical inheritance. In this light, Isaiah 40–55 becomes all the more remarkable, if written in the midst of a refugee community on the eve of their physical return to Jerusalem, as many scholars hold. The prophet calls on them to return *to God* and dreams of a suffering servant of Yahweh who will "bring Jacob back to him [God], . . . that Israel might be gathered to him" (49:5). Granted, the same chapters are richly joyous over the physical return to Jerusalem, but remarkably, in that euphoria there is a clear call for a "repentance" defined as a return to God.

Even so, in the teachings of Jesus, repentance is strictly "de-Zionized." That same de-Zionizing is evident in this parable. The repentance proclaimed is shaped by the shepherd images of the OT, but the return/repentance set forth in our text is without the slightest reference to the political aspirations of any ethnic or political group. C. H. Dodd has written,

> I propose . . . starting from the hint contained in several of our sources—Christian, Jewish and pagan—that the hostility which brought about the death of Jesus was due to the character of his teaching, or, more properly, to fear of its effect on society (*More,* 94).

Dodd also notes,

> It was not clear to those who kept watch upon him that Jesus really cared for the national cause. When he was told about Pilate's slaughter of Galilaeans in the temple, he responded not with indignant denunciation of Roman brutality, but with a warning to his own people to 'repent' (Lu. xiii. 1–2) (*More,* 96).

In his commentary on this parable in Matthew, Montefiore writes that the sayings of Jesus are "of a less nationalist tendency than that of the Rabbis" (p. 261). In like manner, here in Luke 15:4–7 repentance/return has no nationalistic application and is strictly focused on a return to God.

But there is yet another side to the shock of this parable. As noted, by omission, Jesus de-Zionizes repentance. But in addition, positively his definition is a radical redefinition of an idea that already had a clearly delineated content. George F. Moore provides a succinct summary where he writes,

> To the Jewish definition of repentance belong the reparation of injuries done to a fellow man in his person, property, or good name, the confession of sin, prayer for forgiveness, and the genuine resolve and endeavor not to fall into the sin again (*Judaism,* I, 117; cf. 507–34).

The above can perhaps be summarized into three elements. These are

1. compensation offered;
2. confession made;
3. resolve/endeavor not to sin again.

Montefiore notes that a large number of persons were unable to come to Jerusalem to offer the statutory sacrifices. They offered their prayers and their repentance instead (p. 392). He writes,

> Even before the destruction of the Temple [in A.D. 70], it is clear that the ethical substitutes for the sin-offering, which afterwards became all-prevailing, had begun their beneficial influence (ibid.).

Then, after the fall of Jerusalem, when the option of sacrifice in the temple was not open, repentance as a substitute became critically important. So much so that the rabbis affirmed that he who truly repents

> is regarded by God as if he had gone to Jerusalem, rebuilt the altar and offered all the sacrifices of the law (Leviticus Rabbah 7:2, quoted by Montefiore, 393).

From all of the above it is evident that repentance in the Tannaitic period, from before the fall of the temple, was a work which the believer completes which in turn could substitute for the atoning sacrifices. Into such a world Jesus offers a radical alternative. Repentance, as defined by the parable under consideration, is not a meritorious work which the believer completes. Rather it is likened to a sheep who does nothing but get lost. The *shepherd* then in turn must come after that sheep and carry it home. The costly action of the shepherd who finds the sheep and carries it home now defines repentance.

In Western literature Francis Thompson's poem "The Hound of Heaven" magnificently catches this new definition of Jesus. The poet confesses,

> I fled Him, down the nights and down the days;
> I fled Him, down the arches of the years;
> I fled Him, down the labyrinthine ways
>     Of my own mind; and in the mist of tears
> I hid from Him, and under running laughter.

As the poem progresses, the poet, still running, hears heavy footsteps behind him and feels the presence of a dark cloud over him. Finally, he terminates his flight and to his amazement discovers that the "footfall" was that of God seeking him and the darkness was only the "Shade of His hand, outstretched caressingly." He ran away and God came after him. Consciously or unknowingly Thompson has caught much of what is set forth about repentance in the deceptively simple parable under study.

Finally then, what is to be said about those "who need no repentance?" In rabbinic circles there were differing opinions offered. First Kings 8:46 states, "there is no one who does not sin." More to the point is the shepherd/sheep imagery of Is. 53:6 which reads,

> All we like sheep have gone astray;
>     we have all turned to our own way,
> and the LORD has laid on him
>     the iniquity of us all.

Ben Sirach notes, "we are all guilty" (Sir. 8:5; cf. Eccl. 7:20).

In spite of these texts there were voices in the intertestament period that claimed sinlessness for some of the great figures of the past. The Prayer of Manasseh, verse 8 (dated ca. second century B.C. to first century A.D.) reads,

> You, therefore, O Lord, God of the righteous,
> did not appoint grace for the righteous,
> such as Abraham, Isaac, and Jacob,
> those who did not sin against you;

but you appointed grace for me, (I) who am a sinner
(*OTP*, II, 634, trans. Charlesworth).

Sinlessness is claimed for Jeremiah in 2 Baruch 9:1 (dated early second century A.D., cf. *OTP*, I, 623, tran. Klijn). The testament of Abraham in Testaments of the Three Patriarchs (dated first to second century A.D.) is ambiguous. Abraham calls himself a sinner (9:3), and shortly after that God affirms that Abraham "has not sinned" (10:14; *OTP*, I, 886–87, tran. Sanders). Thus some in the NT period thought that the patriarchs and the great prophets lived sinless lives.

This idea persisted through the NT period and appears, in a slightly different form, in the Talmud which reads,

> R. Hiyya b. Abba also said in R. Johanan's name: All the prophets prophesied only for repentant sinners: but as for the perfectly righteous [who had never sinned at all], *'the eye hath not seen, O God, beside thee, what he hath prepared for him that waiteth for him.'* Now he differs from R. Abbahu, who said: The place occupied by repentant sinners cannot be attained even by the completely righteous (BT Sanh., 99a).

If Luke 15:4–7 is read in isolation from the rest of the teachings of Jesus and from the other parables of Luke 15, it could be seen as an early witness to the above view of Rabbi Abbahu. But verse 7 is better understood to reflect the fact that the above discussion was already in process. That is, some of the rabbis already believed there were the "perfectly righteous." Jesus is most likely responding to this developing theological view, but is he endorsing it?

It is extremely difficult to attribute such an opinion to Jesus. In the teachings of Jesus we meet those who "trusted in themselves that they were righteous" (Luke 18:9). But the Pharisee in that parable quickly appears very "unrighteous." Luke 15 is clear evidence of this same view.

Here in the parables before us there are three symbolicly represented sets of contrasts between the "sinners" and the "righteous." These are as follows:

---

|  | **"Sinners"** | **"Righteous"** |
|---|---|---|
| 1. vv. 4–7 | lost sheep | ninety-nine sheep |

| 2. vv. 8–10 | lost coin | nine coins |
| 3. vv. 11–32 | prodigal son | older son |

---

In the first parable, the lost sheep is an animal. The coin is an inanimate object. Thus the reader is obliged to wait until a complete cast of *people* walks on stage in the third story to catch the full meaning of the first two. The *prodigal* will clarify the meanings suggested in the symbolism of the lost sheep and lost coin. In like manner, the *older son* will make precise the meanings implied in the ninety-nine sheep and the nine coins.

At the beginning of the third parable the older son is mentioned but remains silent. But when he appears (v. 25), he displays an arrogant self-righteousness that has no love for his brother and no respect even for his father. In Middle Eastern culture the picture painted of this older son is grim and horrifying. Thus, the "ninety-nine righteous persons who need no repentance" must be seen in the light of the older son who, while offending his father and re-jecting his brother, publically announces that he has never broken his father's law. Obviously *in his view* he has done nothing for which he needs to repent. If nothing else, the older son needs to repent from his attitude of thinking that he needs no repentance!

The bold criticism in 15:28–30 of those who think they need no repentance is very carefully woven into 15:4–7. The ninety-nine are last heard of *in the wilderness*. The point is not that they are aban-doned. Nor is this evidence of a non-Palestinian origin to the parable. But rather this very finely sketched nuance is deliberate. There can be little rejoicing in the village over the ninety-nine, for the simple reason that they have not yet appeared! There is no rejoicing in the banquet hall over the presence of the older son while he is still in the courtyard shouting at his father!

In heaven, the angels (God) can be quietly joyful over the fact that the location of the ninety-nine is known and that they are ex-pected. Full joy will only be possible when they are brought home.

Again, if Jesus is a "simple carpenter" talking to "village folk and children" then we cannot assume these clear, yet subtle meanings. But if a brilliant rabbinic theological mind, highly polished through years of debate, is talking to his fellow theologians, then all of this and more is set forth in the text.

Thus it is clear from the description of the older son that verse 7 rings with irony (Plummer, 369). Indeed the assumption of the universality of sin, affirmed in Is. 53:6, is dominant all through the chapter. Both the "righteous" and the "sinners" need to be brought home to God. In this story one is lost, the others are in the wilderness. The prodigal *and* his older brother offend, break relationships with their father, and must be found, as will be noted in the following chapters.

In summary, the parable displays the following themes: The *original* audience of Pharisees and scribes is pressed to make something of the following decision/response:

> We, the shepherds of Israel, have "lost our sheep" and Jesus, acting in God's place, at great cost has found them. Rather than attack him we should rejoice at the restoration of these lost even if Jesus in the process radically redefines repentance.

The theological cluster of this parable (with its introduction) includes the following:

1. *Failed leadership.* The parable contains criticism of leaders who lose their sheep and do nothing but complain about others who go after them.
2. *Freely offered grace.* The sheep offers no service to the shepherd and in no way earns or deserves his rescue. It comes as a gift.
3. *The atonement.* The shepherd pays a high price both to find the sheep and to restore it to the home. The heart of the atonement is thus found in this parable.
4. *Sin.* Humankind is depicted as lost and unable to find its own way home.
5. *Joy.* The joy of the shepherd and the community at the success of the saving event of restoration is set forth.
6. *Repentance.* Repentance is defined as acceptance of being found. The sheep is lost and helpless. Repentance becomes the act of the shepherd in carrying the sheep back to his home in the village and the sheep's acceptance of that act.
7. *Christology.* Jesus is the good shepherd who is the unique agent of God who restores the sinner to God. (The joy *in the home* of the shepherd is equated in the parable to joy *in heaven*.) This

91

shepherd must personally make the costly demonstration of love/ holiness in order to restore the helpless sheep. Three OT texts stand behind the parable. These are Psalm 23; Jer. 23:1–4; and Ezek. 34:11–16. This OT background strongly hints that the shepherd is more than merely an agent, but in some as yet undefined sense is the very presence of God himself among his people seeking his lost sheep.

This brings us to a consideration of the second parable in the trilogy.

# Notes

1. Compare the account of the parable of the lost sheep in Luke (15:1–10) and in Matthew (18:10–14).
2. Compare Luke 14:15–24 with Matt. 22:1–14. The "man" in Luke appears as a king in Matthew, and so forth.
3. The parable of the great banquet discusses both the *outcast* (the poor, blind, etc.) *and* the *outsider* (those in the highways and hedges, outside the village). Luke 15:1–32 includes only the *outcasts*.
4. Paul's emphasis in Romans "to the Jew first and also to the Greek" (1:16) has expression here as well.
5. Cf. Aleksandr Solzhenitsyn, *The Gulag Archipelago* (1973–76); Nien Cheng, *Life and Death in Shanghai* (1986); Irina Ratushinskaya, *Grey Is the Color of Hope* (1988); Eugenia Ginzburg, *Journey into the Whirlwind* (1967) and *Within the Whirlwind* (1979).

# Chapter 2

# The Good Woman and the Lost Coin

## Luke 15:8–10

This parable also has some suprises. In verse 4 Jesus likens the Pharasaic audience to an "unclean" *shepherd*. Here he likens them to a careless *woman* who has lost a precious coin. In Middle Eastern culture a speaker *cannot* compare a male audience to a woman without giving offense.

Jesus does so. His reasons must be explored. The text is as follows (RSV):

---

### Figure 11

### The Lost Coin (Luke 15:8–10)

| | |
|---|---|
| Or *what woman,* having ten silver coins, | INTRODUCTION |
| 1. if she *loses* one coin, | LOST |
| 2. does not light a lamp and sweep the house and seek diligently until she *finds* it? | FOUND |
| 3. And when she has found it, she calls together her friends and neighbors, saying, *"Rejoice with me,* | REJOICE |
| 4. for I have *found* the coin | FOUND |
| 5. which I had *lost."* | LOST |
| Just so, I tell *you,* there is *joy* before the angels of God over one sinner who *repents.* | CONCLUSION |

---

The previous parable opened with "What *man* of you . . ." (RSV). The audience is Pharisees and scribes who were all men. Jesus begins this parable with "Or what *woman* . . ." He leaves off the final "of you" (v. 4) which would offend to no purpose. The offense is serious enough without intensifying the insult. No intelligent speaker knowingly insults any audience to no purpose. We are obliged to assume, as we did earlier, that the offense is given to make a point. What then is the point?

Ps. 23:5 depicts God as preparing a meal. The text reads, "You prepare a table before me." Thus female activity is used to describe the work of God. In Luke 15:8–10 Jesus likens himself to a woman. The possible dependence of Luke 15 on Psalm 23 will be discussed in detail in chapter 5. Here we would concentrate on the fact that Jesus had men and women followers (cf. 8:1–3; 10:38–42) and is clearly eager to communicate to all his disciples. The particular setting recalled in this chapter is an all male audience. The audience most likely did not include either shepherds or women. Jesus includes both. He specifically intends the material to be remembered and retold in a wider context (Bailey, *Informal*). Because the disciples of Jesus were men and women a significant number of his parables were constructed in doublets with one parable created out of the world of women and a second from the life experience of men. Jesus is rare if not unique in this regard.

In the OT, full story parables such as we find in the gospels are few in number yet can be found (cf. 2 Sam. 12:1–6; Is. 5:1–7). However the OT is *full* of similies and metaphors. Parables are almost nonexistent in the Mishnah (A.D. 200) but plentiful in the Babylonian Talmud (ca. A.D. 400). The rarity of parables in the Mishnah is puzzling. Their reappearance in the Babylonian Talmud is delightful evidence that the authors were authentic Middle Easterners and thus used metaphor and parable extensively.

The Jewish oral torah is over four million words. I have thus far read only half of it. But to my limited knowledge, stretching from the beginning of the OT through to the completion of the Talmud of Babylon, with the exception of Jesus, there is only one author who balances together two metaphors/stories, one male and the other female. This is the author of Isaiah 40–55. This prophetic witness has two cases of this rare phenomenon. The first is Is. 51:1–2 which reads as follows (my translation):

### Isaiah 51:1–2

| | |
|---|---|
| Look to the *rock* from which *you* were hewn, | SARAH THE ROCK |
| and to the the *cistern* from which you were *taken out.* | SARAH THE CISTERN |
|     Look to *Abraham* your father<br>    and to *Sarah* who bore you; | PARABLE OF ABRAHAM<br>AND SARAH |
| for when he was but one I *called* him, | ABRAHAM IS CALLED |
| and I *blessed* him and made him many. | ABRAHAM IS BLESSED |

The Hebrew word *bor* is usually translated in the above text as *quarry* rather than *cistern* and thus the first two lines above are both understood to refer to Abraham. But the clear meaning of *bor* is "cistern" which is pear-shaped, that is womb-shaped. The word rock can be feminine. I am convinced that the first two of the above six lines refer to Sarah and the last two to Abraham. In any case Abraham and Sarah are both mentioned and are in parallel in the center.

The second case of a male-famale parallel is from the same prophet and reads as follows (RSV):

### Isaiah 42:13–14

| | |
|---|---|
| The *Lord* goes forth *like a* mighty *man,*<br>  *like a man* of war he stirs up his *fury;* | THE LORD LIKE A MAN<br>SHOUTS IN ANGER |
| he cries out, he shouts aloud,<br>  he shows himself mighty *against his foes.* | |
| For a long time I have held my peace,<br>  I have kept still and restrained myself; | THE LORD LIKE A<br>WOMAN CRIES OUT IN |
| now I will cry out *like a woman* in travail,<br>  I will gasp and pant. | TRAVAIL |

95

This remarkable text has "God is like a man" and "God is like a woman" side by side. Granted, there are numerous other cases in the OT where female imagery is used to enrich our understanding of God (*IDB,* supplementary volume, P. Trible, 966; cf. also Deut. 32:18; Is. 46:3–4; Ps. 131:1–3). A few borderline cases have male and female metaphors mixed together. But the above texts are unique in the fact that the male and female images are dramatically balanced. The teachings of Jesus may well be the only other place where this remarkable feature appears in all Middle Eastern sacred literature, Christian, Jewish, and Muslim. All the more remakable in the case of Jesus is the fact that a *large number* of texts exhibit some form of balancing of material relating to men and women.

Some cases of male-female doubling in the teachings of Jesus are bold and unmistakable, such as the lost sheep and the lost coin under study. Others are more subtle.

---

## Matthew 5:14–15

| | |
|---|---|
| You are the light of the world. | METAPHOR OF LIGHT |
| A city built on a hill cannot be hid. | WORLD OF MEN |
| No one after lighting a lamp | WORLD OF WOMEN |
|    puts it under the bushel basket, | |
|    but on the lampstand, | |
| and it gives light to all in the house. | |

---

After the initial metaphor of light, the reader is presented with two explanatory images. The first is from the world of men in the first century. Men built cities.[1] The second is from the life experience of women. In Middle Eastern village society, the lighting of lamps is considered to be within the categories of "keeping house" and "preparing food" and thus is the task of women. This assumption is as widespread as the assumption that men build the houses. This practice of women lighting the lamps is specifically mentioned in the Jewish tradition in regard to the Sabbath lights (BT Ber., 31b; Mid. Rab. Genesis, 139 (17:8); *Enc. Jud.,* vol. 14, 566).

Other cases of this doubling of male-female metaphors/parables can be located in both Matthew and Mark. But this feature is especially prominent in Luke. The examples in Luke are of two types. First are those cases of a pair of stories with nearly the same thrust. Second are those cases where the editor (Luke or his source) has chosen two accounts with a similar or identical theme. A man, or something to do with men, is central to one account, while a woman or the world of women dominates the other. A list of such pairs that I have discovered in Luke is as follows:

# Parallel Passages on Men and Women in the Gospel of Luke

## *The Birth Narratives*

1. An angel speaks to Zechariah (1:5–20) and to Mary (1:26–38).
2. Mary sings a song (1:46–55) and so does Zechariah (1:68–79).
3. Simeon and Anna receive Jesus in the temple (2:25–38).[2]

## *The Early Ministry of Jesus and Parallels between the Early Ministry and the Jerusalem Document (9:51–19:48)*

4. The woman of Zarephath and Naaman the leper are set forth as examples of faith in 4:24–27.
5. The parable of the mending of the garment (from the life experience of women) and the making of wine (from the experience of men) in 5:36–39.
6. The raising of the dead: one young man (7:11–17) and one young woman (8:49–56).
7. Two texts demonstrate Jesus' concern for sinners in the face of the harsh rejection of the self-righteous. The first is the account of the woman in the house of Simon (7:36–50). The second is the parable of the publican and the Pharisee (18:9–14). In one case the rejected person is a woman and in the other case it is a man.
8. The band of disciples includes men and women (8:1–3). They all have names.
9. Two people are told, "Your faith has saved you." These are the

woman with the flow of blood (8:43–48) and the blind man (18:35–42).

10. The gospel records two clear cases where Jesus becomes defiled with *midras* (contact) uncleanness: he allows the *woman* with the issue of blood to touch him (8:43–48) and he enters the house and spends the night with a *tax collector* (19:1–10).

### *The Jerusalem Document Exclusively*

11. Martha (10:41–42) and the ruler (18:22) each lack one thing.
12. Two parables on assurance of answer to prayer (the friend at midnight [11:5–8] and the unjust judge and the widow [18:1–8]). The main character in the first is a man, and in the second a woman takes the center stage.
13. The poem on the men of Nineveh and the queen of the South (11:29–32).
14. A concern for justice for men servants and women servants (12:45–46) in the interpretation of the parable of the master who comes home from the marriage feast.
15. Divisions in one house include divisions between men and divisions between women (12:51–53).
16. Two healings on the Sabbath occur in the center of the travel narrative. One is of a woman (13:10–16) and the other of a man (14:1–6). The example of the ox and the ass occurs in each. Other similarities between the two texts also occur.
17. The "daughter of Abraham" (13:16) and the "son of Abraham" (19:9).
18. Two brief parables appear in 13:18–21. One is from the life experience of men (the planting of a mustard seed) and the other from the world of women (the leaven in the meal).
19. Disciples of Jesus must demonstrate loyalty to him above loyalty to male and female family members (14:26–27).
20. The double parables of the lost sheep (15:4–7) and the lost coin (15:8–10).
21. The day of the Son of Man: two men in one bed (17:34) and two women grinding (17:35).

## The Passion

22. In debate with the Sadducees Jesus affirms equality between men and women in the resurrection (20:27–36).

23. A poor woman is made the hero of Jesus' observations of gifts given to the treasury. The grammar allows the conclusion that the rich mentioned are men and women. However the Middle Eastern cultural assumption is that they were men (21:1–4).

24. Strangers who offer aid/support at the cross include Simon of Cyrene (23:26) and the women of Jerusalem (23:27).

25. His acquaintances, men and women, who followed him from Galilee, stand at a distance watching the crucifixion. The women are specifically mentioned (23:49).

26. Those present at his burial include Joseph of Arimathea and the women (23:50–56).

27. The empty tomb stories and the resurrection appearances are focused on the women and the disciples. The initial witness is from the *women* to the *men* (24:1–49).

This list is all the more amazing when the position of women in first-century Jewish life is observed. Jeremias has a carefully researched summary (*Jersualem,* 359–76). A thorough and balanced discussion of the place of women in the Talmud is provided by Judith Hauptman (184–212). The grimmest picture is painted by Ben Sirach of Jerusalem (ca. 195 B.C.), where women are harshly attacked (cf. Bailey, *Women,* 56–73). A low point even for Ben Sirach is reached when he writes,

> For the moth comes out of clothes,
>   and a woman's spite out of woman.
> A man's spite is preferable to a woman's kindness;
>   women give rise to shame and reproach (Sir. 42:13–14).

In regard to religious instruction, women were not taught the Torah. The Mishnah records "R. Eliezer [ca. 80–120 A.D.] says: If any man gives his daughter a knowledge of the Law it is as though he taught her lechery" (Sot. 3:4; Danby, 296). Thus from ca. 200 B.C. through to A.D. 200 harsh antifeminine attitudes are reflected in the tradition.

One further item of rabbinic evidence (second century A.D.)

that is specifically related to the parable under consideration reads as follows:

> Rabbi Pinchas ben Jair ... said: "If thou seekest after the words of the Law as after treasures, God will not withold from thee thy reward. It is like a man who lost a sela, or some other coin in his house, and he lighted a lamp until he found it. If, then, a man kindles many lights seeking that which affords but an hour's pleasure in this world, until he finds it, how much rather shouldest thou dig for the words of the Law which assure thee of life in this world and the next, than for treasures" (Midrash Shir-ha-Shirim, i, I, 79b; quoted in Oesterley, 182–83).

This rabbinic story has its own charm and integrity. A full comparison between this parable and Luke 15:8–10 is beyond the scope of this study. In passing we would only note that a *woman* is the hero of Jesus' story, not a man. The coin in Jesus' parable symbolizes a lost person, not unlearned words of Torah. Has Rabbi Pinchas ben Jair heard Jesus' parable of the lost drachma and given it a male setting? Or has each storyteller composed his own parable out of a known traditional motif? In either case Jesus has deliberately chosen a woman as the central figure of his parable.

In the light of the above it can be said that the words and deeds of Jesus, the interests of the oral tradition community, and the attitudes of Luke are all remarkably affirming of both women and men as full and equal participants in the kingdom of God. The importance of women in the kingdom is clearly on the agenda of both Jesus and Luke. Jesus creates parables in doublets, and Luke selects material where men are central and other similar material where woman are in focus.

In regard to the parable at hand one could conclude that the only important aspect of the story of the lost coin is its gender emphasis. But on closer examination this proves not to be the case. Granted, the parable repeats much of what is said theologically in the previous parable of the lost sheep. Yet the second parable has its own unique nuances.

The building material around the northern end of the sea of Galilee is a beautiful very black basalt. The Franciscans have excavated a part of the ancient city of Capernaum, and the Israeli Department of Antiquities has worked extensively in the city of

Chorazin in the hills just above Capernaum. In each site the build-
ings are almost exclusively constructed of the local black rock. The
great synagogue in Capernaum (fourth century A.D.) is an exception
in that it is constructed of white limestone. But even it is built on
the basalt foundations of an earlier synagogue. The houses of common fisher folk in both towns were, without exception, built of the
local basalt. The first-century homes uncovered by the Franciscans
are generally smaller than a one car garage. The windows on display
in reconstructed houses in Chorazin are about six inches high and
placed in the wall about seven feet above the ground. They are little
more than slits. The ancient building techniques produced ceilings
from slabs of the same black basalt. Particularly in Capernaum the
floors of these early fishermen's homes were covered with flat basalt
stones taken from the lake. Cracks between the stones are naturally
wide. Granted, this trilogy of parables has no specific geographical
setting. Yet, Capernaum and the northern end of the Sea of Galilee
was a major center for Jesus during his public ministry. Father
Corbo, the excavator of Capernaum, has described the flooring in
the first-century homes as follows:

> Almost all the loci which we found had a floor made of black
> basalt stones; ... Also the rather deep interstices between the
> stones are filled up with earth in which were found clay sherds
> and some coins. ... The paving with irregular, roundish stones of
> black basalt with deep interstices makes it possible to understand
> real well the context of the Gospel parable of the lost drachma
> (p. 39).

So the picture that would have formed in the minds of at least
some of Jesus' audience is that of a woman in a small room with
walls, floor, and ceiling of black basalt. The windows are very small
and placed above eye level. She has dropped a small silver coin
between the wide cracks in the irregular stone floor. It is little
wonder that the parable reports the lighting of a lamp, the sweeping
of the house and a diligent search.

The question of the value of the coins and the reason for the
diligent search is often debated. Fitzmyer argues that the first man
is rich (with his hundred sheep) and the woman is poor (with her
10 coins). Semitic languages have no verb "to have." The idiom that
translates 15:4 in Arabic and Syriac is *"to him* a hundred sheep."

101

This phrase can mean "he is responsible for a hundred sheep." Granted, a man who owns a hundred sheep is relatively wealthy in the simple villages of the Middle East. But the shepherd in the parable does not necessarily *own* all of them. John 10:3 describes the scene precisely. Everyone living on the narrow village street has a few sheep. Someone (often a son of one of the families in the alley) agrees to shepherd them. Each morning he leaves his own house (with his own sheep), stands in the narrow street and gives his call. The *gatekeeper* opens the gate, not the shepherd. Obviously the shepherd is not a member of the household where the gate-keeper has to open the gate. Rather, the shepherd stands outside and a member of each house in turn must open each gate to let the sheep out. The point is that generally, anyone *owning* a hundred sheep is wealthy enough to hire someone else to shepherd them. A wealthy man would also naturally want to avoid a "proscribed trade" like "herdsman." Thus the position of the "hired hand" (cf. John 10:12) is well enough known to be useful in metaphorical language about the good shepherd. Rich men do not generally wander across the windswept rocky hills in the heat and cold herding sheep.

Furthermore, the woman is not necessarily the poorest of the poor. She has 10 drachmas. The most natural assumption is that these have been given to her by her husband for the needs of the house. It is possible that the 10 are a part of a necklace, in that coins in Middle Eastern village society are occasionally pierced and used in jewelry. This is more often the case with bedouin women than village women. The parables of Jesus are set in the settled valley, not the trackless desert. Furthermore pierced ancient coins are extremely rare which would indicate that the custom of piercing coins was also rare.[3] The flow of the story more naturally assumes "the household cash box" rather than a necklace. Also, a rich-poor contrast would weaken the impact of the two parables. In each parable Jesus models himself as the one who searches. Is he casting himself as both rich and poor? A rich-poor contrast is most likely not intended. A male-female is. As indicated the coin may have been lost from a veil, a necklace or a cash box. In any case, the 10 coins represent 10 days' wages for a laborer. If we find the "cash box" option the most likely assumption, then the story has a very special thrust. In such a case the woman has lost a part of the monthly "paycheck." The parable would then picture a wife who is trusted with a relatively large sum of money for a modest family. At one time she has in hand one third of the month's income. By contrast Ben Sirach suggests,

> With an interfering wife, it is as well to use your seal, and where there are many hands, lock things up. Whatever stores you issue, do it by number and weight, spendings and takings, put everything in writing (Sir. 42:6–7).

Families that function in this fashion can be found in any society. But this is not the model set before us in this parable. Here is a woman who is trusted with the family's income. She is fully responsible for this money, and does not shirk that responsibility. As we will note the woman is a symbol of Jesus. Thus the first parable presents a picture of a "good shepherd." The second tells of a "good woman." Her sterling qualities set forth in the parable are as follows:

1. As noted, she has financial responsibility in the house. She is trusted.[4]

2. She accepts responsibility for having lost the coin. As noted, the shepherd is specifically blamed for the loss of the sheep. However when he assembles his friends he "saves face" by telling them, "Rejoice with me for I have found my sheep *that was lost*." Among his peers he veers away from admitting fault. Not so the woman. The storyteller holds her responsible at the beginning of the parable. In the middle of the story she accepts responsibility by paying the price to find it. But then, amazingly at the end, when all the neighbors are assembled, unlike the shepherd, she *publicly* admits, "Rejoice with me, for I have found the coin *that I had lost*." This is a brave woman. With the exception of the archaic Greek-to-Arabic, the Arabic versions all turn this last verb into a passive. The Old Syriac and the Peshitta do the same (as does NIV).

3. Her diligence in searching for the coin is spelled out with greater detail than is found in the previous story. Once she discovers that the coin is lost, she lights the lamp, sweeps the house, searches diligently until she finds it. In the case of the shepherd, no details of the search are listed. Thus the theme of the *cost* of the *search* has greater emphasis in the second story. The shepherd does pay a high price for *restoration;* a theme that disappears in the second story. Once the coin is found it is automatically restored. Yet the

woman, like the shepherd, does pay a price, only for her it is in her search.

4. She shares her joy and affirms her integrity in a community setting. But her situation differs from that of the shepherd. The friends and neighbors of the shepherd know he has lost a sheep because he does not return to the village at the accustomed time and he will be noted returning alone with one sheep. But the neighborhood does not necessarily know that she has lost a coin. If a coin has fallen from a necklace or veil they will most likely notice. But if a day's wages are lost out of the cash box they certainly will not. In traditional village society wealth is hidden, not displayed. This traditional secrecy is also fine-tuned into the story. The listener/reader knows she had 10 coins. But the neighbors in the parable are not given this information. The woman does not say, "I had 10 coins and lost one." She merely asks her friends to rejoice that she found a coin. (By contrast the villagers know so-and-so herds a hundred sheep.) Thus the woman's public celebration has more self-revelation than that of the shepherd. She could have kept the entire event secret.

Furthermore sheep do wander off. Coins do not! Thus by merely having a party she admits fault. Then, to the amazement of all, she *publicly* admits fault to her friends. Yet she too affirms her integrity. Trusted by her husband, she calls in her friends to hear the story of her diligence in the fulfilment of her responsibilities. "Rejoice with me for *I have found* ..." Like the shepherd's party this celebration is in her *honor.*

5. The worth of a coin is undiminished because it is lost. The sheep may be wounded or the wool damaged. The prodigal may be "messed up" as a person by his experiences in the far country. But the coin loses nothing of its value by being lost. This may be a partial explanation as to why this kind of an inanimate object was chosen by Jesus for such a theme. In human terms "the lost" almost universally consider themselves worthless. This parable specifically denies that assumption.[5]

As in the first parable, we are obliged to reflect on the reason for the search. Why does the woman seek the coin? If the necklace theory is followed, then the evident answer is that this particular piece of jewelry has sentimental value. She loves it. Its beauty is critically damaged if a coin is missing. So she goes after it. But if our cash-box suggestion is followed then the affirmation of her own integrity becomes an important theme. If a piece of her jewelry has a coin missing, she will be saying to herself,

> My beautiful necklace! It will be ruined if I don't find that missing coin!

But if a day's wages are missing from the cash-in-hand, she will reflect,

> I have lost a day's wages. I have not been out since I last knew I had it. It is in the house. It *can* be found. I am *always* careful of our meager resources. The "good woman" of the book of Proverbs *"provides* food for her household," and "she does [her husband] good, and not harm, all the days of her life." This is who I am. I *will find* the lost drachma.

This latter possibility reflects the "for his [own] name's sake" of Ps. 23:3 and the holiness theme of Ezek. 36:22–23.

A part of what drives her is that she *knows* it is in the house. In the parable there is no hint of a possible search of the street or the neighbor's courtyard. With sufficient effort she *can* find it. This theme is stronger in the second parable than in the first. The lost sheep is out there in the open spaces of the wilderness and may be devoured, stolen or never found. Not so the coin. This self-respecting woman will not cease the search until it is located. The Dominical conclusion (v. 10) is similar to that of the previous parable (v. 7). Again the joy of the neighbors over the coin found is a mirror of the joy of heaven over a found/repentant sinner. Jesus is thereby saying to his Pharisaic audience,

> The angels in heaven (God) rejoice when a sinner is found. Surely you the *haberim* can join us! If *heaven* rejoices, is celebration so impossible for you?

Again repentance = being found. What then is Jesus saying in this parable?

No two metaphors have exactly the same nuances. Yet the theological cluster of this parable includes some themes that are nearly identical to those noted in the previous text. These include the following:

1. *Costly grace.* A good woman pays a high price to find the lost coin.

2. *Atonement.* The above mentioned grace *finds* the coin. Without this effort the coin will be lost forever. It will not find itself nor can it cooperate in the process. The search is successful. The theme of the atonement is unmistakably present.

3. *Sin.* Humankind is here likened to a lifeless coin, lost and nearly hidden on the floor of a dark room.

4. *Joy.* Again the friends and companions (*haberoth*) rejoice with the woman. The possibility that they might sit in judgment over her for her saving efforts is absurd. Heaven itself rejoices! How could the *haberim* fail to do so?

5. *Repentance.* The lost coin is completely inanimate and yet is a symbol of repentance. The sheep's bleating provides *some* help to the shepherd who seeks his lost one. But here the total un-qualified weight of the rescue operation is on the actions of the woman. Thus again repentance is being found.

Other themes in this parable seem to move significantly beyond the parable of the lost sheep. Among these the following can be noted:

6. The undiminished *worth* of the coin has a unique emphasis in this parable as noted.

7. *Christology.* The first story presents "Jesus the good shepherd." Here the text reflects on "Jesus the good woman." The church historically has chosen to recognize and proclaim the first while ignoring the second. This traditional attitude can be seen as disloyal to the teachings of Jesus. The question must be asked: Has not the church sustained a significant loss of potential spiri-tuality as a result?

8. *Holiness/love* as a spring of saving action. If anything, the holi-ness theme is here dominant. The woman acts primarily "for her own name's sake."

9. *The worth of women.* The reader of Luke's gospel has just read where Jesus likens himself to a mother hen (13:34). Here he is a good woman. Prior to Jesus, Ben Sirach wrote, "the birth of a daughter is a loss" (Sir. 22:3b). Relatively soon after the time of Jesus, the rabbis were praying each day thanking God that they had not been created women (Hauptman, 196). In the first parable Jesus boldly says, "You should be like this 'unclean' shepherd." In his parable he affirms, "I am like this woman! I

search for the lost. What about you?" In the process Jesus elevates the worth of all women by his choice of imagery.

10. *The hope of success in finding the lost*. This theme is clearly intensified as noted. The outcome of the shepherd's search, in spite of his determination, is uncertain. The woman's diligence is assured success.

Again, a bold picture alive with bright colors reflecting great theological themes was created by Jesus with the briefest of strokes. The chapter then moves on to the climax of the trilogy.

# Notes

1. The NRSV (as above) reads "a city *built* on a hill." The verb *keimai* literally means "lie, recline, or place." The intent in this text is certainly "built" as appears in the NRSV. This appropriate meaning was also chosen by the translators of the famous Vatican Arabic 13 (eighth century A.D.).

2. Anna does not speak. So why is she mentioned? Luke apparently had her name, but no recorded speech in his sources. Yet he recalls her presence in the account. Luke it appears had a deep concern to affirm that Jesus had come for *men and women,* and so Luke included Anna in his gospel even though no word from her was available to him.

3. The Mishnah reads, "If a *denar* had become defective and was fashioned for hanging around a young girl's neck, it is susceptible to uncleanness" (Kel. 12:7; Danby, 622). This text is interesting in that it mentions coins made into a necklace, but they are *defective* coins. There is no hint in our parable that the coins are damaged. The Mishnah also mentions a veil worth 12 hundred *denars* (B.B. 9:7; Danby, 379). In this case precious stones would be assumed to be sewn into the veil. I have seen bedouin women with veils displaying perhaps two hundred coins but not more.

4. The insistence that women are to be trusted with finance also occurs in the story of Mary's anointing of the feet of Jesus in John 12:1–8. Judas bluntly affirms that her money was ill-spent. The assumption of his remark is, "If we men had controlled this money, waste like this would not have occurred!" Jesus replies by insisting that such is not the case and that she is to be left to make her own financial decisions about her own resources. Luke 8:1–3 also mentions women who are responsible for finance. By mentioning them in this manner the tradition offers indirect praise and gratitude for their financial contributions to the ministry of Jesus. Again a sharp contrast can be found in Ben Sirach who affirms, "Bad temper, insolence and shame hold sway where the wife supports the husband" (Sir. 25:22). Behind Ben Sirach, in the book of Proverbs the good wife is deeply involved in finance. She buys real estate (31:16), engages in business (31:18, 24), and gives to the poor (31:20). That good woman, like the good woman of our parable, is *trusted* by her husband (31:11). Thus Jesus

appears to be returning to positive affirmations about women available to him in the tradition.

5. One consideration might slightly modify this aspect of the parable. The Mishnaic discussion of *Toharoth* (purity) discusses things lost and says,

> If a man lost aught and found it the same day, it remains clean. If he lost it during the day and found it during the night, or lost it during the night and found it the next day, or lost it on one day and found it on the next, it becomes unclean. This is the general rule: If a night or part of a night has passed over it, it becomes unclean (Toh. 8:3; Danby 727).

If the woman has these considerations in mind, her inner pressure to find the coin would be intensified. She would want to find it before it becomes unclean. Yet, even if rendered unclean by the passing of a night, it could be purified and restored to full value.

# Chapter 3

# The Good Father and His Two Lost Sons

## Part 1: The Younger Son
## Luke 15:11–24

Thomas Carlyle once described his *History of the French Revolution* as having come "direct and flaming from the heart of a living man" (Stewart, 148). Clearly Carlyle's stance in regard to his subject was not that of a dispassionate objective observer. With no intent to hint at lofty comparisons, I am obliged to say that some such language describes my attitude toward this matchless parable. For over 30 years, in Arabic and in English, in the Middle East and across the Western world, it has been my privilege to study and teach this great text. The goal has always been to rediscover its authentic Middle Eastern cultural assumptions and to understand its theological content in the light of those assumptions. What appears below is an attempt to display the flame that across the centuries has kindled many hearts and in these latter decades has set fire to my own as well. The reader alone can judge the success or failure of the effort.

The parable is divided into two halves. The text of the first half is found in figure 12 (my translation).

As in previous chapters, the summary words to the right of each stanza attempt to show the inverted parallelisms of the story. Any Middle Eastern son who requests his inheritance from a healthy father is understood to want his father to die. Such a son is indeed *dead* (1) to the family. At the conclusion of this section the father affirms that the prodigal was indeed *dead* (1) but that now he is *alive* (8). The two stanzas form a pair.

I have labeled stanza 2 *all is lost*. He loses everything in two ways. First he loses his family by radically breaking relationships

109

## Figure 12
## Two Sons Have I Not—Part 1 (Luke 15:11–24)

There was a man who had two sons;

| | | |
|---|---|---|
| 1. | A. and the younger of them said to his father,<br>"Father! *Give me* the share of the *property* that will belong to me."<br>And he divided his property between them. | DEATH |
| 2. | B. Not many days later the younger son *sold all* he had,<br>traveled to a distant country,<br>and *wasted* his *property* in extravagant living.<br>And when he had *spent everything,*<br>a severe famine took place in that country<br>and *he* began to be in *need.* | ALL IS LOST |
| 3. | C. So he went and joined himself<br>to one of the *citizens* of that country.<br>And he *sent him* to his fields to *feed* the *pigs.*<br>And he would gladly have filled himself with the pods<br>that the pigs were eating,<br>and *no one gave him anything.* | REJECTION |
| 4. | D. And when he *came* to *himself* he said,<br>"How many of my father's *craftsmen*<br>have *bread enough* and to spare,<br>but here I am dying of *hunger!* | THE<br>PROBLEM? |
| 5. | D. I will *arise* and *go* to my *father* and say to him,<br>'Father, *I* have *sinned* against heaven and before<br>you<br>and am not now worthy to be called your son.<br>Fashion out of me a *craftsman.'* "<br>And *he arose* and *came* to his *father.* | THE<br>SOLUTION? |
| 6. | C. And while he was still at a *great distance,*<br>his *father saw* him<br>and had *compassion* and *ran*<br>and *fell* upon his *neck*<br>and *kissed* him. | ACCEPTANCE |
| 7. | B. And the son said to the father,<br>"Father, I have sinned against heaven and before you<br>and am *not now worthy* to be called your *son."*<br>And the father said to the servants,<br>"Bring quickly the *best robe* and put it on him,<br>and put a *ring* on his hands and *sandals* on his feet; | ALL IS RESTORED |
| 8. | A. and bring the *fatted calf* and kill it,<br>and let us eat and celebrate,<br>for this my son was *dead* and is *alive,*<br>he was *lost* and is *found."*<br>And they began to celebrate. | RESURRECTION |

(Revised from Bailey, *Poet,* 159–60)

with it, as we will see. He then loses everything again in the distant country. In stanza 7 *all is restored* by the actions of the father. The father does this by ordering the servants to dress him in the father's own best robe, by instructing them to give him a signet ring and by ordering a banquet. Again the two form a pair. The next pair of scenes, labeled *rejection* and *acceptance,* are even more striking. On the one hand (3) the prodigal is reduced to feeding pigs and begging. The contrasting scene (6) is the turning point of the entire story.[1] In the center the prodigal analyzes his problem (4) and projects his own solution (5). In the opening scenes, the dominating figure is the prodigal (1–5). Starting just past the center, the last three scenes focus on the father (6–8). With this overall structure in mind, we turn to the details of the text.

---

There was a man who had two sons;
1. A. and the younger of them said to his father,
   "Father! *Give me* the share of the *property*
   that will belong to me."
   And he divided his property between them.          DEATH

---

Some have argued that the two halves of this parable are actually two separate parables. The first is thought to be exclusively about the prodigal while the second focuses on the older son.[2] Such is not the case. Here in the opening scene the older son appears twice. The text announces a story about a father and *two* sons (15:11), and the father divides the property between *them* (v. 12). Thus all three major characters in the parable appear in the opening verses. The same can be said for each of the two previous stories.

The first parable (vv. 4–7) is not two stories, one of which tells of the lost sheep and a second which focuses on the ninety-nine. Rather the interaction between the shepherd, the lost sheep, and the ninety-nine is an integral part of the tension of the story (as a whole) from its beginning. The same can be said of the second parable. The woman, the lost coin, and the nine coins *together* make up the story. So here, the older son enters the story (off stage) at the very beginning. The tensions between the three are critical from the start. Through verse 10 the "righteous" (*haberim*) and the "sinners" (*'am ha-'arets*) have been represented by animals and coins. Now *people* appear, and each of the three major characters is mentioned twice in the two opening verses.

After the list of main characters is announced (v. 11), the Middle Eastern mind automatically attributes the following rank to the three:

First: father
Second: older son
Third: younger son

Thus the reader is startled to hear the opening speech delivered by the lowest ranking member of the family. But the real shock is the speech itself. As noted, in Middle Eastern culture, to ask for the inheritance while the father is still alive is to wish him *dead*. A traditional Middle Eastern father can only respond one way. He is expected to refuse and drive the boy out of the house with verbal if not physical blows.

It is illuminating to observe commentators from West and East as they reflect on this opening thrust of the parable. B. T. D. Smith writes,

The request of the younger son, with which the story begins, is evidently not to be regarded as blameworthy, nor yet his journey abroad after having realized his share of the property (p. 194).

Oesterley finds the request "quite in accordance with the conditions of the time" (p. 183). Plummer notes, "We may say, then, that the younger son was not making an unheard of claim" (p. 372). Fitzmyer argues that Ben Sirach's caution *against* a father giving his inheritance to his children while he is alive (Sir. 33:19–23) is evidence "that it must have been common enough" (*Luke*, II, 1087; Marshall does not discuss the problem, p. 607). This view of Ben Sirach as a key to understanding the prodigal's request was set forth by T. W. Manson in 1937 (p. 287). I find the logic faulty. Are we to conclude from Shakespeare's play *King Lear* that Elizabethan fathers, while in midlife, commonly surrendered their property to their children? If an Armenian father raises his children with the admonition, "Don't trust the Turks!" are we to conclude that Armenians commonly trust Turks and thus a caution against doing so is expressed by an Armenian father? If the decalog is displayed in a Jewish synagogue, does this mean that the congregation is full of idoloters, idol makers, blasphemers of the name of God, breakers of the Sabbath, murderers, adulterers, and thieves? Or rather does it mean that the community is publicly announcing, "These are the standards we live by"? The sage of the Middle East does not focus on "solving contemporary problems" but rather records the wisdom of the ages as distilled from centuries of human experience. Thus Ben Sirach's words are best understood as a reflection of community standards rather than the words of a moralist trying to reform community errors. What then of Eastern Christian commentators?

Ibn al-Tayyib comments on the prodigal's request as follows:

> This is an illegitimate request! The son has no right to make such a request. There is no evidence that such a gift was even possible under Jewish law. Granted, Abraham divided his inheritance among his sons while he was still alive. But he did this *out of his own choosing* [emphasis mine] to keep the family from splitting apart (Gen. 25:5–6). But this son has made his request for his own physical pleasures (*Tafsir,* II, 267).

Ibn al-Salibi describes the views of the prodigal in this opening scene as "despicable and childish" (p. 153). Neither of these classical authors belabors the point. To do so would be like explaining snow to the Eskimos. What everybody understands and accepts needs no extended clarification and defense. Ibrahim Sa'id, an Egyptian protestant scholar of the last generation, writes,

> "Give me the portion that falls to me." This means the younger son considered it a misfortune to live under his father's roof and that he tired of obedience to his father, choosing rather separation and pleasure. For indeed, sin in its origins is the seeking of distance from God (p. 396).

Again Sa'id evidences no need to defend or explain his point. He, like Ibn al-Tayyib, is triggering universally known, time-honored attitudes in our Middle Eastern world. Lachs, a modern American Jew, writes, "Here the younger son requests immediate possession of what would normally have come to him only at the death of his father" (pp. 307–8). This point of culture is a watershed. Ibn al-Tayyib, Ibn al-Salibi, and Sa'id take the interpreter one way and the

Western commentators mentioned above lead another. My own 35-year search for Middle Eastern literary parallels from any age and in any Semitic language has produced nothing. Two cases from contemporary life have already been reported.[3] Both affirm the deep sense of shock and rejection that such a rare request occasions here in the Middle East. Levison ably summarizes the matter by saying, "There is no law or custom among the Jews or Arabs which entitles the son to a share of the father's wealth while the father is still alive" (p. 156).

Thus if such a request is made, the father is expected to explode with anger and refuse. As noted, Ben Sirach's advice was, "when death is approaching, is the time to distribute your inheritance" (Sir. 33:23). The Babylonian Talmud identifies "he who transfers his property to his children in his lifetime" as among those who "cry out and are not answered" (B.M., 75b). Furthermore, both of these texts offer advice to the *father* and tell him not to distribute his wealth while he is alive. But the case of a *son requesting* the inheritance is not discussed. It is too unthinkable to contemplate. The prodigal makes such a request. The father's granting of the request makes clear that the character of the father in the parable is not modeled after a traditional Middle Eastern patriarch. As Sa'id has written,

> The shepherd in his search for the sheep, and the woman in her search for the coin, do not do anything out of the ordinary beyond what anyone in their place would do. But the actions of the father in the third story are unique, marvelous, divine actions which have not been done by any earthly father in the past (p. 396).

On three different occasions the father in this parable clearly violates the traditional expectations of a Middle Eastern father. This is the first of them. An awareness of the redefinition of the word *father* that takes place in this story is critical for the theology of Jesus in general and for the theological content of this parable in particular.

The use of the word *father* in reference to God appears in the OT (cf. Deut. 32:6; Ps. 2:7; 89:26; Is. 63:16; 64:8; Jer. 3:4, 19; 31:9; Mal. 1:6; 2:10). Jeremias argues for the uniqueness of the use of this word by Jesus. The tradition uses the word father to *describe* God. Jesus alone *addressed* God as an individual with the title *Abba*

114

(*Promise,* 9–30; *Theology,* 61–68). Jeremias' point is well made. However this parable seems to be adding a different dimension to the topic. Jeremias focused on *how* Jesus used the word (as an individual using *father* as a title). This parable sheds critical light on what Jesus *meant* when he used it. Responsible theologians and philosophers define their terms. I am convinced that Jesus not only called God "Father" but spelled out his meaning. As noted above, the Western world expects definitions in abstract concepts. Jesus, as a metaphorical theologian, has defined the term *father* in a story—this story.

The current Western discussion of how to name God seems to assume that the word *father* in the Bible is always modeled after an ancient Middle Eastern patriarch. The literature refers constantly to the "patriarchal" model, or metaphor for God. As such, the term is now seen by some as a major ideological force throughout Christian history that has denied rights and freedoms to women.[4] The literature on this subject is enormous and the contemporary debate beyond the scope of this study. However, a clarified understanding of the central figure of this parable as seen in the light of Middle Eastern culture may be relevant for many aspects of that debate. Two lists appear to be emerging. They are as follows:

| **Male** | **Female** |
| --- | --- |
| rule | love |
| order | compassion |
| discipline | suffering |
| rationality | sensitivity to feelings |
| judgment | new birth |
| authority | gentleness |
| power | kindness |
| | patience |
| | forgiveness |
| | yearning for reconciliation |
| | creativity in new relationships |

As the characteristics of the father in this parable are demonstrated it will become increasingly evident that key items in each list contribute significantly to this central figure in the parable. The lists themselves are not helpful. The dominant characteristics of some women and some men can be found in the first or the second list.

As regards our subject, the nature of a Middle Eastern father is unimportant, except as Middle Eastern Christians take it as a model for God, which this parable does not justify. Likewise the nature of a Western father is irrelevant except as Western Christians have historically taken their own cultural perceptions of a father as a model for God, which is also disloyal to the intent of Jesus. What is of major importance is that Jesus does not merely name God "Father," but goes on to define his term. The primary title for God chosen by Jesus can only be historically and scientifically evaluated after a careful examination of his own definition of that same title. As the story progresses, the picture of the father emerges slowly like a photo in the developer. Yet its bold outlines can be seen from the beginning.

Rather than strike the boy across the face for his insolence, the father *grants* the request. The father is able to extend this costly form of grace because he is willing to endure the agony of rejected love. This agony is the most painful form of suffering known to the human spirit. The greater the love, the greater the pain when that love is not accepted. It is out of his rejection of his father's love that the prodigal makes his request. It is out of the father's costly love that he grants that same request. In the process the father grants the ultimate form of freedom, namely the freedom to reject the offered relationship. Thus in this first scene the prodigal receives grace in three interrelated forms. These are as follows:

1. He is assigned his share of the inheritance.
2. The father's willingness to act out of his love rather than out of his pain is a second gift of which the prodigal is not (apparently) aware.
3. The freedom to break his relationships with the family by selling and leave town *with his inheritance* is yet a third gift.

This third gift makes clear that the son presses for a second unimaginable privilege.

The Jewish law of inheritance is carefully spelled out in the Mishnah. The critical text is as follows:

> R. Jose says: If a man assigned his goods to his son to be his after his death, the father cannot sell them since they are assigned to

116

his son, and the son cannot sell them since they are in the father's possession. If his father sold them, they are sold [only] until he dies; if the son sold them, the buyer has no claim on them until the father dies. The father may pluck up [the crop . . .] and give to eat to whom he will, and if he left anything already plucked up, it belongs to his heirs (*B.B.* 8:7; Danby, 377).

This text provides the legal framework assumed in the parable. The rabbi quoted is Jose ben Halafta (A.D. 140–65; cf. Danby, 827). Thus the text is early and can be considered as reflecting the legal attitudes of the period. The assumptions of the above text are clear. The *father* will (of course) initiate the discussion. The sons will have the right to *dispose* of the property only *after* the father dies. In the meantime the father can spend the income from the estate as he chooses. What the father does not spend is added to the capital. So in our story, the father at the end of the parable has the full right to butcher the (young) fatted calves. But if the father entertains infrequently and modestly, then the capital of the estate will gradually increase *to the older son's eventual benefit*. This is an important part of the tensions of the story at the end of the parable. But the legal description of the Mishnah noted above has *no* provision for a younger son pressing for a division of the inheritance. No culture sorts out legal precedence for social situations that will (naturally) *never* happen. If they do happen they will be dealt with automatically. The wisdom tradition may offer some advice but laws are unnecessary. The boy (of course) will be thrashed and denied his request. So the above Mishnah text indirectly heightens the unthinkable nature of the prodigal's request.

But the Baba Bathra legislation, noted above, is significant for another reason. It is clear that the son cannot finalize the sale of the property until the father dies. The son may sell, but the buyer does not gain control over his purchase until the father is gone.

In the parable the reader is told that the son "gathered all he had," which the NEB rightly translates "turned the whole of his share into cash" (Marshall, 607–8; Fitzmyer, *Luke,* II, 1087). So the text specifically tells the reader that the prodigal initially presses for the right of *possession* as regards his inheritance. But the text then assumes that he also manages to pressure his father into allowing him to *dispose* of that same inheritance. Granted, the Mishnah allows for the son to sell but, as noted, the buyer must wait for the death of the father to gain control over the purchase. Such legislation would be meaningful when a father was in his last days. But it is hard to imagine a buyer willing to tie up his capital for what might prove to be decades. The parable specifies a younger son and assumes a *healthy, active* father who directs servants and hosts great banquets. This is not a tottering old man in his last days. The prodigal is presumably unmarried and thus under 20 years of age (Jeremias, *Parables,* 129). His father is in the prime of life. The clear assumption of the story is that the prodigal manages (with his father in good health) to extract from his father the full right to dispose of his inheritance. Only if he did would he be able to sell and take the money with him.

Why then does the father do this? Godet provides a simple and yet profound answer where he writes, "God gives such a man over to his folly" (p. 376). Godet finds a parallel in Romans 1:24, 26, 28, where Paul wrote, "God gave them up." A deeper reason is that such an action grows out of the father's nature. He is willing to grant ultimate freedom: the freedom to reject the love offered to him by a compassionate father (cf. Donahue, 160–62).

Scott makes the interesting point that the younger son in the OT is often the favored son (pp. 111–13). Abel, Isaac, Jacob, Joseph, Benjamin, Moses, David, and Solomon were all younger sons. However, in their youth, these worthies were generally not rogues. Jacob is the clear exception, who does manage to get a rich blessing out of his father through devious means. But he has to *trick* the father to get it. Furthermore what he gets is a blessing to which he had no right, neither then nor at the death of his father. So the parallel is relatively weak. The other younger sons were generally favorites but not prodigals. However Scott's thoughtful observation opens three interesting possibilities.

1. If the audience assumed a younger favorite son, they would have been all the more suprised at the total lack of response to that favoritism on the part of the prodigal. Rather than basking in his special privileges, he verbally attacks his father with the cultural equivalent of "Why don't you drop dead?" What then (the audience would ask) is the father going to do with *this kind* of a favorite son? Surely he will be put in his place for gross ingratitude! Joseph may have been a bit proud, but his loyalty to his father was complete! Isaac's blessing was not granted knowingly to Jacob, who then was

obliged to flee for his life! The prodigal is open and blatant. The father is not deceived. Surely some harsh disciplinary action will be inevitable! Such would be the audience response if the "favorite son" theme is introduced. Thus the actions of *this* father become all the more remarkable.

2. There is a further possibility. In the parable, *this* younger son is a symbol of the audience's opponents, the sinners. If the prodigal is intended to be a "favorite son," then Jesus could be saying to his audience,

> Favorite younger sons are *great* men in the tradition—so I tell you a story of a favorite younger son. Jacob was less than perfect. Why do you so despise these people?

3. Finally, if the "favorite younger son" is an intentional under-current of the parable, the audience would watch with interest and understanding when the father welcomes the younger son home. The question in their minds would then be, "Will the father show *similar* love to his nonfavorite older son?" As we will see, the father does just that. Thereby, if there are any "favorite son" thoughts lingering in the minds of the audience, at the end of the story, they would evaporate when the father offers the same costly love to the older son as he extended to the younger son.

To conclude, the possible "favorite son" theme appears to evaporate as the parable comes to its conclusion.

So the prodigal requests his portion of the family estate with his father in the community enjoying good health. In a costly demonstration of unexpected love the Father grants the request. Hurt and anger are reprocessed into grace. The text simply reads, "he divided his *life* [*bios*] between them" (my translation). The primary meaning of *bios* in Biblical Greek is not *living*, but *life* itself (cf. Luke 8:14). The archaic Greek-to-Arabic translation has "he divided his *life* between them" (not "his living"). Ibn al-ʿAssal and Vatican Coptic 10 do the same. This detail is fully authentic to our Middle Eastern world. The family inheritance is *life* for that family. Naboth will die, but he will not sell the land of his fathers, even to the king (1 Kings 21:1–16).

The American musical *Oklahoma* reflects similar attitudes with the words,

We know we belong to the land,
and the land we belong to is grand!

The singer does not say, "the land belongs to us." If such were the case it could be sold and other real estate purchased. But if *we* belong to the *land,* our identity is irrevocably tied up with the land itself. Even so today, each of two communities in the Holy Land cries out, "Give us the land of our fathers!" Neither can accept other land somewhere else without loss of identity. Such is the deep attachment to the land in traditional Middle Eastern culture. In the parable, the father gives away his very *life* when he acquiesces to the heartless pressure from his younger son. The form of the inheritance becomes the next question.

The parable depicts a wealthy family. There *is* an inheritance to divide. They have fatted calves and slaves. At Middle Eastern banquets, meat is butchered on the basis of the number of guests. So the picture painted at the end of the parable is that of a family with a banquet hall large enough to accommodate the two hundred or more people required to eat a fatted calf. They can afford paid entertainers who will provide music and dancing (v. 25). A landed estate is the assumption all through the parable. The boy is given deeds to property, which (as noted) he proceeds to sell.

Deut. 21:17 stipulates that the older son receive twice the portion of the younger. This was modified by the rabbis who wrote,

> If a man apportioned his property to his sons by word of mouth, and gave much to one and little to another, or made them equal with the firstborn, his words remain valid (M B.B. 8:5; Danby, 377).

Thus we cannot determine with any certainty how much of the estate was assigned to the prodigal. But it is clear that the estate itself is sizable. In any case the prodigal receives enough to finance the journey into a far country and to sustain himself there for a fairly long time (*great* famines do not happen over night). So what happens in the home village when the prodigal offers his inheritance for sale? This brings us to scene 2. The text is as follows:

2. B. Not many days later the younger son *sold all* he had,
traveled to a distant country,
and *wasted* his *property* in extravagant living.
And when he had *spent everything*,             ALL IS LOST
a severe famine took place in that country
and *he* began to be in *need.*

Again, with the briefest of strokes, Jesus paints an entire picture. The prodigal sets out in the village to sell his own life/land/inheritance with his father in good health and living in the village! The town is outraged! This is demonstrated by the fact that the prodigal completes all transactions in "not many days." The settling of an estate is a slow process anywhere in the world. Sale of land in the Middle East takes months and often years. This young man sells quickly. Someone in the community buys. But the community at large is horrified! The prodigal is selling his own soul and insulting his father publicly by making public what has happened between them. The hostility of the community dictates his haste.

Ben Sirach declares "slander by a whole town" to be a terror worse than death (Sir. 26:5). This slander can be endured for only a limited time. So he quickly sells and leaves. But he leaves with a Damocles sword hanging over his head. This sword is the *qetsatsah* ceremony.

The Aramaic word *qetsatsah* means "cutting off." The ceremony is described in Midrash Rabbah, Ruth (7:11 on 4:7) and in the Jerusalem Talmud (Ket. 2:10; Kidd. 1:5). The Ruth Rabbah explains that if a man "sold his field to a gentile," the relatives would bring parched corn and nuts, place them in a jar and break the jar in front of the people as they proclaimed, "So-and-so is cut off from his inheritance." The tractate Ketuboth 2:10 (JT) does not mention the Gentile. It affirms that if a man sold to *anyone,* the ceremony could be enacted. Only restoration of the land could revoke the "cutting off" of the offending person. If we take this earlier Jerusalem Talmud text as more likely to repesent the first century, the threat is even

121

stronger. The prodigal has sold the land. Now he goes into a far country with the proceeds of the sale in his pocket. If he returns and rebuys, all will be forgiven. But how will the village react if he loses all the money and adds insult to injury by doing so *among the Gentiles?* If the *qetsatsah* ceremony was not enacted when he left, surely it will be performed if he dare return under these latter unthinkable circumstances. He must succeed.

A final note is made by Jesus through silence. The older son, as noted, is specifically mentioned in the opening verses. He too has his inheritance assigned to him. But he is silent. Middle Eastern culture has a traditional role for him that he refuses to play. As soon as his brother makes the outlandish request for his inheritance, the older son is expected to be galvanized into action. When serious breaches in relationship occur, a mediator is selected or often naturally emerges in the community. This mediator is always the person with the closest relationships to both sides. The mediator moves from one party to the other in this "Kissinger diplomacy."[5] The older son is already mentioned in the story. The listener fully expects him to begin this classical and very effective process. His silence announces to all that the older son has poor relationships with both his brother and father. If he does not like his brother, he will yet fulfill this duty for the sake of his father. Rather we see an older son who will take but will not give. He accepts the apportionment of his inheritance but will not move himself to prevent the disaster of his brother's actions in selling a part of the estate and by that sale announcing to the community that the members of the family are at odds with one another. Thus all three major characters are clearly delineated. The reader understands the prodigal by what he does, the father by what he gives, and the older son by what he does not do. The prodigal is on his way.

The story moves ahead with no unnecessary verbiage. The prodigal journeys to an unspecified far country. He spends his family's life in extravagant living. The Greek word *asōtōs* is derived from the word *sōzō* ("to save") and has an alpha privative. In early Greek this word means "incurable" (Foerster, *TDNT,* I, 507). Later, the person who is *asōtōs* is a glutton. Foerster concludes,

> In terms of the general Gk. usage, *zōn asōtōs* at Lk. 15:7 [*sic*] speaks of the dissipated life of the Prodigal without specifying the nature

of this life. . . . It is simply depicted as carefree and spendthrift in contrast to the approaching dearth (ibid.).

With the one exception of the Old Syriac, our Syriac and Arabic versions for 1800 years have consistently translated "expensive" or "luxurious" or "spendthrift living," with no hint of immorality. A colorful set of expressions dot the Arabic version landscape across the centuries. Ibn al-'Assal has "spendthrift" in the text. His margin offers the following:

[Unidentified marginal note:] trouble free
Some Syriac and Greek: A life full of entertainment and
    amusement
The Arabic copies say: Love of luxury, splendor

Bar-Hebraeus, patriarch of the Syrian Orthodox Church (d. A.D. 1286), wrote regarding this text,

And he went to a far country . . . and there wasted his possessions (Greek: his own being) living luxuriously (Greek: wastefully) (122).

Thus in the East both translators and commentators found no immorality implied in the language of the text.

At the end of the story the older brother specifically accuses the prodigal in public of immorality. But that same older brother has had no contact with the prodigal in his absence and makes this accusation without having talked to him after his return. Nor has he received any report about him beyond the bare fact that the prodigal is home and that a celebration ordered by the father is in progress (v. 27). The older son, in his self-righteousness, projects what he *thinks* his brother has been doing all that time. The accusation of immorality stems from the imagination of the older brother, not from the narrator of the story. The King James was imprecise with "riotous living." The RSV remained on the fence with "loose living" and the NRSV reads "dissolute living." If the latter word (dissolute) is taken in its older sense of "lax, slack, careless, negligent, remiss," it is on target. But if the modern nuances of "lax in morals, licentious, profligate, debauched"[6] are insinuated, then we have agreed with the older brother against the narrator of the story. The text gives no details of the prodigal's lifestyle in the far country.

The "phenomenon of spilling" may have influenced traditional Western understanding and translation. The older brother's speech in verse 30 has "spilled" into verse 13. To allow this "spilling" is to blur the older son's deliberate attempt to discredit his brother in public by manufacturing damaging details out of thin air.

As noted, among the Eastern versions only the Old Syriac succumbed to this temptation. Since the appearance of the Peshitta in the fourth century, Eastern Christians have universally read the text as "expensive living." Thus, with a Greek word that carries no necessary implications of immorality, the irresponsible wastefulness of his life in the far country is most certainly the intent of Jesus. The prodigal "threw the money away." Was it in moral or immoral ways? The reader is not told. Jeremias records 10 famines in the Holy Land from 169 B.C. to A.D. 70 (*Jerusalem,* 140–44). In the days of international relief agencies and satellite communications it is difficult for a modern person to catch the terror of a famine. The first audience would have known such events in recent memory if not in fact. The Mt. Sinai Greek-to-Arabic version translates "he was overwhelmed by need and privation." As a person who lived in Beirut, Lebanon, through 10 years of war, I know that in the Middle East, when life becomes desperate, everyone turns to the extended family for safe shelter, protection, and food. The extended family is usually large, resident in the same geographic area, and pulls together in any emergency. But this young man is a stranger. He has no extended family in the city or district! The text is emphatic. *He* began (*autos ērxato*) to be in want! That is, inspite of his considerable resources, at last he *also* fell victim to the famine. This phrase can also mean he *especially* was in want, because he was alone and could not join a family clan to struggle through the famine to the next harvest. In either case the prodigal is singled out as a victim of the famine. Ibn al-'Assal translates "he also began to be in want." Others fell victim to the famine. Finally it caught up with him also (cf. Bailey, *Poet,* 170, n. 118). Now penniless and alone in the midst of famine in a strange country, his very survival is threatened. If there were a Jewish community to turn to, he perhaps could have gotten up to three meals, but not more (M Pe'a 8:7; Danby, p. 20). What is he to do?

At this crisis point in the story the natural thing for the prodigal to do is to return home. However, Middle Eastern cultural life is governed by honor and shame. Abstract principles of law are not the touchstone for behavior. Rather the child is carefully trained to do that which is honorable and to avoid shame at all costs. The Talmud gives eloquent testimony to this value system when it cautions against shaming anyone in public. The text reads,

> R. Zutra b. Tobiah further said in the name of Rab—according to others, R. Hanah b. Bizna said it in the name of R. Simeon the Pious, and according to others again, R. Johanan said it in the name of R. Simeon b. Yohai: It is better for a man that he should cast himself into a fiery furnace rather than that he should put his fellow to shame in public (BT, Ber., 43b).

The remarkably long list of rabbis to whom this statement is attributed is in itself significant. Honor and avoidance of shame is so critical that many rabbis seem to have made this strong statement. So if the prodigal returns to the home community he subjects *himself* to public shame. This will take three forms. These are as follows:

1. He is ashamed primarily before his father. Returning as a failure is obviously not what he had in mind when he left home. He was given his inheritance. He planned to manage somehow. He failed. Returning to his father will be painfully humiliating.
2. All that is left in the house is now the inheritance of his brother. If he goes home, his maintenance will use up profits of the estate that his brother would eventually own if they were not spent on him. His brother will not be pleased at his return.
3. The fear of the community is likely his greatest concern. If they did not formally enact the *qetsatsah* ceremony when he left, they will surely now perform it.

Scene 3 tells of his next move.

---

3. C. So he went and joined himself
       to one of the *citizens* of that country.
       And he *sent him* to his fields to *feed* the *pigs.*
       And he would gladly have filled himself with the pods
       that the pigs were eating,
       and *no one gave him anything.*                           REJECTION

---

Rather than the public shame of a return to his father's house in rags, he attaches himself to an influential member of the community who still has food. As Ibn al-Tayyib notes,

> The son [at this point] when he was hungry should have returned to his father's house. But he was ashamed to do so because of his pride (*Tafsir,* II, 268).

The word for "joined himself" is more literally "glued himself." The desperately poor in most societies are reduced to this humiliating ploy. They select someone who can provide food or shelter and try to become literally "hangers on" to that person. Not everyone in a Greek *polis* was a "citizen." Only members of the town council qualified. This specific political meaning most likely does not apply (Strathmann, *TDNT,* VI, 534). Yet the prodigal has clearly selected a man who at least owns a herd of pigs and thus has food. Furthermore he is able to hire someone to herd the pigs. He does not herd them himself. Some Arabic versions read "one of the great ones of the city."

Godet suggests that this humiliating service to a foreign master is an allusion to the tax collectors and their defiling service to Rome. He writes,

> We can hardly avoid seeing, in the ignoble dependence into which this young Jew falls under a heathen master, an allusion to the position of the publicans who were engaged in the service of the Roman power (p. 377).

The citizen is a Gentile, for he owns pigs. This notable most likely wants to get rid of the young stranger and so assigns him a task the citizen knows the stranger will refuse. The stranger is a Jew! He came with wealth and is thus from a family of means. Surely he will not herd pigs! He does.

At this point in the story the interaction between the storyteller and his audience must be noted. As observed, in the West we do our thinking in concepts. If the debate between Jesus and the Pharisees were a Western debate, we would be reading the following:

Pharisees: Rabbi Jesus, we don't think your doctrine of sin is serious. If it were, you would not be eating with sinners.

Jesus: Gentlemen, I see that I have been misunderstood. I am sorry you think I have a faulty doctrine of sin. Please allow me to explain myself. In my view, sin is a very serious matter. The faults of sinners are not to be taken lightly. Perhaps an illustration will make my views clear. I think that sin and the sinner are like a young Jewish boy who tells his father to die by asking for his inheritance. He then sells his portion of the family estate with his father in good health and resident in the village. Beyond that, he travels to a far country, looses the inheritance money to the *Gentiles* in a Greek city *and ends up feeding pigs! This* is my view!

Pharisees: Amazing! We had no idea! This young rabbi has a *magnificent* doctrine of sin. He has not set up a "straw man" to knock down. He has presented our theological position on the matter better than we could have done ourselves. This is *exactly* the way we feel about sinners!

From this point on in the parable the reader of the gospel of Luke is observing "participation theater." The Pharisaic audience is no longer a group of objective observers. Rather they have been drawn into the parable as participants. For his first-century audience, Jesus has indeed presented a powerful and repulsive picture of evil.

Ibn al-Tayyib writes,

The son sought to rid himself of very easy service to his father and ended up offering very difficult service to a foreigner. . . . The result of his lostness was that he exchanged living in his father's palace for living in the wilderness, and the companionship of his family for the companionship of pigs, and the good food of that palace for karobs, and plenty for famine (*Tafsir,* II, 168–69).

In this same vein Godet remarks, "He sought pleasure, he finds pain; he wished freedom, he gets bondage" (p. 377). At the same time, the evil set forth in the story is *primarily* in terms of broken relationships, not broken laws. There is no specific legislation against a son requesting his inheritance from a relatively young healthy father. The son could also not expect to receive the right of disposal of that property. But there is nothing formulated that says the father is legally forbidden to make such a gift.

The OT only forbids the eating of the meat of pigs and the touching of the carcass (Lev. 11:7; Deut. 14:8). Nothing is said about herding pigs for Gentiles. The Amish of Pennslyvania cannot own tractors but they can drive them while working for their "English" neighbors.

The Talmud records the colorful remembrance of some occasion when the Hasmonean house was divided and at war. Hyrcanus (d. 105 B.C.) was inside the city of Jerusalem and Aristobulus (d. 104 B.C.) on the outside. Each day those inside let down a basket of money. The appropriate animals for the sacrifices were then returned in the basket. After some time an old man (outside) told the besiegers that they could not conquer the city unless they stopped the daily sacrifices. So the next day, when the daily basket of denarii was lowered, a pig was put into it. The text records,

> When the swine reached the centre [sic] of the wall it stuck its claws into the wall, and Eretz Yisrael [the land of Israel] quaked over a distance of four hundred parasangs by four hundred parasangs. It was proclaimed on that occasion: Cursed be the man who would breed swine (BT B.K., 82b).

A *parasang* was a Persian measure that is reckoned to be three to three and a half miles. The hyperbole of the story is evidence of how deeply abhorrent swine were for the Jewish community of the Middle East at the time. So the community may curse you if you *breed* pigs, but, as noted, the Torah does not expressly forbid herding them for a Gentile. If the prodigal does not eat the meat and refuses to touch a carcass, he can stay within the precise requirements of the Torah. Or can he? He would have had a very hard time making this point to the later rabbis who forbad even feeding pigs (BT Shab., 155b). No doubt Jesus' audience saw the prodigal as a law breaker. But his larger problem is that he does things that are *unthinkable* and *deeply offensive* to the family and community and thereby breaks relationships with them. Thus, as the story unfolds, often overlooked aspects of the nature of evil are expounded.

Jeremias has noted that the verb *epethumei* ("would gladly") represents an unfulfilled wish (*Parables,* 129, n. 75). The pods mentioned are most likely carobs (Bailey, *Poet,* 171–72). If the sweet variety is assumed, this type is harvested, crushed, and boiled for a carob treacle that is extracted. But no one can "fill himself" with the pods. The Talmud refers to carobs being chopped up for cattle feed (BT Shab., 155a). If Jews fed them to cattle it is easy to assume that Greeks fed them to pigs. It is quite possible that after the carob molasses was extracted the coarse pulp was thrown to the pigs. Or the pigs ate the carob pods that fell from distant unharvested trees.

In either case the prodigal longs to have the kind of stomach that could digest such things, for then he too could "fill himself." Thus, the prodigal, a Jew, is reduced to *wishing he were a pig!* The pigs can eat until they are satisfied. He cannot.

A final desperate condition is reached with the telling phrase, "no one gave him anything." Either he tried begging and failed, or he was given part of the pig when the master butchered and he could not bring himself to eat it. Otherwise no one gave him anything. A number of the early Arabic versions read, "No one gave him any [of the carobs]." In short, the pigs had food. He did not.

So his attempt to avoid the shame of a penniless return to the village and to his father's house failed. But he has not yet given up. There is one card left in his hand. He hopes it will be an ace. Playing it will be painful. Thus he has left it to the last. The next two stanzas expose that final card.

---

4. D. And when he *came* to *himself* he said,
   "How many of my father's *craftsmen*
   have *bread enough* and to spare,
   but here I am dying of *hunger!*

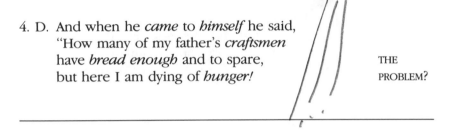

THE
PROBLEM?

---

In this stanza the prodigal presents his understanding of his problem. He is hungry. In the next stanza (5), he will propose a solution. What is intended by the critical phrase "And when he came to himself he said ..."? This opening line merits careful scrutiny. Material already published needs no repetition (Bailey, *Poet,* 173–80). Aspects of the topic previously overlooked may be worthy of note. The traditional understanding of "he came to himself" is "he repented." This supposed new awareness of himself, his journey home, and his confession have usually been interpreted as symbolizing repentance. However, this view overlooks a critical aspect of the chapter as a whole. As noted, in the parable of the lost sheep Jesus redefines repentance as "acceptance of being found." Neither the lost sheep nor the lost coin find themselves. Rather, the shepherd and the woman, at great cost in time and effort, *find* their lost sheep and coin. Repentance is thus something done for the believer. It is not something the believer does for himself/herself. Are we now to understand that in the third parable Jesus is *violating* the definition of repentance that he has just set forth in the first and second stories? Is Jesus saying,

> Repentance is acceptance of being found. The lost sheep and the lost coin are symbols of this repentance. On second thought, repentance is a case of leaving the far country and resolutely tramping home alone and unaided. The lost one needs no help. He can make it home on his own. Don't take the first two stories seriously. What I really mean is set forth in the third. Actually, I am confused on the matter so I will leave you with both options and you can take your choice.

Surely such is not the case! How then is this phrase to be understood?

In the English language the phrase "he came to himself" is reflected in popular idiom with the remark, "so-and-so hasn't found himself/herself yet." This is usually said of young people who have not sorted out their long-term commitments and have no direction in life. I am convinced that the idiom comes from this parable. In any case, the modern idiom now appears to influence perceptions of the parable in the minds of most Western Christians. The assumptions are as follows:

> Like young people we have known, the prodigal feeding the pigs "has not yet found himself." Then comes the magical moment of insight. He comes to himself. That is, he repents. From that point on his life begins to mend.

The obvious difficulty with this widely held view is seen above. Such an interpretation creates an unreconcilable conflict between repentance as defined in the first two parables and as (supposedly) set forth in the third.

The Greek phrase *eis heauton de elthōn* occurs in the Codex Bezae of Luke 18:4, but in that text the judge is not repenting; he is merely trying to get rid of the widow who is giving him a headache. Acts 12:11 appears in English to be a parallel, but a different word for "came" appears in the Greek and, in any case, Peter is not repenting. At the end of the first century, the Stoic philosopher Epictetus uses this phrase as he talks to an over-dressed young man. The slave philosopher tells the young man that when he "comes to himself" he will discover that "to follow the best nature of man" he will need an adjustment in his values (*Discourses*, III, 1, 15). Much less than the Biblical understanding of repentance is implied. Strack and Billerbeck suggest rabbinic parallels (Str.-B., II, 215). But on close scrutiny the texts listed do not carry the meanings suggested for them (Bailey, *Poet*, 173–75). What then can be made of this phrase in Luke 15:17?

Rather than artificially creating an irresolvable conflict within the trilogy of stories, what happens in the far country can best be seen as one more attempt on the part of the prodigal to solve his problem. The key to understanding may be Psalm 23:3.

In the first chapter we observed Psalm 23:3a, "he restores my soul," in some detail. This same phrase is significant here as well. In the case of the psalmist *God* is the actor and the return of the *nephesh* (the self) is to God. The Syriac and Arabic versions of Luke 15, with one (Arabic) exception, always use the word *nephesh* (Arabic: *nafs*) in the translation. The almost universal Arabic translation of 15:17, for more than a thousand years, is "he returned to his *nafs* [himself]." So the following comparison between the two texts can be made:

Luke 15:17: "He came to *himself* [i.e., to his *nephesh*]."
    In the case of the prodigal:
        The actor = the *prodigal*
        The direction of movement = to *himself* (to his *nephesh*)

Psalm 23:3: "He brings me [my *nephesh*] back."
    In the case of the psalmist:
        The actor = *God*
        The direction of movement = to *God*

So the prodigal *acts* to return to *himself.* In the case of the psalmist, *God acts* to return the psalmist to *God.* The key word *nephesh* appears in each text. The phrase "he came to himself" in Hebrew, Aramaic, Syriac, and Arabic naturally translates with the word *nephesh.* We can be assured that in the original Middle Eastern telling of the parable this word was used. If Jesus is a simple village carpenter who teaches fishermen, farmers, and children, what we are suggesting is not plausible. However, if he is a metaphorical theologian of the first rank, defending his views to a group of intellectuals, the invocation of Psalm 23 and its significance will appear. Jesus has already clearly invoked Psalm 23 in the first parable. Both texts open with a story about a shepherd. Here again the great psalm is significant. Jesus is not violating his own definition of repentance. Rather, in the far country the prodigal *still* thinks he will save himself. He will save his *nephesh*. Unlike the psalmist who knows that God must bring him back, the prodigal returns to *himself* and no one else. This possibility of interpretation is significantly reinforced by the fact that the motive of the young man is in the text.

If the traditional view is correct and the prodigal actually repents at this point in the story, we are obliged to ask, "Repents of what?" If a genuine repentance is intended by Jesus then the Middle Eastern listener would expect one of the following motives to appear.

- "I have shamed my father before the community."
- "I have impoverished the entire family by losing a significant portion of the inheritance."
- "I have rejected my father's love and caused him great pain."
- "I have sold and now lost my own soul."
- "I have caused great pain in the hearts of all the family by my extended absence."
- "I have cared for nothing and no one but myself."

Nothing of the above is mentioned or even hinted. The prodigal *wants to eat* and says so. Why should he die of hunger when there is an alternative? Obviously, any impoverished return to the village is deeply humiliating. Thus it was not considered earlier. But when desperate enough, even this card can be played. It is his last. If there was still money in his pocket, he would not think of going home. The famine came. He ran out of money and needed food. He tried one way to get food. He went off to feed pigs. It didn't work. Now he will try this!

In the Arabic versions it is possible to identify two points of view. Ibn al-'Assal seems to have held the traditional view that the prodigal repented in earnest in the far country. Thus his text reads, "When he returned to his heart." But his margin reads, "Some Syriac: 'He took an interest in himself.'" Then Sinai Arabic 68, 101, and 112 read, "he thought to himself." This latter translation continued on and appears in the first two printed versions of the Arabic gospels in A.D. 1590/91 (Rome) and 1616 (Leiden). The Arabic text of the great eight-language London Polyglot of A.D. 1657 translates the entire phrase with one word, *tafattan* (he got smart). Thus there is a substantial stream of translators in the Christian Arabic tradition that took seriously the stated motive of the prodigal. These scholars did not think the prodigal repented in the far country. Rather he was "looking out for number one," namely himself. Surely his stated motive is the key to his intentions. He is hungry and wants to eat. So what can he do?

---

5. D. I will *arise* and *go* to my *father* and say to him,
 'Father, *I* have *sinned* against heaven and before
  you
 and am not now worthy to be called your son.
 Fashion out of me a *craftsman.*' "     THE
 And *he arose* and *came* to his *father.*    SOLUTION?

---

His solution is clear. He will try to convince his father to have him trained as a free, self-supporting craftsman. He will not live at home, and not join the family. He will pay his own way. First he must convince his father to support the plan. Thus the opening line, "I have sinned against heaven and before you. ..." This is what Pharaoh confessed to Moses and Aaron during the plague of locusts (Ex. 10:16). The comparison is significant. When Pharaoh offered this confession he was trying to "work" Moses. Pharaoh had no remorse and demonstrated no "change of heart." He simply wanted to get one more plague stopped. In like manner, the prodigal's announced intent is to check his hunger. To do this he must "work" his father a bit.

Ibn al-Tayyib translates the next phrase, "I am therefore not *now* worthy to be called your son." There is a subtle difference between his reading of the text and our Western tradition. When we translate, "no longer worthy to be called your son," there is a clear implication of "I am not now worthy and will never again be worthy to be called your son." The banker steals from the bank and when caught says, "I am no longer worthy to run this bank!" He means, "Never again can I be trusted with this responsibility." Ibn al-Tayyib's text means in Arabic, "I am not *currently* worthy. *Today* I am not worthy. I will say nothing about *tomorrow*." This fits precisely into what we perceive to be the prodigal's plan. He is not *now* worthy because he owes the money. Tomorrow (after he has paid it back) he will again be worthy to enter the house as a son. He plans to earn the restored status (as his next sentence makes clear). Ibn al-Tayyib's suggestion is very thoughtful. But can it be justified on the basis of the Greek text?

The word I have translated "not now" is *ouketi,* a non-Lucan word. In the NT it has two meanings. These are as follows:

1. Adverb of time meaning "no more, no longer."
2. A logical meaning. BAGD states, "In Paul there is found a usage that takes *ouketi* not temporally, but logically" (p. 592; cf. Rom. 7:17).

This latter meaning loses its temporal frame. It means because of X-Y-Z I am not (*ouketi*) this or that. If applied to Luke 15:19 it would read, "accordingly I am not worthy . . . ," or "I am not now worthy," which is precisely Ibn al-Tayyib's translation.

The source for Ibn al-Tayyib's insight is the Syriac Peshitta. This is clear because, in the parable, the opening part of the prodigal's prepared speech appears twice; once as a soliloquy in the far country (v. 19) and a second time as delivered to the father at the edge of the village (v. 21). The Greek word *ouketi* ("no longer" or "therefore not") in the Old Syriac is *makil* and appears in both verses. In the Peshitta however *makil* appears in verse 19 but is *missing* from verse 21. As a Syriac word *makil* also has two meanings. J. P. Smith describes these as follows:

1. Adverb of *time:* "thence forth, after this."
2. Illative adverb (i.e., adverb of inference): "therefore, so now."

Burkitt translates *makil* in the Old Syriac of verse 19 as "I am henceforth not worthy," and Lamsa renders the Peshitta of the same verse as "no longer worthy." Thus both translators chose the first of the above options. Ibn al-Tayyib looked at the same Syriac word and chose the second alternative. Ibn al-Tayyib's selection makes eloquent sense out of the Peshitta text in front of him. It gives a clear reason for the Peshitta's ommission of *makil* (no longer/not now) in verse 21. As seen in Ibn al-Tayyib's Arabic, the prodigal intends to communicate to his father, "I lost the money, *therefore* I am *not now* worthy to be called your son. *But,* give me a few years working as a skilled craftsman and I will be!"

Then, when faced with the outpouring of his father's love in verse 21, this carefully constructed plan evaporates. This is evidenced from the omission of the phrase "fashion out of me a craftsman." The Peshitta further emphasized this point by omitting the word *makil* in verse 21 and thus left that verse reading simply "not worthy," rather than "not now worthy." Ibn al-Tayyib caught this latter emphasis in his Arabic translation of the Peshitta.

Granted, Ibn al-Tayyib is working with the Peshitta which is a translation. But the second alternative for his Syriac word *makil* mirrors a second alternative for the Greek word *ouketi*. Thus Ibn al-Tayyib's Arabic is a legitimate option for the original Greek and not merely an option in Syriac. It appears that the translators of the Peshitta caught this nuance and reinforced it by the omission of *makil* in verse 21. Ibn al-Tayyib preserved this fine-tuning in his Arabic NT. Even if not reinforced by the omission in verse 21, this interpretation of *ouketi/makil* is a valid option that reinforces the picture of the calculated self-interest which the prodigal verbalizes in the far country. The archaic Greek-to-Arabic version leaves *ouketi* out of both verses as does Ibn al-'Assal and Vatican Coptic 9. The Mt. Sinai Greek-to-Arabic version omits the first (v. 19) and translates "I am *also* not worthy" in verse 21. Thus it is only in the Peshitta (as translated by Ibn al-Tayyib) that this thoughtful legitimate translation option is preserved.

In summary, finding this subtle nuance from Ibn al-Tayyib a legitimate translation of the Greek text, I have adopted it in both of the prodigal's speeches. However, in Ibn al-Tayyib's Arabic/Peshitta translation, the prodigal in the far country says, "I am not *now* worthy to be called your son" (meaning: give me time and I will be!). Then in response to his father's love, the prodigal drops this preposterous hope and merely says, "I am not worthy to be called your son." But the Greek text has the identical wording in each occurrence of this first part of the prepared speech. The question thus becomes this: Can Ibn al-Tayyib's insight be legitimately affirmed for both speeches? Does this translation make sense in the far country and in the presence of his father? I think it does.

The speech in the far country can be translated with Ibn al-Tayyib, "I am not *now* worthy" (meaning: I am not worthy today, but tomorrow I will be!). This idea is reinforced by the fact that he plans to then say, "Fashion out of me a craftsman," which is how he intends to *become* worthy! Then after his father's demonstration of costly love, the prodigal uses the same language, but with a different meaning. The prodigal repeats, "I am not *now* worthy" (meaning: now, in the light of this stunning outpouring of love, I am not worthy and can never become worthy). He says the same words, but they have a different ring. This different ring is also reinforced. In this case, the reinforcement is seen in the fact that he does *not* say, "Fashion out of me a craftsman."

The rabbis created a story similar to the parable under consideration. It is as follows:

> A king's son fell into evil courses. The king sent his tutor to him with the message, Repent [*hazara*], my son. . . . But the son sent to his father to say, How can I (literally, with what face can I) return (or repent)? I am ashamed (to come) before thee. Then the father sent to him to say, Can a son be ashamed to return to his father? If you return, do you not return to your father? So God sent Jeremiah to the Israelites who had sinned against him. He said to Jeremiah: Tell my sons to return (repent). They replied, How can we (with what face can we) return to God? Then God said to them: My sons, if you return, is it not to your Father that you return? (Deut. Rabbah 2:24; quoted in Montefiore, 356).

The king's son in this story is a noble man. He is filled with remorse and has no "bright ideas" as to how he can manage once he returns. The only return he imagines is to the palace. Not so the prodigal. The key to his plan is the phrase "fashion out of me a craftsman." This phrase also requires careful scrutiny.

The prodigal is not planning to live at home. His soliloquy affirms only that he is hungry and that on return he anticipates being paid for his services. He specifically remembers the "good money" the craftsmen earn. What he thinks to himself and what he intends to say to his father (to gain his father's consent for a new venture) are not the same. What then are the details of the prodigal's plan?

He will go home and try to talk his father into financing his training as a craftsman. A key word (occurring twice) in his soliloquy is the word *misthos,* which is often translated "hired servant" but can better be rendered "craftsman." He does not plan to become a slave (*doulos*) or a table waiter in the house (*diakonos*) but rather a *misthos* (a craftsman). What is the significance of his choice?

Ibn al-Tayyib is again helpful. He observes that those who serve fall into three categories. He describes these as follows:

1. The *son* who serves in his father's house without needing to be urged and without expecting any return.
2. The *craftsman* who expects to be paid for everything he does.
3. The *slave* who serves out of fear of punishment.

Ibn al-Tayyib then alludes to Rom. 8:15 and writes,

We do not take the spirit of slavery in fear but the spirit of adoption, so it is our duty to do good like the son who serves in his father's house (*Tafsir,* II, 270).

His father's house has slaves (*douloi*). He does *not* offer to join them. He is yet too proud to do so. But he has a more important reason for refusing to consider such a lowly status. Slaves do not get paid. He needs money for his plan. From his prepared speech, it is clear that he thinks it *quite impossible* to be reinstated as a son. Thus, then starting with his mentality in the far country, becoming a paid craftsman and working for wages *is his only option.*

As noted, the rabbis were "blue collar" craftsmen. Thus a craftsman was a respectable person in the community and was in no way despised (Bailey, *Poet,* 176–77; Heinemann). Furthermore the prodigal specifically remembers that the craftsmen on his father's estate were *well paid.* They had "bread enough and to spare." This is a Middle Eastern way of saying that these craftsmen were able to feed their families, pay their bills and their taxes, and *still* have something left over. So here is the meaning of this last card which the prodigal now prepares to play. If he can talk his father into training him as a *craftsman,* he too will have money left over which could accumulate. Then *one day* he would have enough to restore his honor in the community by settling his "account" with his father. He is still young and his health is not broken (as the story itself affirms; cf. v. 27). He can yet learn a profitable trade. He will indeed "come to himself" and save face before the family and the community.

The Palestinian rabbis had a proverb, "When a son [abroad] goes barefoot [through poverty] he remembers the comfort of his father's house" (Lam. Rabbah 1:7 [53b]; quoted by Lachs, 308). The prodigal only appears to fit this parallel. He does not remember the comforts of his father's house but rather the comforts of the houses of his father's paid *craftsmen*. He intends to acquire a skill and pay his own way in the village or in some nearby village. He is not going home, not yet.

At this point we must observe the intense intellectual debate that is taking place in the telling of the story. The audience was no doubt pleased at the repulsive picture of sin painted by Jesus in the pig herding scene. So now again the theological position of the audience is authentically represented. We have already observed that repentance for the rabbis included three elements. To recapitulate, these involved the following:

1. Confession of sin
2. Compensation for the evil done
3. Sincerity in keeping the law previously broken

These expectations the prodigal plans to fulfill. He prepares a confession. As a craftsman he can eventually make financial compensation to the family. In the meantime his sincerity in his new law-abiding lifestyle will be on display to all. He will fulfill the law and "salvation" will be his. With this plan in mind he starts home.

His greatest problem is the reception he knows awaits him in the village. His brother's now intensified hostility will have to be endured. The father must be persuaded to send him somewhere to become an apprentice to a craftsman. Negotiations may be difficult. Not every craftsman will want him. He is not well thought of in the community. Without his father's support the plan will be stillborn. But the greatest problem is no doubt the village community. If the *qetsatsah* ceremony was a part of the village tradition, they will surely enact it now, even if it was omitted when he left. He has not only lost the inheritance, he lost it to *Gentiles* who keep pigs! Somehow they will find out. Close-knit village societies are never kind to wayward prodigals who return having *failed*. Furthermore, he did not just leave the community on his way to make his "fame and fortune." He consciously offended the community on a very deep level before departing. So after this offense and his all-too-evident failure he *now* contemplates returning.

Everything that happens in a traditional Middle Eastern village is everybody's business. We are not dealing with isolated nuclear

138

families, each dwelling alone in apartments or individual dwellings. The average size of the ancient Middle Eastern town was about six acres. Streets are traditionally only wide enough to allow a loaded camel to pass. The old sections of Jerusalem, Bethlehem, Aleppo, Damascus, and Cairo preserve the narrow streets with houses and shops wall-to-wall, crowding their edge. Evidence for such towns and streets is also available in the Mishnah. In the tractate Shabbath there is a discussion of where you can carry food on the Sabbath. To carry food out of the house is forbidden, but if your balcony is opposite your neighbor's balcony across the street, and if a man "stretched out or threw aught from the one to the other," that was judged acceptable (11:2; Danby, 110). One could also put a board across from one balcony to another and take food to the neighbor across the street (M Erub. 7:4; Danby, 131). The picture is that of balconies certainly no more than eight feet apart across the street.

The Talmud has a discussion of the case of a camel loaded with flax passing through a street. The flax overflows into a shop, catches fire from the shopkeeper's lamp and the shop is destroyed. The rabbis ruled that if the lamp was *inside* the shop, the camel driver was not responsible. If the lamp was hanging *outside* the shop, the camel driver was responsible (BT Shab., 21b). The picture is that of a loaded camel making its way through a narrow street carrying flax which is light and bulky. The load inevitably extends some distance on each side of the camel and brushes against the walls of the shops on both sides of the street, and even protrudes *into* the shops themselves as the camel struggles by. In the case under discussion the flax catches fire from a shopkeeper's lamp. The flax may even be ignited from a lamp *inside* the shop. Our interest is in the fact that the street assumed in the discussion cannot be more than eight feet wide at the most.

The assumption all through the rabbinic literature is that *everyone* lived in a town. Some were walled, some not. Even farmers lived in towns and then went out each day to work their fields. They slept on their land (in booths) only at harvest time to guard the crop. Mishnah tractate Megilla discusses when to read the book of Esther. Everyone must read it and specific suggestions are made for walled cities, villages, and towns. These three categories encompass the entire population (1:1–3; Danby, 201–2; cf. also M B.B. 1:5;

Danby, 366, where the unedited text of the Mishnah again assumes that everyone lives in a town).

In a traditional village the streets are narrow and crowded with village life. Friends sit and talk, business is transacted, goods are displayed and sold, the news of the day is passed—all in the street. The street is the "commons" of the community. It is through such a street that the prodigal must make his way to reach his father's house. As noted, the parable is about a family living *in* a community, not a family dwelling in grand isolation on the top of a hill. The guests at the banquet, the older son's friends, the servants, the musicians, the dancers, the young boys in the courtyard all affirm the presence of the community in the story. The gauntlet the prodigal must run to reach his father's house is intimidating if not terrifying. We have already noted Ben Sirach's terror of the slander of a whole town (Sir. 26:5). Because of this terror the prodigal first exhausts *all other options,* hoping against hope that he will not have to return in humiliation to the town and make his way home through one of its streets.

The phrase "he arose and came to his father" must not be overlooked. He is making a move in the direction of the village and the ancestral home. But on what basis is he returning? The answer is already given in the previous phrase where he plans to ask to be trained as a craftsman. He sees himself potentially as a *servant/ employee* of his father, not a son. As a son he will not be paid, so he opts for becoming a wage-earning craftsman. The issue Jesus is here powerfully raising is, Is the *primary* relationship between the believer and God that of a servant before a master or that of a child in unbroken fellowship with a compassionate parent? If the problem is the money (the broken law) and the only relationship open to the prodigal that of master-servant, then his plan to become a craftsman is a good one.

So are the believers children or servants? The OT witness is divided. On the one hand the boy Samuel in the temple prays, "Speak, for your servant [*'abd*/slave] is listening" (1 Sam. 3:10). On the other hand, the vision of Hosea is that "it shall be said to them, 'Children of the living God' " (Hos. 1:10). The post-Biblical rabbinic discussion reflects both attitudes. On the one hand the Talmud records,

Raba removed his cloak (when he prayed), clasped his hands and prayed, saying '[I pray] like a slave before his master.' R. Ashi said: I saw R. Kahana, when there was trouble in the world, removing his cloak, clasp his hands, and pray, saying '[I pray] like a slave before his master' (BT Shab., 10a).

In contrast Rabbis Abaye and Raba argue that God's people are sons of the living God when they "behave as sons," but "if you do not behave as sons, you are not designated sons." In the same text Rabbi Meir insists that in both cases they are sons of God (BT, Kidd., 36a; Lachs, 308).

Both of these themes can be found in the teachings of Jesus. On the one hand the parable of Jesus about the obedient servant in Luke 17:7–10 admonished the disciples to see themselves as "slaves." On the other hand, it is clear that Luke 15:11–32 is working on the other side of the coin of the God-believer relationship. The house has slaves/*douloi* (cf. v. 22 [NRSV]). The prodigal does not want to join them. In the far country he has already rejected the master-slave relationship exhibited by boy Samuel in the temple. He wants to be a free craftsman. The issue in the parable from this point onwards is, Will the father be *satisfied* with a master-(paid)servant relationship? The audience had the master-slave, master-craftsman, and the father-son models in their background. In this parable Jesus is strenuously arguing for the third. In the tensions of the story up to this point the master-craftsman relationship is the *most* the prodigal dare ask for, and some form of that relationship is the *most* the father dare give if he follows traditional cultural patterns.

We noted that the audience's abhorrence of *sin* is built into the story. Now their views on *salvation* appear. If the prodigal "repents" in the manner outlined in his speech in the far country (reasons the audience), he will, after careful negotiations and appropriate compensation, be accepted by his father. Even so, the sinner who fulfills these requirements will be accepted by God. Thus the "participation theater" becomes almost complete. The audience is by now fully "on the stage." Their view of the problem (sin) and their understanding of the solution (salvation) are each authentically represented in the parable up to this point. Thus they can be confident of the parable's ending.

The audience would expect something of the following. The

FINDING THE LOST: CULTURAL KEYS TO LUKE 15

boy returns. He is badly treated by the town. The feared *qetsatsah* ceremony is most likely enacted. After unspeakable humiliation and insult, he reaches the family home. After the delivery of his prepared speech and *considerable* negotiation, he *finally* convinces his father to trust him yet once more and to send him away from the estate for training in a craft. Once trained, he may work on the estate but as a paid craftsman. He will not live there. Years later he anticipates coming home with enough money to recover the lost inheritance. This will achieve reconciliation with the family and the village.

But this is not what happens. The list of electrifying suprises is not complete. The climax of the story appears just past the center of the rhetorical structure in the following text.

---

6. C. And while he was still at a *great distance,*
    his *father saw* him
    and had *compassion* and *ran*             ACCEPTANCE
    and *fell* upon his *neck*
    and *kissed* him.

---

When a passage of Scripture exhibits inverted parallelism, there is often a critical point of turning just past the center of the rhetorical construction.[7] This feature appears here. Four stanzas are completed and the fifth parallels number 4. With stanza 6, the reader starts (as it were) down the other side of the rhetorical mountain. Here in stanza 6, a point of turning appears. This point of turning breaks into the parable like a bolt of lightning. Why then are the father's actions so startling?

The audience's expectations, as best we can reconstruct them, are set out above. But rather than remain aloof in the family home, waiting to see what the young man has to say for himself, the father sees him at a distance, has compassion, runs, embraces, and kisses. Each of these responses needs examination.

1. *The father sees him at a great distance.* Again the picture is not that of a father looking out through the windows of a pillared mansion on the top of a hill who just happens to look up and see

the approach of the long lost boy. Rather we have the picture of a home in the middle of a traditional village facing on a narrow street. The father, for months or years, has been watching the distant road as it approaches the town gate and becomes a village street. He knows his son well and knows that he will fail. He also knows that the boy is arrogant and will not return until all is lost. Thus he will appear in rags and will be *badly treated* by the village. So the father has a plan. He is determined to reach the boy *before the boy reaches the village.* He alone can protect the boy from the hostility of the town. So from some vantage point the father watches the road. He must see him "at a great distance" to give time to reach him and carry out his plan.

The word *makran* occurs twice in the story. The boy leaves home for a distant (*makran*) town (v. 13). Now he is yet afar off (*makran,* v. 20). He is physically closer to home, but his real distance from his father remains.

2. *The father has compassion.* The Good Samaritan responds in a similar manner (10:33). In each parable this response comes from a person who is not expected to show compassion. A traditional Middle Eastern patriarch is expected to uphold the honor of the family. To do so he must exhibit indignation and anger once it is evident that the money is gone. He has the full right to have nothing to do with the boy. He may well guess that the boy is planning to "work" him for some further privilege, and indeed he is! None of this appears. The father acts only out of his compassion.

The compassion shown here is also in harmony with the image of God set forth in Hosea. Hosea prophesies for God saying:

When Israel was a child, I loved him, . . .
Yet it was I who taught Ephraim to walk,
   I took them up in my arms; . . .
I led them with cords of compassion,
   with the bands of love (11:1–4 RSV).

Jeremias includes this text among those in the OT that show God as a father (*Message,* 13). The language could refer to a mother but yet profoundly fits the picture of the father created by Jesus in our parable. The compassion is dramatically demonstrated in the father's next action.

3. *The father runs.* Middle Eastern gentlemen do not run in

public. Young boys run, owners of estates do not (cf. Bailey, *Poet,* 181). Ben Sirach, probably writing from Jersualem in about 195 B.C., notes, "A man's manner of walking tells you what he is" (19:30). Further west in the Greek world, Aristotle observed, "a slow step is thought proper to the proud man, . . . and a rapid gait [is] the result of hurry and excitement" (*Nichomachean Ethics,* book IV, chap. 3, 1125, 10–15).

So at this point the Greek and Semitic worlds met. People of prominence did not and do not run in public. The verb *trekhō* ("to run"), in various forms, appears 12 times in the gospels. The people run to bring their sick to Jesus for healing (Mark 6:55; 9:15). The Gerasene demoniac runs to Jesus (Mark 5:6). A bystander at the cross runs to bring vinegar (Matt. 27:48; Mark 15:36). Excitement at the resurrection triggers running (Matt. 28:8; Luke 24:12; John 20:2, 4). Simple folk can run when excited for one reason or another. All of these occasions fall into that category. With one possible exception, only here and in the story of Zacchaeus do we have a prominent person running. Yet Zacchaeus is *protrekhō*, he is running *ahead*. The people at the parade are focused on Jesus. Running ahead, Zacchaeus is confident he will not be seen. Furthermore, he climbs into one of the few broad-leaved trees in the Holy Land—a sycamore fig. Again, he clearly tries to hide. His running even then is striking and signals intense agitation. Thus our text is the only occasion in any of the gospels where a prominent person deliberately runs in public and makes no attempt to hide his action. Mark 10:17 may be the exception that proves the rule. Yet, even there, a reason for the running is stated in the text. Jesus "was setting out on a journey," and a man ran up, apparently to catch him. In Luke, the man is called a ruler, and he does *not* run (Luke 18:18). As noted, Aristotle cautioned against running because a "proud man" does not hurry. Middle Easterners have an additional reason.

One of the main reasons why Middle Easterners of rank do not run is that traditionally they have all worn long robes. This is true of both men and women. No one can run in a long robe without taking it into his/her hands. When this occurs the legs are exposed, which is considered humiliating. This can be seen in Is. 47:1–3 where the prophet symbolizes Babylon as a virgin daughter and paints a picture of her humiliation as follows (my translation):

144

For you shall no more be called
    tender and delicate.
Take the millstones and grind meal,
    put off your veil,
tie up your robe, *uncover your legs,*
    pass through the rivers.
Your *nakedness* shall be *uncovered,*
    and your *shame* shall be *seen.*

Clearly exposure of the legs was considered shameful. The robes themselves reached the ground. The Talmud likens the tabernacle to a woman who goes in the street, in that each had skirts that trail the ground (BT Shab., 98b). The same was true for men. A quaint ruling for the Sabbath states that if a bird crawls under your robes on the Sabbath, you may not catch it. The suggested alternative is to sit very quietly and wait for sundown and then seize the bird (BT Shab., 107a). Thus the robes were long enough that they reached the ground. On the Sabbath you could smooth out your robe to make it look nice but could not lift it up (BT Shab., 147a). If your robe did not reach the ground and you did not have a longer one for the Sabbath, you should lower the hem of the one you have. Also one should not jump or take long strides. One foot should be on the ground at all times (BT Shab., 113a). The reason for this last ruling is to assure that no part of the leg is ever exposed. Rabbi Hisda, while walking between thorns and thistles, would lift up his garments to keep them from being torn, and in the text he offers a defense of this unacceptable exposure of his legs (BT B.K., 91b). In another tractate Abba Hilkiah lifts his robes to avoid thorns while walking in the country and he is asked to explain "these mysterious acts of yours, which are bewildering to us?" (BT Taan., 23b). Outer robes themselves are called "that which brings me honor [*mkbdut'*]" (BT B.K., 91b; my translation). Priests making the sacrifices were not allowed to lift their long robes to keep them out of the blood on the pavement (BT Pes., 65b). On one occasion a man was complaining about his forced servitude to the king. He is told not to complain because he is, after all, serving the king! Rabbi Johanan then comments, "A man should always be eager to *run* to see the kings of Israel" (BT Ber., 9b). Clearly one should be willing to suffer public humiliation for the privilege of even *seeing* the kings of Israel.

    The slow stately pace of the Middle Eastern gentleman moving about in public is still an important part of traditional Middle Eastern life. At the same time, on television I have never seen a Western public figure running in a business suit. The American president, for example, may "jog" in a track suit. But he is not seen running with coat flying trying to catch a cab! In the Middle East today Eastern Orthodox Christian leaders and Muslim sheikhs still wear the traditional long robes. They do not run in public!

The reluctance on the part of the Arabic versions to let the father run is amazing. The three Syriac translations record the running of the father. Not so the Arabic. These latter render "he went" (Ibn al-Tayyib, Paris Ar. 86) or "presented himself" (Arc. Gr.-Ar .) or "hastened" (Si. Gr.-Ar.) or "hurried" (Ibn al-'Assal; Sinai Ar. 68, Vat. Cop. 10). For a thousand years a wide range of such phrases were employed (almost as if there was a conspiracy) to avoid the humiliating truth of the text—the father *ran*! The explanation for all of this is simple. The tradition identified the father with God, and running in public is too humiliating to attribute to a person who symbolizes God. Not until 1860, with the appearance of the Bustani—Van Dyck Arabic Bible, does the father appear running. The work sheets of the translators are available to me and even in that great version the first rendition of the Greek was "he hurried," and only in the second round of the translation process does *rakada* (he ran) appear. The Hebrew of Prov. 19:2 reads, "He that hastens with his feet sins" (my translation). The father represents God. How could he *run*? He does.

In the case of the father and the prodigal it is bright daylight, as evidenced by the fact that the father can see a long distance. The people are about. The village street is crowded. From some vantage point in the house the father has been watching. He now takes his robe in his hands and in a humiliating public demonstration takes upon himself the form of a servant and *runs* down the village street to the boy. As noted, *he wants to reach the boy before the boy reaches the village!*

4. *The father falls upon his neck and kisses him.* The prodigal is expected to fall upon his face and kiss the feet of his father. Rather the father embraces *him* and kisses *him*. Men in the Middle East greet each other with a kiss on the cheek or mouth. This kiss is a gesture of acceptance and friendship.

In Gen. 32:24–32, at the ford of the Jabbok, Jacob wrestles with "a man" until dawn. He is approached by Esau with four hundred men. Jacob is returning with great wealth. He was successful in his far country. He bows to the ground seven times before his brother. Esau then "ran to meet him, and embraced him, and fell on his neck and kissed him, and they wept." Two *brothers* are involved. The scene is in the open country. There are witnesses but they are only the family and servants of the brothers. Jacob's obeisance is total. There are points of overlap and critical points of divergence between the two stories.

In Gen. 45:14–15, Joseph "fell upon his brother Benjamin's neck and wept. . . . And he kissed all his brothers and wept upon them." Again brothers are involved. Moreover the scene is in private and Joseph assures himself of the remorse of his brothers before he offers the kiss of reconciliation. These two accounts identify the parable as verbally steeped in the OT tradition. But the self-emptying actions of the father remain unique.

Ibn al-Salibi writes, "He kissed him on his two unclean lips" (II, 157).

Vatican Coptic 9 and 10 place the kiss "on the mouth." Ibn al-'Assal notes this latter in his margin and identifies it as "Coptic only." Ibn al-Tayyib explains, " 'He kissed him' means forgiveness, peace, and love" (*Tafsir,* II, 272).

In traditional Eastern society, after the morning Eucharist in a Christian community, the village priest is often kissed on the hand by his parishioners. When relationships are good, a son will kiss his father on the hand as a sign of respect. Abraham Rihbany, who grew up in a Lebanese village toward the end of the 19th century, has this to say about his own relationship with his parents,

> Upon coming home from a journey I always saluted my parents
> by kissing their hands, as a mark of loving submission (p. 335).

But with the prodigal, relationships are broken by his actions and failures. A kiss on the hand is no longer good enough. He must now kiss his father's feet. Rather, the *father* falls upon the neck of the prodigal and kisses his face. What does this mean for the son?

After steeling his nerves for the harsh treatment he knows awaits him in the village, suddenly the son sees his father *running the gauntlet for him!* Indeed, the father again offers a costly demonstration of unexpected love. The father's previous offer of costly love was at the beginning of the story. However, on that occasion his pain was not on display. It was internal. Here the father has truly taken on the form of a suffering servant as he endures the humiliation of running in public through the streets. The father thus makes the cost of his love *visible* in a public drama. I am convinced that at this point Jesus is talking about himself and about the meaning of his suffering.

We observed above that the Pharisees' complaint was, "This fellow [Jesus] welcomes sinners and eats with them" (v. 2). Put into conceptual language, Jesus' reply would look something like the following:

> Gentlemen, I understand that you accuse me of eating with sinners, with the *'am ha-'arets*. You are correct, that is exactly what I do. But I do not merely allow them to eat with me. And I not only invite them, but like a good shepherd searching for a lost sheep and like a good woman looking for a lost coin and like this father running through the village to welcome his boy, I go out with costly love seeking these *'am ha-'arets* whom you so despise. I am ready to pay *any* price to win them and to bring them home to eat with me.

As observed, in the first parable the shepherd first symbolizes a "bad shepherd" who *loses* his sheep. The same figure in the story then represents the "good shepherd" who pays a price to go after them. In like manner the woman is initially irresponsible. She *loses* her coin. She then becomes a good woman and goes after it. So in each of the first two stories Jesus presents a central figure (the shepherd and the woman) each of whom first symbolizes the Pharisaic audience who have lost the outcasts of their society and then presents himself as he seeks those same lost.

In the third parable there is no hint that the father is responsible for the prodigal's departure. Unlike the two previous parables, the third story does not open with the picture of a bad father who loses his sons. Rather, a good father with costly love grants ultimate freedom. Thus the father at the opening of the story no doubt symbolizes God as father. But here in stanza 6, while he is "still at a great distance," the father comes to the prodigal, even as the shepherd came to the sheep and the woman to the coin. The speech of the father reinforces this aspect of the father's action. He does not announce, "This my son was lost and at last *has made his way home!*" Rather he says, "This my son was lost and *is found.*" The interpreter is obliged to ask, Found by whom? At the edge of the village he is still lost and in grave danger of wandering yet further away with his self-serving plans. As he approaches the village, he is as desperately in need of someone to find him as was the sheep and the coin. He is found by the father.

The very phrase "still at a great distance" has a special connotation, as noted. The phrase is nuanced with the meaning, "still at a great distance" in spirit. The prodigal journeyed into a *far* country. He is still *far* off. The reader knows the boy's soliloquy expressed *no remorse!* His planned address to his father included "I have sinned." If he does not say at least this much, his hope for new job training is lost! But his expressed *motive* is a desire to eat. The prodigal returns home planning to save himself by his labor as a craftsman. If he is allowed to proceed with his plan, there will be no authentic reconciliation, for any genuine reconciliation will require the prodigal's awareness of the real meaning of what he has done. Only when that awareness dawns on him will he be able to see that he *cannot* solve the problem he has created. The very assumption that he can pay money and compensate for the agony of rejected love is to cheapen the reality of that pain. A broken window is not like a broken heart. A new sheet of glass and the broken window is a thing of the past. Not so a broken heart. Thus, if the father allows the prodigal's plan to proceed, the end result will be two "older brothers" in the house rather than one. Genuine reconciliation can only be achieved by the father's self-emptying costly love.

This dramatic scene at the edge of the village contains three theological themes. Hints of the *incarnation* is the first. The father must come *down* from the house and move *out* into the street in self-emptying humiliation (like a servant) if the prodigal is to be reconciled. In this move the incarnation can at least be "overheard." If Jesus is the shepherd who seeks and finds and if Jesus is the woman who seeks and finds, is Jesus (at the edge of the village) not also the father who comes to the lost one seeking and finding? Jeremias writes,

Jesus vindicates his revolutionary conduct by claiming in the parable, 'God's love to the returning sinner knows no bounds. What I do represents God's nature and will.' *Jesus thus claims that in his actions the love of God to the repentant sinner is made effectual.* Thus the parable, without making any kind of christological statement, reveals itself as a veiled assertion of authority: Jesus makes the claim for himself that he is acting in God's stead, that he is God's representative (emphasis his; *Parables,* 132; cf. Marshall, 604).

Granted, the parable makes no *conceptual* Christological affirmation. But do we not find a *metaphorical* Christological statement? Ibn al-Tayyib believes we do. He writes,

> From this action [the father's kiss] we learn the extent and scope of the joy with which Jesus rejoices at the repentance of the sinner and the scope of His willingness to accept him and of His love for the sinner whom He monitors through all of his lostness. In this expression also is a sign of the sending by God of His Word from heaven to this world to redeem the human race. The kiss is indeed a sign of reconciliation (*Tafsir,* II, 272).

Ibn al-Tayyib, with a Middle Eastern mind, finds a clear Christological statement in the *story* because for him metaphors are primary forms of theological articulation.

The second theme here set forth is the *atonement.* The costly demonstration of unexpected love made by the Father in his reconciling action as a suffering servant is surely a setting forth of some of the deeper levels of the meaning of the cross. This action has indescribable redeeming power. Its unqualified nature is reinforced by the fact that this costly love is offered *before* the confession of the prodigal. On the "story line" side, the father does not know what the boy will say. The costly love of the father (in a different form) preceded the boy's departure from the house at the beginning of the story. Now it appears again, and it precedes his confession and restoration. St. Paul conceptualizes the same meaning when he writes, "While we still were sinners Christ died for us" (Rom. 5:8). Isaiah 57:19 reads, "Peace, peace, to the *far* and to the near, says the LORD; and I will heal him" (RSV). Paul builds on the Isaiah text and writes, "But now in Christ Jesus you who *once were far off* have been brought near in the blood of Christ" (Eph. 2:13 RSV; cf. also Acts 2:39). The same language and theology is also reflected in this parable.

The third theme is *repentance*. As noted above, in the first two parables, Jesus redefined repentance as "acceptance of being found." Yet the sheep and the coin are imperfect examples of this theme. The sheep can only partially express gratitude and acceptance for being found. The coin is inanimate. Thus these first two stories affirm repentance as simply "being found." In this third parable the definition of repentance as set forth by Jesus finds its finest and most complete expression. The prodigal *accepts* being found as his revised speech makes clear. Thus, in the far country the audience's understanding of repentance is operative. Here at the edge of the village the new definition of Jesus bursts into life. Because the parable has become "participation theater" for the audience, there is thereby the possibility of both the understanding and the acceptance of Jesus' view.

Some of the same theological meaning here created by parable is affirmed in other NT writings using other language. In the parable the father as head of the house and the father at the edge of the village are one person. In John's gospel Jesus says, "The Father and I are one" (10:30). Also in the parable the father becomes a suffering servant in order to reconcile his son to himself. St. Paul writes, "God was in Christ reconciling the world unto himself" (2 Cor. 5:19 KJV). What is said *conceptually* in John and in 2 Corinthians appears *metaphorically* in Luke 15.

Returning to the parable, the prodigal's response is formative for the next scene.

---

7. B. And the son said to the father,
  "Father, I have sinned against heaven
    and before you
  and am *not now worthy* to be called your *son*."
  And the father said to the servants,
  "Bring quickly the *best robe*
    and put it on him,                    ALL IS RESTORED
  and put a *ring* on his hands
    and *sandals* on his feet;

---

151

Western readers need to note that there is (of course) an audience. Nothing out of the ordinary in a traditional Middle Eastern village takes place without an audience. In this case a part of the audience appears in the text. After greeting the son and hearing his response, the father turns immediately to the servants/slaves and orders the banquet. No time lapse to return to the house is suggested or implied. The servants/slaves are naturally a part of the crowd that has followed the master down the street. Everything that is said and done will be repeated in every home in town within 30 minutes at the most.[8] The father *wants* witnesses because he is sending a signal to the community. After his offer of costly love *there can be no* qetsatsah *ceremony!* No one can now suggest its enactment. If the key person offended (the father) has "withdrawn his case" against the prodigal, who would dare agitate for it? As noted, the parable opens with the agony of rejected love (v. 12). But in that verse the pain of the father's heart is invisible. It has no effect on the prodigal. It is because of the village community that the father's pain at the end of the story is *visible*. The son can now see, "He is getting hurt because of what he is doing for me!" If there is no one watching, then the humiliation evaporates and so does the powerful effect on the prodigal. Granted, if the welcome has no witnesses, then the prodigal can still be impressed with the fact that his father has come to him. But in that case, he could easily be on guard for some kind of a trick. (What is father trying to do? Lure me into the house to imprison me?) Rather it is the sudden shock of his father's humiliation *in public* to protect him from the village that triggers the authentic reconciliation that takes place and renders the above mentioned suspicion impossible. The costly love is *visible* and the prodigal is transformed.

Scene 7 opens with the son's response. The planned speech was composed of three parts (cf. 5). At the edge of the village the son delivers only the first two. He omits "fashion out of me a craftsman." For centuries Western commentators have assumed that the father interrupted him. Middle Eastern commentators do not agree. Ibn al-Tayyib notes the omission and comments,

> He [the prodigal] did not complete what he was planning to say which was "make out of me one of your paid craftsmen" ... because he saw from the running of his father to him and the grace-

152

filled way his father met him and embraced him that there was no longer any place for this request to be a craftsman. For if after such acts he had made such a request, it would have appeared that he doubted the genuineness of his father's offered forgiveness (*Tafsir*, II, 272–73).

Ibn al-Salibi observes,

> Why did he [the prodigal] not say to his father, "Fashion out of me one of your paid craftsmen," when he had planned to say it? The answer is that his father's love outstripped him and forgiveness was everflowing toward him (II, 157).

These two giants of Biblical interpretation in the Syriac tradition make clear that the issue is not an interrupted speech, but a new speech made from a liberated heart.

The prodigal is overwhelmed with the scene before him. Granted, the first two parts of the confession are prepared. But as noted, they now have a new meaning. In the far country, I "am not now worthy to be called your son" meant "I have lost the money and I hope to impress you enough (with a good speech) to win your favor for yet another privilege. Give me a chance! I will yet become worthy!" He expected a private discussion. Now he must respond in public. His confession now means, "I am unworthy of this stunning public costly demonstration of unexpected love which has just unfolded before my eyes!" As the prodigal throws away his last "card," he is abandoning any attempt at solving the problem himself. Nothing forces him to change his mind. He can still proceed with his original plan of asking to be trained as a craftsman and live away from the family until the money is paid. The son now offers *no suggestion* for his ongoing relationship to his father. Suddenly the problem is no longer the money lost but rather the heart broken. For the first time this broken heart with all of its pain becomes known to him. He may learn a craft and repay the money lost. How much shall he pay to mend the broken heart? The failure of the Law to redeem opens his heart to the Gospel. Like Paul before the Damascus experience, the Law was an attractive solution as to how he would relate to his father *until* he was confronted with the word of grace incarnate. Then suddenly the Law was powerless to save because the problem was then seen for the first time in its full dimensions. Now for the first time costly grace was perceived, accepted, and became for him a life-changing power.

Henri J. M. Nouwen describes his pilgrimage from professorships at Notre Dame, Harvard, and Yale to life with the mentally-handicapped L'Arche communities in Toronto. Among the mentally handicapped no one had read his books and he could not "impress anyone" Nouwen writes,

> These broken, wounded, and completely unpretentious people forced me to let go of my relevant self—the self that can do things, show things, prove things, build things—and forced me to reclaim that unadorned self in which I am completely vulnerable, open to receive and give love regardless of any accomplishments (pp. 15–16).

Although traveling quite different paths, Nouwen's words eloquently describe the prodigal's resurrection at the edge of the village. The father's brokenness obliges the prodigal likewise to let go of his relevant self. He must surrender his plan to "do things, show things, prove things, build things." On doing so he becomes for the first time "completely vulnerable, open to receive and give love regardless of any accomplishments."

When the son confesses *only* his *sin* and his *unworthiness* and offers no more "bright ideas" about how the broken relationship can be mended, the father knows that his costly love has been accepted. The prodigal, lost long before he left home, is now at last found. The father then makes two decisions.

The first is to order the servants to *dress* the prodigal. He is not told to go and get cleaned up. Rather the servants are instructed to dress him with the best robe, a ring, and sandals. Ibn al-'Assal attaches the word "quickly" to the dressing rather than to the bringing and thus translates, "Bring the best robe and dress him quickly." This can only mean "I don't want anyone else to see him in these rags! Dress him quickly! He is to be honored here, not humiliated!" This point is implied in the Greek word order. Ibn al-'Assal simply gives it emphasis. Ibn al-Tayyib adds thoughtfully, "The father treats him as though he had never left" (*Tafsir,* II, 273).

The best robe is the father's robe. The NEB translates, "Fetch a robe, my best one." When seen dressed in the robe the father wears on major feast days, all who meet him will respect him because of the clothes he wears, if for no other reason. The ring may be the

154

signet ring of the house, we cannot be sure (cf. Bailey, *Poet*, 185). Free men wear sandals. The prodigal has traveled a long way. Yet obviously he has returned without sandals. In the Talmud a certain Sadducee notes a rabbi without shoes and tries to insult him with the following remark,

> He [who rides] on a horse is a king, upon an ass, is a free man, and he who has shoes on his feet is a human being; but he who has none of these, one who is dead and buried is better off (BT Pes., 118a).

In another text Rabbi Judah said, "one should always sell [even] the beams of his house and buy shoes for his feet" (BT Shab., 152a).

So the prodigal is given honor (the best robe), trust (a signet ring), and self-respect (sandals).

The second decision is spelled out in the final stanza of this first half of the parable and is as follows:

---

8. A. and bring the *fatted calf* and kill it,
    and let us eat and celebrate,
    for this my son was *dead* and is *alive,*    RESURRECTION
    he was *lost* and is *found.*"
    And they began to celebrate.

---

The father anticipates a banquet with enough guests to consume a fatted calf. In traditional village society, meat is kept alive until it is eaten. The amount of meat butchered is an important clue to the size of the banquet. It would take perhaps two hundred people to eat a fatted calf. A grand occasion is anticipated. The extended family and all the prominent people in town will be present. The father is not just expressing his personal joy, he is formally reconciling the prodigal to the entire family and village. For the sake of the father (after such a grand banquet), no one will stand aloof from the prodigal. The contemporary indication of a great banquet is the butchering of a sheep. One person says to a good friend, "When such-and-such happens, I will have a banquet and butcher a sheep."

The occasion could be a marriage feast, the visit of a famous person, the dedication of a building, the return of a native son from a pilgrimage, or the like. I have never heard of the offer of a calf for a banquet.

In the OT the killing of a calf signals a very special occasion. Abraham offers a calf to his three angelic visitors (Gen. 18:7). King Saul and his servants have a calf butchered for them (1 Sam. 28:24–25). Amos condemns those who "are at ease in Zion" and who feast on calves from the midst of the stall (Amos 6:1, 4). Clearly a calf is fare for kings, princes, and *very* special guests. Yet there are two critical differences between these banquets and the feast in the parable under consideration. These are as follows:

1. On these occasions a lesser person butchers a calf for someone of higher rank. The meal/banquet is in honor of that high ranking person. (In the case of the prodigal the high ranking person [the father] offers the banquet with a lower ranking person as a guest [the prodigal]).

2. In the OT examples the guests have not offended the hosts. (The prodigal has deeply offended his father in a variety of ways and returns in failure and disgrace.)

Thus the banquet spread by the father is *very* unusual. Its unusual circumstances are one more affirmation of the costly grace that the father is extending to his son. In the process Jesus is making a statement about the meaning of his table fellowship with sinners. At the same time the father is the key figure at the banquet, not the prodigal. The celebration is not "in honor of the prodigal." When a great king hosts a banquet for his courtiers, the king is the central figure at the banquet, not the courtiers. We have noted that the shepherd's party is not in honor of the lost sheep, nor is the woman's celebration in honor of her coin. So here, the banquet is in honor of the father and the reconciliation he has achieved at such great cost. The father will be congratulated. The son is formally, but not warmly, accepted for the sake of what the father has done. The father is assuring this acceptance in the community. Acceptance in such circumstances is not easily achieved—thus the great banquet with a butchered calf. The banquet is a celebration of joy in honor of the father and his life-saving costly love.

As noted in verse 12, the figure that emerges is not that of an oriental patriarch. No Middle Eastern father will act in this manner.

## Figure 13
## Isaiah 66:10–14

| | |
|---|---|
| 1. *Rejoice* with *Jerusalem,* and *be glad* for *her,*<br>all you who love her;<br>*rejoice* with her in *joy,*<br>all *you who mourn* over her; | REJOICE FOR JERUSALEM<br>JOY WITH JERUSALEM<br>(mourning ended) |
| 2.     that you may nurse and be satisfied<br>from *her consoling breast;*<br>that you may *drink* deeply with delight<br>*from her glorious* bosom. | PARABLE OF<br>JERUSALEM = MOTHER<br>(Jerusalem consoles) |
|     For thus says the LORD:<br>3.     Behold, I will extend to her<br>*peace like* a *river,*<br>and *like* an *overflowing stream*<br>the *glory* of the nations; | PARABLES OF RIVER/<br>STREAM |
| 4.     and you shall *nurse,*<br>and be *carried* on her [*hip*],<br>and *dandled* upon her *knees.* | PARABLES OF<br>JERUSALEM = MOTHER<br>(Jerusalem loves) |
| 5.     As a *mother comforts* her child,<br>so *I* will *comfort you;*<br>you shall be *comforted* in Jerusalem. | GOD = MOTHER<br>(God consoles) |
| 6. You shall see, and your *heart* shall *rejoice;*<br>your *bodies* shall *flourish* like the grass;<br>and it shall be known<br>that the hand of the LORD is *with his servants,*<br>and his *indignation* is *against his enemies.* | REJOICE FOR YOURSELVES<br>FOR GOD IS WITH YOU<br>(enemies opposed) |

A traditional oriental patriarch *might* accept to have the prodigal trained as a craftsman and go somewhere else to live. Even this would be very difficult to negotiate. After all, why should the father trust such a son again? It is clear that Jesus has shaped the character of the father in the story after his understanding of *'Abba' di bish-mayya'* ([Our] Father in heaven [Aramaic]; Matt. 6:9). So Jesus creates a unique compassionate figure and names him "Father." Are there any hints in the tradition that could have been sources for him?

The "our Father" as a metaphor occurs in Is. 63:16 and 64:8, as we have noted. But nearby in Is. 66:10–14 another striking image appears. The text is shown on figure 13 (stanza 3 is my translation).

Isaiah is again composing stanzas that interrelate in an inverted pattern. The pattern is quite simple and is summarized by the extra words to the right of each stanza. When seen together the major repetitive themes are as follows:

1. Rejoice for/with Jerusalem
2.    Jerusalem is your mother
3.       River/stream parables
4.    Jerusalem is your mother
6. Rejoice for yourselves

At the same time, again just past the center (stanza 5), there is a dramatic new image. In stanzas 2 and 4, Jerusalem is the mother and the people suck at her comforting breasts. But suddenly in stanza 5 God says,

> As a mother comforts her child,
> so I will comfort you;
> you shall be comforted in Jerusalem.

Jerusalem is now the *place* where this act of motherly love is to take place, and the mother is God, not Jerusalem. But the word *mother* does not appear as a title. The text has a simile (as) for the mother, but not a metaphor. God is not called "our Mother" in the fashion that God is called "our Father." So the concluding chapters of Isaiah offer the reader a metaphor for God who is called "our Father" and that same God comforts his people with the compassion of a mother comforting a newborn child. Why then does Isaiah use a male metaphor (father) for God but female imagery (mother) appears only as a simile?

If the prophet had called God both Mother and Father, two disastrous consequences would have most likely followed. First, sexuality inevitably would have been projected into the understanding of God in the mind of the reader. With the idol-worshiping Canaanites and Babylonians, sexuality and their gods were a single package. The gods did not create the world; they copulated and gave birth to it. Worship involved "sacred" prostitution and so forth. Isaiah is careful to avoid that pitfall. Second, if God is mother and father, the unity of God is critically compromised. The prophecy of

Isaiah calls God *father* and at the same time it enriches the community's understanding of God by describing that Father God as having the compassion of a *mother*. All of this is a part of the spiritual heritage of Jesus of Nazareth. What then happens in Luke 15?

A Middle-Eastern father is expected to sit stern and aloof in the house when word reaches him of the approach of his wayward son. The mother of the house might throw caution to the wind, run down the road, and shower the boy with kisses. Mothers are like that (the village would say). But the *father*! No traditional village father would act in such a publicly disgraceful manner, especially for such a son! So in this parable Jesus can be seen to be following the example of Isaiah. Here also a father acts with the tender compassion of a mother. Ibn al-Tayyib notes the highly charged emotion of the father when he writes, "The grief of the father over the boy was like grief over the dead" (*Tafsir,* II, 275).

The absence of the figure of the mother in the story is not due to a male-dominated environment that thinks little of women. Rather, following the prophet Isaiah, the single metaphor preserves the unity of God and the finest qualities of father and mother are built into that unity. Indeed the father who acts with the tender compassion of a mother displays that compassion from the beginning of the story until its end. It is the visible love in suffering of this compassionate father that makes possible the resurrection of his wayward son. The father thus says, "My son was dead and is alive, he was lost and is found."

The father found him, and the father brought him to life. Probably related to this parable, the oldest Arabic versions translate *Savior* with *muhyi* (the one who brings to life).

When the father says, "My son was dead *and is alive,*" the verb in verse 24 is *anazaō* and can be translated "up and alive" (cf. Robertson, 571) or "has come to life" (Marshall, 611). King James and other English versions have translated, "and is alive again." The father's nearly identical speech to the older brother in verse 32 has the verb *zaō* without the prepositional prefix *ana*. The compound word *anazaō* appears only three other times in the NT (Rom. 7:9; 14:9; Rev. 20:5). Rom. 7:9 carries no connotation of "alive again," but 14:9 can have that meaning. Rev. 20:5 is unclear. The text here in verse 24 obliges the making of a significant interpretive decision. Does the father mean:

The prodigal was alive when he was with us in the house before he left. In the far country he was thought dead. Now returned, he is alive again.

In this case the verb *anazaō* in verse 24 will be understood as meaning "alive again" (NRSV) or "come back to life" (JB). In the case of NEB, this was clearly the decision of the translators who then proceeded to translate both *anazaō* in verse 24 and *zaō* in verse 32 as "come back to life." But if the father means:

The prodigal is *now* alive. He was "dead" to the love of his family from the beginning. That is why he demanded his inheritance, sold it, and left. At the edge of the village he was still "far away." Now, in a very deep sense, for the first time he is "alive" to our love and this accounts for our joy.

If this latter understanding is what the text intends, then the *zaō* in verse 32 will be seen as critical and the *anazaō* of verse 24 will be translated with Marshall as "come to life." The two great Christian Semitic languages of the Middle East, Arabic and Syriac, have from the second century onward consistently translated both verses 24 and 32 he "was dead and is alive." This may be partly because the two phrases

[he] was dead and is alive
he was lost and is found

form a perfectly balanced Semitic couplet which would be extremely awkward in Syriac and Arabic if the word *again* were added. We can safely assume this same awkwardness in the Aramaic of Jesus.

Furthermore Semitic languages cannot add prepositions to verbs as is common in Greek. Thus it is very likely that the two phrases (verses 24 and 32) in the original telling of the parable were identical. It is also possible that the Middle Eastern exegetical tradition perceived that the prodigal was "dead" before he left home and thus at the conclusion to the story he comes "alive" but not "alive again." Therefore they translated both verbs in the light of *zaō* in verse 32. In any case, I am convinced that the thrust of the entire story leads us to the second option set forth above. The prodigal was *always* dead to his father's love. Paul affirms that "even when we were dead through our trespasses, [God] made us alive" (Eph. 2:5). In like manner the prodigal comes truly alive for the first time at the edge of the road when he accepts the freely offered costly love of his father. Indeed out of his lostness he left the house and now for the first time he is *found* and *resurrected.*

The first half of the parable ends with the beginning of the celebration. Ibn al-Tayyib writes, "The joy of the father is parallel to the joy of the shepherd and of the woman" (*Tafsir,* II, 276). The archaic Greek-to-Arabic version translates this final phrase, "Bada'u yatahallalu" (They began to celebrate with hallelujahs). I am sure they did!

The *Alternative Service Book* of 1980 of the Church of England has within it a prayer for after Communion. The prayer opens with the following eloquent lines:

> Father of all,
> we give you thanks and praise,
> that when we were still far off
> you met us in your Son
> and brought us home.

The prayer is composed by Dr. David L. Frost of St. John's College, Cambridge. In this first sentence, Frost had the parable of the prodigal son specifically in mind.[9] In a mere 26 words Frost has brilliantly illuminated the parable. The prayer addresses the *Father.* While we were *still* (at the edge of the village) far off, you (the Father) met us in your Son, Jesus, and through him brought us home. Indeed, so he has.

(The theological cluster of the entire parable is considered at the end of chapter 4.)

# Notes

1. Quite often when the Biblical author uses inverted parallelism as a structure, the point just past the center of the material is a point of turning. The material comes to some kind of a focus. Then, as the themes start to repeat either in the very center or more often just past the center, something very dramatic happens which makes all the difference. We have observed this over two hundred times in Old and New Testament texts. This feature also appears here.

2. J. T. Sanders (*NTS,* 15 [1968–69], 433–38) has argued for the secondary nature of verses 25–32. His linguistic arguments were fully answered by J. Jeremias (*ZNW,* 62 [1971], 172–89). A. Julicher, R. Bultmann, J. M. Creed, F. Hauck, J. Fitzmyre, H. Marshall, and many others understand the entire parable as authentic to Jesus of Nazareth (cf. Fitzmyer, II, 1085; Marshall, 604–6).

FINDING THE LOST: CULTURAL KEYS TO LUKE 15

3. One case in contemporary life was that of a Syrian farmer's son who asked for his inheritance. The father drove him out of the house. The second was the story of a medical doctor whose son asked for the inheritance. The shock of the request brought on a heart attack (cf. *Poet*, 162, n. 73).

4. For a good summary of some of the main lines of the discussion cf. Sallie McFague, "God the Father: Model or Idol?" (pp. 145–92).

5. In the mid 1970s then American Secretary of State, Henry Kissinger, came to the Middle East. He shuttled between Cairo and Tel Aviv negotiating a peace agreement between Egypt and Israel after the Yom Kippur War. He did not ask Begin and Sadat to sit down together, but rather, in classical Middle Eastern manner, went from one party to the other until agreement was hammered out. The grass roots response expressed to me at the time was, "At last we see a Westerner who understands our way of making reconciliation."

6. Cf. *Compact Edition of the Oxford English Dictionary*, vol. 1, pp. 765–66.

7. This feature was first noted by Lund. He called it "the law of the shift at the centre [*sic*]" (p. 41).

8. I have on numerous occasions observed this phenomenon in the Old City of Jerusalem. If the Israeli military enters any one of the gates, word is shouted from shop to shop down the narrow streets of the nearly mile-square city, and every Arab shop within the walls is informed almost instantaneously. I have noted the same kind of effective communication taking place in many other Middle Eastern traditional towns much smaller than Jerusalem.

9. R. C. D. Jasper and P. F. Bradshaw, *Companion to the Alternative Service Book,* (London: SPCK, 1981), p. 243.

# Chapter 4

# The Good Father and His Two Lost Sons

## Part 2: The Older Son
## Luke 15:25–32

The participation theater discussed in the previous chapter now comes to its climax. The audience heard their views on sin and salvation authentically presented in the speech and actions of the prodigal in the far country. They observed him return confident that after considerable negotiation he would manage to get the backing of his father to become a craftsman and earn his way. Then suddenly and dramatically the father breaks into the story to offer costly love to the undeserving son. As he accepts that costly love the prodigal is reconciled. He abandons the plan to become a craftsman. The banquet is ordered and all eagerly expect a grand occasion.

Now the participating audience is given a voice. In the person of the older son their response to Jesus' welcome of sinners is expressed in words. Again the parable authentically represents the views of the audience as the parable rushes on to its climax. The text is found in figure 14 (my translation).

The overall structure of the material is nearly identical to the first half of the parable. There is one significant change. This second drama is incomplete. It has seven stanzas. There should be eight. The last is missing because the audience, now on the stage, must finish the unfinished play. The cultural details of this critical second half of the story will need to be examined with care.

Yet a word in passing on the structure may be meaningful. In stanza 1 the older son stands aloof rather than enter the banquet with joy. The hoped-for missing final scene I have tried to recon-

# Figure 14
## Two Sons Have I Not—Part 2 (Luke 15:25–32)

Now the elder son was in the field,

1. and when he came and approached the house,
   he heard music and dancing.
   And he called one of the boys      HE STANDS ALOOF
   and asked what this meant.

2.      And he said to him,
        "Your brother has come,      YOUR BROTHER—PEACE
        and your father has killed the fatted calf      (a feast)
        because he recovered him with peace."      ANGER
        Then he became angry and refused to go in.

3.      So his father came out      COSTLY LOVE
        and began to plead with him.

4.      But he answered his father,
        "Listen, for all these years,
        I have been working like a slave for you,
        and I never disobeyed your commandments,      MY ACTIONS
        yet you never gave me even a young goat      MY PAY
        so that I might celebrate with my friends.

5.      But when this son of yours came back,
        who has devoured your living
        with prostitutes,      HIS ACTIONS
        you killed the fatted calf for him!"      HIS PAY

6.      And the father said to him, "Beloved son,
        you are always with me,      COSTLY LOVE
        and all that is mine is yours.

7.      And to celebrate and rejoice was necessary,
        for this your brother was dead      YOUR BROTHER—SAFE
        and has come to life,      (a feast)
        he was lost and has been found."      JOY!

8. And the older son embraced his father
   and entered the house
   and was reconciled to his brother      ????????????
   and to his father.      ????????????
   And the father celebrated together with his *two* sons.

(Bailey, *Poet,* 191)

struct at the end in the above figure (stanza 8). This is the ending the father longs for. Stanza 2 is a report of the return of the prodigal, the father's response to the return, and the celebration now in process. The parallel stanza 7 discusses the same themes and argues that such a response was right and necessary. As we will note, the father's *demonstrated love* in coming down and out to his older son in stanza 3 is even more costly than the welcome he offered to the prodigal earlier in the day. The father's love is then expressed in words in the parallel stanza 6. The center of the first half of the parable was a speech by the prodigal. In like manner, here the only speech by the older son appears in the center. The two sections of the speech (4–5) are obvious and need no comment. We turn then to the details of the text.

---

Now the elder son was in the field,
1. and when he came and approached the house,
   he heard music and dancing.
   And he called one of the boys         HE STANDS ALOOF
   and asked what this meant.

---

    This second half of the parable opens with a very subtle touch. Each brother starts a journey back to the family home from "the field." The comparisons between the two brothers will become clearer as we proceed. A full list of parallels between them is discussed below. Here this finely crafted hint in the story signals the beginning of the list. The reader awaits with interest to see what will happen when this son arrives at the house "from the field."

    The older son could have been at home when the prodigal arrived. But Jesus has deliberately chosen to have this older brother arrive from the field. This small detail highlights the coming comparisons between the two sons noted above. Looking at the story from a human relations point of view I have often been asked, "Why was the older son not notified at once?" What is said theologically (through the parable) from this point onward is only really possible if the older son also starts some distance away and returns to the house. Omitting the notification is unavoidable from the point of view of the storyteller's theological intent.

The older son hears music as he makes his way through the narrow streets of the village to the family home. Traditional Middle Eastern instruments include a flute and a mandolin, but it is the drum that dominates any performance. The musicians and dancers are paid entertainers. The picture is not that of a quiet mandolin and a Japanese kimono-draped traditional singer and dancer gently and quietly performing her routine. This is a loud, boisterous, joyous celebration. The drum can be heard at a considerable distance and the rhythm of the beat announces to the entire village that there is a party. The fact that the older brother can also hear the dancing assures for the reader that the party is in full swing with lots of clapping and loud laughter. Ibn al-Tayyib writes, "[the music and dancing] are evidence that everything has been done to assure a joyous and happy occasion" (*Tafsir*, II, 276). The Peshitta reads, "He heard the voice of many people singing." Ibn al-'Assal has this reading in his margin. Although not in the Greek text, this interpretive translation indicates that the translators of the Peshitta visualized a large, boisterous party.

The natural reaction for any such son would be to enter the banquet hall at once, respond to the welcoming cheers (they have been awaiting his arrival), and greet each guest with a handshake and an exchange of compliments. He could withdraw briefly to change his robes and then rejoin the celebration. But his reactions are of a very different nature.

The older son calls one of the *paidos* and requests information. Ibn al-Tayyib is again right on target as he writes,

> He asked for the reasons for the banquet as though the family had no right to set up such a banquet in his absence, whereas he should have entered the hall and shared the joy of those who were rejoicing (*Tafsir*, II, 276).

Thus the initial response of the older son leaves the reader uneasy. It is not a natural response and hints at presumption. The *paidos* he talks to can be a young slave/servant, young boy, or son. Son obviously does not fit. The servants/slaves are busy in the house with the banquet. But in the courtyard of the home there is a large crowd of very excited young boys who are clapping, singing, shouting, and playing in their own boisterous manner. They are too young to enter the banquet hall but can participate in this manner. As indicated, everyone knows everything in a traditional village, thus any witness can report the events of the day (Bailey, *Informal,* 48–49). If this young boy were a servant/slave he would have said, "My master has done so-and-so." He doesn't. Rather he says to the older brother, "Your *father* has done so-and-so." This makes it almost certain that a young boy is pictured rather than a servant/slave. The Old Syriac and some of the early Arabic versions caught this picture and translated "one of the lads" (Bailey, *Poet,* 193).

The second scene is a brief conversation between the older son and this boy and is as follows:

---

2. And he said to him,
   "Your brother has come,                    YOUR BROTHER—
   and your father has killed the fatted calf   PEACE
   because he recovered him with peace."        (a feast)
   Then he became angry and refused to go in.   ANGER

---

The young boy informs the older brother of all the critical details. First, he announces that the prodigal has returned. He then tells of the grand nature of the banquet. Third, he gives the community understanding of the father's motive. When important events take place in a traditional Middle Eastern village, in a very few hours the community mind condenses the incident and people all across the village report its main outlines in the same manner (cf. Bailey, *Informal*). What then is the community perception in this case?

The young boy reports that the father recovered his son. Our traditional "received him" makes the father passive. Such is not the case. The word *apolambanō* can be translated "receive" but BAGD lists the second usage of the word as appropriate for this text and translates it, "he has gotten him back" (p. 94). The boy states clearly that the father has been *active* in restoring the prodigal to the family.

The last word in the boy's speech is the most important. Just how did the father receive the prodigal? The common translation of *hugiainō* is "safe and sound." *Hugiainō* as a Greek word clearly refers to good health. There is a discussion in the interpretive literature as to whether the prodigal is in physical or spiritual good health. Plummer opts for physical health, because a servant would not be in a position to comment on the prodigal's spiritual health (p. 377). Nor would a young boy! But if the story was originally told in Aramaic or Hebrew, then more is involved. NT Greek usage is deeply influenced by the Greek OT (LXX).

In the LXX the verb *hugiainō* almost without exception translates the Hebrew word *shalom* (peace). It was a good choice because a part of the meaning of *shalom* is "good health." Von Rad writes, "in many . . . instances *shalom* really signifies bodily health or well-being and the related satisfaction" (*TDNT,* II, 402). Traditional phrases such as "Peace be with you" (Dan. 10:19 RSV) and "Go in peace" (Ex. 4:18) sometimes use our verb *hugiainō* to translate *shalom.* Texts referring to physical health do the same. Joseph is sent by his father to find his brothers with these words, "Go now, see if there is peace to your brothers and peace to the flock" (Gen. 37:14; my translation). Again *shalom* appears in the Hebrew, and the LXX uses the Greek word *hugiainō.* Later in the same story (in Hebrew), Joseph, (now prince of Egypt) talks to his brothers and asks about his father saying,

And he [Joseph] inquired about their peace [*lahem leshalom*] and said, "Is your father with peace [*ha-shalom 'abikem*], the old man of whom you spoke? Is he alive?" And they said, "There is peace to your servant [*shalom le'abdka*] our father, he is alive" (Gen. 43:27–28; my translation).

Each appearance of the word *shalom* in the above text is translated with *hugiainō* in the Greek OT. Joseph obviously wants to know whether his father is alive and in good health. He does so by inquiring about his *shalom* and then asks specifically, "Is he alive?" because *shalom* has so many nuances. Other texts where *shalom* is translated by *hugiainō* are Gen. 26:6; 1 Kings 25:6; and 2 Kings 14:8.

Many Arabic versions of the past 1,000 years have translated Luke 15:27 "because he received him *saliman,*" which means "in good health." These versions do not translate "with peace," but yet a derivitive of the root *s-l-m* is used.

One could object that the Greek of Luke 15:27 literally reads, "well, [*hugiainonta;* accusative case] he brought him back." There is no preposition *with.* If the phrase means "with peace he recovered him," would there not be a Greek *en* to represent a Hebrew *b* or *l?* Not necessarily. The word *shalom,* even when it means "good health," is not always the object of a preposition as Gen. 43:27–28 demonstrates. Joseph asks, "Is your father *with* peace?" but the Hebrew reads, *"ha-shalom 'abikem?"* which literally says, "Peace your father?" The Aramaic of Targum Onkelos has the identical grammatical construction (*Targum,* I, 75). In their response the brothers say, "There is peace to your servant [*shalom le'abdka*] our father." In this latter case the preposition "for" (*li*) appears. Thus *shalom* can be applied to the physical health of a person with or without a preposition. In Luke 15:27 the clear surface meaning refers to the prodigal's health, and (as noted) this is one of the major meanings of the word *shalom.* Thus our traditional translations are correct. But with the weight of the Hebrew, Aramaic, and Greek OT texts behind us, it is fully possible to translate the young boy's speech, "because he recovered him with *peace.*" Literally translated (following Luke's word order) the text reads, *"Shalom* him he recovered." The wide usage and comprehensive nature of the word shalom allows this construction to make sense. This possible translation adds important nuances otherwise missed.

In describing the word *shalom* von Rad writes,

> Seldom do we find in the OT a word which to the same degree as *shalom* can bear a common use and yet can also be filled with a concentrated religious content far above the level of the average conception (*TDNT,* II, 402).

The "common use" in our text is obviously "good health." But is there a "concentrated religious content" also implied in the text? Von Rad goes on to discuss "the great number of passages in which *shalom* denotes a relationship rather than a state" (ibid.). The father has already proclaimed, "Let us eat and celebrate." The father has brought the prodigal back with *peace.* He is alive, found, and in good health. But more than that, now his *relationship* with his father is restored. There is shalom between the prodigal and the family.

The village and the reader of Luke know that this restoration of relationships has happened because of the father's costly love displayed and accepted in the town that day. Indeed it was that display of love, and the prodigal's acceptance of it, that created authentic *shalom* between them.

Failure to note the probable use of *shalom* in the original telling of the story greatly cheapens the declared motive for the banquet. Has the father killed the fatted calf and thrown a party for his family and friends merely because of a good health report? If the prodigal had arrived weak or with a broken arm, would there have been no celebration?

Furthermore, we could ask, Was he actually in such good shape? The prodigal admits in the far country, "I am dying of hunger." After the long hike home with nothing to eat and without sandals, is he really in good health? From yet another perspective, his health is overlooked in the telling of the story. At the edge of the village the father calls for a robe and sandals and thus implies that the prodigal arrived poorly dressed. But the father makes *no* comment about his health. Thus he may have been in poor health, but in any case his health is not observed. How then could the prodigal's good health become the publicly perceived reason for the banquet?

The young boy in the street is not offering his personal reflections, like an official interviewed by a television reporter. Rather the boy is mirroring what is being said in the community about the party. The community witnessed the costly reconciliation. Thus it is perfectly natural to find them affirming through the young boy that *shalom* has come upon the house and that this *shalom* is the comprehensive reason for the party!

Furthermore, if the party is merely a celebration of the prodigal's return in good health, the older son could have accepted the party and maintained his clearly expressed views. It would be inhuman not to be happy that the prodigal was alive and in good *health*. In such a case, the future position of the prodigal in the house would be yet undetermined. Appropriate punishment and hard labor could still be demanded in a family debate. But if *shalom* is what has happened, then it is a very different matter. If the father is *reconciled* to the prodigal and that *reconciliation* is being celebrated at the banquet, then the major decisions about the prodigal's future status in the house are already made. In this latter case, the older son's response is consistent with his expressed views. The archaic Greek-to-Arabic translation reads, "He received him *sahihan*." The word means both "in good health" and "truly, genuinely." So the text means, "He received him in good health" and "he truly and genuinely received him." The Diatessaron has "*sadafahu sahihan*" (he *genuinely/in good health* found him). This choice of words carries the precise freight I am suggesting. The older son is not upset over the health report but at the evidence of reconciliation.

With the above meaning of *hugiainonta* as a clear possibility for the Hebrew or Aramaic (?) behind the Greek text, the older son's response flows naturally and dramatically. After this announcement the inevitable question for the older son is:

> Your *father* extended his *shalom* to your brother! How will you receive him?

This brings us to the dramatic close of scene 2. The text bluntly affirms, "he became angry and refused to go in." The shock of this public action is beyond description. The equivalent in Western society might be some case of a wealthy leading figure in a Western community who has a candlelight formal banquet for his most important friends and associates. In the middle of the banquet his unshaven son appears without a shirt or shoes and verbally attacks his father in the presence of the seated guests. Such a scene would be excruciatingly painful for the father. It would show *utter* disregard for the feelings and personal dignity of that father on the part of his son. Such a scene can hardly be imagined in the modern West where family relationships are less formal than in the past. How much worse then is it in the East where the public respect of the father is virtually never withheld?

We have already noted the rabbis' admonition regarding anyone who shames his *fellow* in public: "It is better for a man that he should cast himself into a fiery furnace rather than that he should put his fellow to shame in public" (BT Ber., 43b). The older son has not shamed his *fellow* but his *father.* It is not merely in public, but at a formal banquet hosted by that father! So what is the meaning of this refusal in the *East* when an *older* son deliberately insults his father in public at a banquet?

Ibn al-Tayyib offers an answer. He writes,

> [In his refusal to enter,] the older son demonstrated maliciousness of character and meanness. He has no love for his brother and no appropriate respect for his father. His position in this regard is equivalent to the grumbling of the scribes and Pharisees against the Christ for his acceptance of sinners" (*Tafsir,* II, 186).

Ibn al-Tayyib's strong words are a clear indication of the offense he feels at the refusal of the older son. Also Ibn al-Tayyib finds Christology in the person of the father.

The parable does not inform the reader as to how the news reaches the father in the banquet hall. It does not need to. Word passes almost instantaneously across the courtyard of the family home and enters the banquet hall. In seconds the entire assembled crowd knows of the public crisis forced on the father by the shameful act of the older son. The music and dancing stops and the banquet is brought to a standstill, awaiting the father's response.

Before turning to examine that response, a number of clear implications can be discerned from the older son's action.

1. This insult cuts more deeply than that of the prodigal at the beginning of the story because it is delivered at a public occasion hosted by the father. The two brothers (in different ways) each put the father through the "torture of the damned." Yet here the father suffers more than he did at the beginning of the story. The prodigal insulted his father in private. The older son did it in public.

2. A traditional Middle Eastern father in the past would immediately order the slaves to overpower the disobedient son in the courtyard and drag him by force into a side room and lock him up. A grim-faced father would then proceed with the banquet. After the guests had left, the older son would be brought out, held down by the slaves, and beaten.

3. Now for the third time in the parable the person of the father is not shaped by the traditional image of the Middle Eastern patriarch. Again, Jesus is defining his term and is presenting a father whose fatherhood is expressed in remarkable ways.

4. In keeping with our suggested translation of *shalom* for *hugiainonta* in verse 27, it is the *reconciliation* proclaimed by the banquet that upsets him, not the return of the boy in good (?) health.

5. The prodigal at the banquet can well say to the father, "You prepare a [banquet] before me in the presence of my enemies." This raises again the question of the relationship between this trilogy of parables and Psalm 23, which will be discussed below.

Scene 3, in all of its simplicity and wonder, is as follows:

3. So his father came out                    COSTLY LOVE
   and began to plead with him.

The *father,* in *very painful* self-emptying love, leaves the seated guests and proceeds to the courtyard. A hundred people or more are watching and listening. The assembled guests, servants, entertainers, and young boys observe in stunned silence as the father goes out to his son. As usually happens in a village quarrel, each side is "playing to the audience," knowing that everything said will be remembered and repeated to their shame or credit for a long time to come.

So now for the second time in the same day the father deliberately chooses to take upon himself the form of a suffering servant and offer a costly demonstration of unexpected love. Ibn al-Tayyib waxes truly eloquent as he describes this scene. His Arabic is deeply moving. Only a part of its meaning can be captured in English. He writes,

> Look at the heart of this father! It is full of tenderness and love in that he left the banquet, the guests, and his younger son to plead with his older son to come in. It is as if his own joy is incomplete as long as one of his children is grieving. He does not rebuke the older son on his hardness of heart or his inappropriate sensitivities. In like manner the heavenly Father desires the entrance of the scribes and Pharisees into the kingdom of heaven as much as the tax collectors and sinners. Thus he demonstrated long suffering and intense desire for them to come to him even as did this earthly father (*Tafsir,* II, 277).

Plummer observes that the father, "treats both sons with equal tenderness" (p. 378).

In his translation of the Diatessaron, Ibn al-Tayyib adds another interpretive slant to the material. He translates, "His father came out *searching* for him." The word chosen is *'iltamasa* (searching), which is used also to describe the searching of the shepherd and the woman. Ibn al-Tayyib rightly saw the internal connection between

173

the actions of the three people. Each paid a price to search for that which was lost. The Mt. Sinai Greek-to-Arabic version has, "He came out speaking tenderly to him [*yulatifahu*]." Ibn al-'Assal translates, "He came out urging him to accept the invitation (*yistad'ih*)." Literally the Greek carries the meaning of "He came out seeking to reconcile him." All of the above texts attempt to catch the painfully and beautifully tender moment of this father who now again acts out of his sorrow and not out of his anger as he reaches out to his boy. What does the father hope to accomplish by such a move?

Earlier that day a similar costly demonstration of unexpected love turned a self-seeking prodigal (who saw himself only as a potential employee) into a son who could receive life-changing grace. Will it happen again? The village people observed the earlier events of the day and are asking the same question. But on the theological level something else is being affirmed.

In the first parable of this trilogy, the ninety-nine sheep, safe in the herd, were seen to symbolize the Pharisaic audience. That same audience was again represented by the woman's nine coins that were never misplaced. Here in the third parable, animals and coins have become people. Furthermore, in the far country the audience's views of both sin and salvation were authentically represented. As noted, at that point in the story, the audience was inevitably drawn into the parable. So here, at the climax of the entire parable, and indeed of the trilogy, a *person* represents the audience. That person appeared briefly at the beginning of the story but was silent. Now he is at the center of the stage and is *talking*.

In addition, I have suggested that Jesus, as God's unique representative, is the figure of the father in the form of a suffering servant on the road and now in the courtyard. The father in the house as host of the banquet is a symbol of the *Abba* (Father) of the prayers of Jesus (Jeremias, *Parables,* 132). But the father in the stance of a suffering servant in the courtyard, humiliated before all the village, is a symbol of Jesus himself, as Jeremias and Ibn al-Tayyib have indicated (Jeremias, *Parables;* 132; Ibn al-Tayyib, *Tafsir,* II, 273 [quoted in chapter 3]). Thus the storyteller (Jesus) and the listening audience to the telling of the parable (the Pharisees and scribes) are *both* on the stage when the father as servant descends to the courtyard of the house. At this point in the telling of the parable, the participation theater comes to its climax in that the playwright enters the play and argues directly with the audience, which by this time has mentally also made its way to centerstage. The first action of the father is described without recorded words. He "came out and began to plead with him." As in the first half of the parable (vv. 11–24), the person "lost" gives a speech of two parts in the very center of the rhetorical structure. How then will the older son respond to this costly love?

---

4. But he answered his father,
   "Listen, for all these years,
   I have been working like a slave for you
   and I never disobeyed your commandments,        MY ACTIONS
   yet you never gave me even a young goat          MY PAY
   so that I might celebrate with my friends.
5. But when this son of yours came back,
   who has devoured your living
   with prostitutes,                                HIS ACTIONS
   you killed the fatted calf for him!"             HIS PAY

---

Some plays are so freighted with powerful emotions and dramatic turns that to watch them is exhausting. But if it is the right play, such emotional and intellectual involvement can also be cathartic for the viewer. This parable is such a drama. After empathizing with the father's humiliating walk out to deal in public with what Bishop Craig has called "lawlessness within the law," the reader must now try to absorb the older son's response.

Each of the above lines needs brief comment.

1. "Listen, for all these years, I have been working like a slave for you." The older son opens with the omission of a title. All through the parable the father has been addressed respectfully as "Father." Now he is spoken to with no title. This reflects bad manners and borders on insult.

There is a famous incident recorded in the Talmud of a Gentile who first asks Shammai and then asks Hillel to make him a proselyte.

175

The omission and then addition of titles reflects first rudeness and then respect as the story unfolds (*BT Shab.*, I, 31a). The archaic Greek-to-Arabic version omits the title "O father" in the prodigal's speech at the beginning of the parable as well as this omission by the older son at the end. Thus the two insulting speeches (one by each brother) are brought into even closer parallel in that version. Each son insults his father and the reader knows it.

The older son then claims to have slaved for his father. Ibn al-Tayyib, Ibn al-'Assal, and the Diatessaron all emphasize this point by translating, "How many years I have served you in slavery." The prodigal never considered this option. What is pathetic about the older son's claim is that the father, by his actions all through the parable, has made clear that he does not *want* any such service. No master passes out an inheritance to a servant. No master would ever humiliate himself in public for a *slave*. And no slave would *dare* challenge his master in this manner in public. The dullness of spirit that the older son here exhibits is amazing and tragic.

But an even more startling aspect of this opening volley is the older son's claim to have slaved *for the father*. The story assumes only two sons. Thus this older son knows that one day he will inherit the remainder of the estate. He cannot work on the estate without working on property he already owns and will one day be free to manage. Particularly from the day the prodigal sells and leaves, any effort the older son puts forth to maintain or improve the estate *is to his own direct material benefit*. When he claims he has worked like a slave *for the father* he is deceiving no one (except perhaps himself)!

2. "And I never disobeyed your commandments." Ibn al-Tayyib finds close parallels between this speech and the prayer of the Pharisee in the parable of the Pharisee and the publican (Luke 18:9–14). Each feels they have more than fulfilled all requirements.

Here the reader sees the actions and hears the views of the "ninety-nine righteous persons who need no repentance" (v. 7) because they have *always* kept the law!

The older son claims to have never disobeyed his father's commandments. But he says this in the midst of an insensitive action that shames his father in public! He has not broken the law, but he has shattered his relationship with the source of that law. On Good Friday those who sent Jesus to Pilate would not enter the praetorium

176

"so that they might not be defiled" (John 18:28), but they sensed no defilement in what they were there doing. So all through history, in every major religious tradition, very religious people have committed evil acts in the name of that religion, confident that by so doing they are fulfilling its highest demands. Jesus is here depicting a classical "insider" in any legal/religious system who can destroy the deepest and most sacred relationships in the process of the keeping of the law expected of an insider. In the process, Jesus is defining critical aspects of the nature of evil that can never be understood, controlled, or overcome by any system of law, however good.

3. "Yet you never gave me even a young goat." This is a blunt accusation of favoritism. It says, "You love him. You don't love me! He gets the fatted calf. I don't even get a goat!" Everyone knows that the entire estate is now given to the older son, who will take possession at the death of the father. This older son, by his silence at the beginning and by his speeches at the end, is sharply critical of the prodigal. However, in this part of his speech the older son is showing frustration over the fact that he is not able to dispose of the assets of the estate *as he chooses*. Ah! So does he *also* want his father dead? Then he would have full control over the estate and be able to throw banquets at his pleasure! He could then butcher a goat or a calf every night until the herd was eaten if he so chose! So, who now is the sinner and who now has the right to be angry with whom? In the process of judging his brother and father, more of the unredeemed areas of his own life are revealed than he intends. His speech is a classical example of "Do not judge, so that you may not be judged" (Matt. 7:1).

Yet there is more. The father has just demonstrated for the older son the same quality of compassionate self-giving love that he demonstrated earlier in the day for the younger son. In this public demonstration for the older son, the father offers a gift that is of far greater worth than any goat or calf. In wrath he remembers mercy (Hab. 3:2). Another painfully sad aspect of the son's response is that *as the father is making this great gift,* the older son is accusing his father of failing to love him.

4. "So that I might celebrate with my friends." Apparently for the older son, having a goat to eat with his friends is a cause for celebration. The welcome of a long lost brother back to the home

is not. Furthermore in this phrase, the older son reads himself out of the family. His father, brother, extended family, and family friends are at the banquet. But these are not *his* friends. His friends are a different set of people. He awaits the chance to throw a party for them. His primary community does not include his family.

5. "But when this son of yours came back." For centuries it has been noticed that he refuses to say "my brother." The circumlocution "this son of yours" is used to avoid the distasteful (?) word *brother*. The same avoidance of "unpleasant" words is seen in the parable of the Good Samaritan. At the end of the parable the Samaritan acts with compassion and rescues the wounded man. Jesus then asks the lawyer, "Which of these three ... was a neighbor to the man who fell into the hands of the robbers?" (Luke 10:36). The lawyer avoids pronouncing the hated word *Samaritan* by replying, "The one who showed him mercy." There and here a statement is being made about hate and unjustified anger.

6. "Who has devoured your living with prostitutes." Plummer notes succinctly, "This is mere conjecture, . . . to make the worst of his brother's conduct" (p. 378). It is also gross exaggeration. The archaic Greek-to-Arabic version emphasizes the exaggeration by translating, "he has devoured *everything you own*." If the *living* (*bios*) still belongs to the father in the eyes of this older brother, then why did he quietly accept his portion at the beginning of the parable? Why did he not speak up and say,

> No, no, father, may you live a hundred years! I will *never* accept my portion of the inheritance while you are in good health with many years (God willing) to live!

No such speech was forthcoming from his lips. The older son accepted. Now all of a sudden the lost inheritance is "your living." He is caught in a contradiction. If the portion given to the prodigal is not "his living" but still the father's, then is he denying the validity of the oral will that gave him *his* portion?

As observed, the word *asōtōs* in verse 13 has to do with spendthrift living. No hints of immorality are necessarily implicated in what we know about the prodigal's lifestyle in the far country. The story tells us nothing and *asōtōs* is morally neutral. This older son knows so little. He did not even know there was a party in progress or even that his brother had returned. So now suddenly he is announcing in public the private details of his brother's intimate life in a distant, unknown country. The older son obviously has not heard about the pigs, or he would certainly have shouted about them in this angry speech. The fact that the pigs are omitted is clear proof that he has no "hard news" and is improvising.

The accusation is made in public. It is a very, very serious accusation. If believed, no respectable family in the village will give their daughter in marriage to the unmarried prodigal.

Furthermore, the audience in the courtyard knows that the prodigal was gone long enough to spend his considerable inheritance. The family is wealthy. It has goats, fatted calves, and slaves and hosts great banquets with professional musicians. The fact that he lived among the Gentiles will soon be discovered. Is the older brother accusing the prodigal of having slept with *Gentile prostitutes*?[1] Villagers from Spain to Iraq have for centuries killed each other over such accusations. Foreign *wives* were forbidden centuries before by Nehemiah (13:23–27). What then of foreign *prostitutes*? The older son is raging! What is he trying to accomplish?

The older brother *knows* that the celebration will seal reconciliation between the prodigal and the community. The father has already recovered the prodigal with *shalom*. The father wants *shalom* to also govern the relations between the prodigal and the community. That is precisely why the prodigal is dressed in the father's finest robe and is wearing a signet ring of the house. For the sake of the father, the community will accept the prodigal whom otherwise they would despise. This is why the older brother is screaming. He wants to *destroy* the purpose of the celebration. Rather than *shalom* between the prodigal and the community, he wants permanent and uncompromising rejection. Deut. 21:18–21 commands that a rebellious son be stoned. The Mishnah reads, "These are they that are to be stoned: . . . a stubborn and rebellious son" (Sanh., 7:4; Danby, 392). The older son may be trying to define the prodigal in these terms in order to destroy him. At least he wants no reconciliation for the prodigal with the father or with the village.

Jesus in the process is giving a picture of the distortions of perception that he faces among those opposed to his ministry among the lost. The parable allows the audience an objective view of themselves. Jesus offers a brilliant analysis of how a self-righteous spirit can dominate and poison any person.

This is perhaps a part of what St. Paul meant when he defined love as that which "does not rejoice in wrongdoing, but rejoices in the truth" (1 Cor. 13:6). Often the Talmud has high praise for those who consistently attribute high motives to people who are engaged in suspicious-appearing activities. By contrast this older son wants his brother to look as disgusting as possible. Having shamed his father in public, he now proceeds to do the same to his brother.

Ibn al-Tayyib again catches the scene in his comments on this speech. He writes,

> This is the language of scorn and degradation. Because he is unwilling to humble himself and call him "my brother," he intensifies his scorn and says, "who devoured your living with harlots." The older son intends by these words to cause his brother to be hated in the eyes of the father even though the prodigal has repented and received forgiveness. The older son has no right to be angry (*Tafsir*, II, 177–78).

7. "You killed the fatted calf for him." The older son erroneously concluded that the banquet was *for* the prodigal and that the fatted calf was killed *for him*. Too many commentators to note have unfortunately agreed. Such is not the case. This banquet is the third in a series. The lost sheep was certainly not the "honored guest" at the simple party the shepherd hosted for his friends when he returned to the village carrying that same lost sheep. Nor did the guests at that celebration "make a fuss" over that lost sheep. The guests may ask, "Where is that rascal who caused you all the trouble?" The shepherd may then point out the lost sheep, perhaps tied in the courtyard. Rather the shepherd and his friends celebrate the *success* of the *shepherd's* costly efforts! Joy at success seeks company. The shepherd wants to celebrate his success at finding his sheep and so calls in his friends.

The woman's lost coin (when found) is not the center of attention at the woman's party. It may be on display, but her women friends have entered her house for the express purpose of congratulating *her* on the success of *her* costly efforts. The celebration is not "in honor of the coin," but rather in celebration of the *woman* who searched the house until she *found* her coin.

In like manner the party (vv. 25–32) is *not in honor of the prodigal*! The party is taking place because the *father* recovered his son with *shalom!* The *father* is the center of attention at the banquet, not the prodigal. As indicated, the community will somewhat reluctantly accept the prodigal because of what his father has done for him and because of the robe he is wearing. Otherwise he would be ostracized. But by no stretch of the imagination is he the "honored guest." No congratulations will be offered to him. *God* will be praised that he is back. No more will be said to him! They will not embarrass him with questions about his absence. By contrast many words of congratulation will be extended to the father. The banquet is in *his honor!*

The older son has completely misunderstood the purpose of the banquet. This misunderstanding is in keeping with everything else he says and does. For, as he makes these complaints, he is in process of misunderstanding the father's costly search for *him.* In keeping with this misunderstanding, he also distorts the meaning of the banquet that celebrates his father's costly love for *his brother!* Positively, if he lets himself understand how his father has reached out in love for the prodigal, the door will be open to finding the meaning of the father's pain as he stands there in the courtyard entreating *him* to be reconciled. So here Jesus allows the Pharisees their center stage soliloquy. Their complaints against him are reflected in the attitudes and actions of the older son as he rejects the father's words and actions.

Many of the early church fathers allegorized the parable and identified the prodigal as the Gentiles and the older son as the Jews. For that to be the case the prodigal could not have started from his father's house. He would need to have come in as a Greek from the far country.[2] Other commentators have seen the older son as representing "the rabbis" or Judaism in general. Such is also woefully inadequate. Jesus is addressing the human predicament. Every religious community has its insiders and outsiders. The first at least appear to keep the accepted patterns of faith and life, the second break them. For the insiders the very keeping of the rules can create an ultraorthodox mentality that fosters a sense of superiority and a judgmental attitude toward all others. For Jesus, the Pharisaic audience before him fits this classical pattern, which he strikingly portrays in the speech and actions of the older son. The specific reference to the fatted calf tells us something about the older son's priorities. As noted, the older son knows he already owns the rest of the estate. Until his father dies, the father *does* have the full right to spend the profits of the estate as he chooses. But *if* the father cuts back on the "entertainment budget," then the capital of the estate will gradually increase to the older son's eventual material benefit!

The older son's speech is now complete. Before we look forward to the next scene, a detailed comparison beween the two sons is perhaps useful. The older son now appears remarkably similar to his brother. The following points of comparison can be made.

1. Each son at a critical point starts from the field.
2. Each makes a movement to return to the house but as a *servant* (the prodigal as a craftsman, the older son claiming to be a slave).
3. Each expects to be paid for services rendered. The prodigal anticipates becoming a *misthos* precisely because they are paid. The older son argues that he *has* worked and has not been adequately compensated—he has received no goat!
4. Each insults the father and thus breaks the relationship with him on a very deep level. (The older son's break with his father is more profound because the insult is public.)
5. Each at some point tries to manipulate the father in order to serve his own interests.
6. Each wants the money of the estate for his own pleasure. (The prodigal *disposed* of his portion and spent it in the far country. The older son expresses anger that he does not have the freedom to *dispose* of the goat herd as he pleases.)
7. Each searches out and finds a primary community separate from the father and the family. (The prodigal does this in the far country. The older son speaks of "my friends" who are not present at the banquet. They are not a part of the extended family and its friends and associates. The older son wants his *own* party with *his* friends somewhere else.)
8. For each, the father makes a public costly demonstration of unexpected love.
9. Each tries to break up the family by rejecting primary relationships within it.
10. Both are equally welcome at the banquet.

There is a well-known Arabic phrase which says, "Each one of them is worse than the other." This phrase applies magnificently to these two brothers.

The father's deeds and words here in the courtyard of the home are the second demonstration of costly grace in a single day. Earlier in the day, the father offered costly love to the prodigal who in turn was stunned into a complete reversal of his self-understanding and his understanding of his father. Here the father has just offered even more costly love to the older son. Sadly the response to that love is a barrage of public criticism.

Breathlessly all await the father's next response. If the father was not initially outraged by the older son's refusal to enter the banquet hall, he will now certainly order a thrashing for the son! His public honor is at stake! The listening guests, family, musicians, slaves, and young boys will cheer him on if he raises his walking stick and brings it down with a resounding crack over his son's back after this second public outrage! What then does the father say?

---

6. And the father said to him, "Beloved son,
   you are always with me,                               COSTLY LOVE
   and all that is mine is yours."

---

This response also staggers the imagination. Again, a human metaphor is used and shaped by Jesus to carry the heavy freight of his theological intent. Scenes 3 and 6 are parallel. Scene 6 is the point of turning. As noted, often something very critical happens at this point in a rhetorical structure composed of inverted parallelisms. This feature appeared in the story of the prodigal. It appears here as well. The first costly appeal for reconciliation was primarily a dramatic action, and it was reported without words. Now the father's words are recorded. What do they mean?

In the previous speech the older son failed to use any title for his father, thereby insulting him. So the father responds with "beloved son." The word *huios* (son) appears eight times in the parable. Here the text has *teknon* (my beloved boy). Once more the anger of the father is reprocessed into grace at great cost. The Mt. Sinai

183

Greek-to-Arabic version translates, *ya waladi*. If *abba* is a tender word in first-century Aramaic speech used by a young boy as he addressed his father, then *ya waladi* is an equally tender response of a loving father addressing a beloved son. It expresses *teknon* magnificently. To respond in such a manner to such hostility in such circumstances is unimaginable! Yet it happens. So after this initial gracious title what more does the father say?

The father understands the "lostness" of the older son with the same perceptiveness that he exhibited in his dealings with the prodigal. The father knows the older son is concerned for his "rights." Thus the father continues, "you are always with me, and all that is mine is yours." Very gently the father reminds the older son that he, the father, has provided for all his son's needs all his life—you are always with me! Furthermore the older son has enjoyed these privileges in an uninterrupted fashion. The father then again very gently and subtly reminds the older son that he has been serving *himself* with all of his hard work, because the rest of the estate is already his.

He also assures the older son that he (the father) will not now take a part of the older son's share and give it away to the younger brother, for "all that is mine is yours." This signals to the older son that he, the father, *knows* the older son is worried about "what will happen to my share now?" The deeper answer here given is that the older son can relax and needs only to enter the banquet hall and be reconciled to his father and brother because *all* his rights and privileges are intact.

They are not lost nor compromised because the prodigal is back. The older son thinks there is not enough for both of them. As Plummer writes, "like the first laborers in the vineyard, he supposed that he was being wronged because others were treated with generosity" (p. 378).

Ibn al-Salibi reflects on what the father could have said. He writes,

> Notice the reasons the father could have given to the older son in defense of his dealings with the younger son. We will summarize them in four points.
>
> First: "My son, who is able to see someone who is dead and comes to life and not have his heart moved with compassion for that

184

person? Your brother came to life, and my heart carried me along to do what I did."

Second: "When your brother met me, he said to me in a voice full of remorse, 'I have sinned, before heaven and before you,' and my deepest feelings were stirred to mercy and compassion even as my heart is always inclined towards mercy and therefore I kissed him and did what I did."

Third: "I did not divest you of what is yours. I did not strip you of your robe in order to put in on him! I did not take a ring from your finger to put on his! From my own resources I have given to him even as from my grace I gave to you."

Fourth: "Even as I am your father even so I am his father. I extended favor to you by reason of your nobility. I showed compassion to him by reason of his restoration from his lostness and his resurrection from the condition of misery and moral death that was ruling over him" (II, 161–62).

Ibn al-Salibi makes one common, yet critical error in his interpretation. The father runs to greet his son, embraces him, and kisses him *before* the son offers his confession, not after. The father is not stimulated to offer grace by the actions of the prodigal. The demonstration of love precedes the son's confession. Only the announcement of the banquet follows the prodigal's contrite words. In spite of this lapse, the above passage perhaps demonstrates why this great father of the Syriac Church has been so highly regarded for so long. Few exegetes, East or West, have caught the tenderness of the father addressing the older son with such sensitivity.

The father continues:

---

7. "And to celebrate and rejoice was necessary,          YOUR BROTHER—
      for this your brother was dead                                SAFE
      and has come to life,                                              (a feast)
      he was lost and has been found."                          JOY!

---

Plummer notes a distinction between the two words for joy in

185

the opening line above. The first (celebrate) indicates the exterior festivities. The second (rejoice) refers to the true inner feelings of the people involved (p. 379). But the question the text raises is this: Who precisely is obliged to rejoice?

Three choices are available to us in the wider Christian exegetical tradition.

First: The Greek text gives no answer. The Harclean Syriac and the RSV (as above), preserve this silence.

Second: Many translations have added an interpretive slant to the text and rendered some form of "*We* should make merry." Translations that have chosen this option are as follows:
Syriac: Peshitta
Arabic: Mt. Sinai Greek-to-Arabic; Ibn al-'Assal
English: KJV; JB; TEV; NEB; NIV; NRSV; and many others

Third: Some Eastern versions read, "*You* should rejoice . . . for this *your* brother was lost." This reading can be found in the following:
Syriac: Old Syriac
Arabic: archaic Greek-to-Arabic; Sinai Arabic 68; Diatessaron; Rome 1590/91; Leiden 1616

Each reader, translator, and interpreter is free to choose between these options. The first has the weight of the Greek original. We can only suggest that if interpretation is to be added to the text *at all,* does not the early Eastern Christian alternative of "you should rejoice" commend itself as much as the popular Western option of "we should rejoice"? In this final speech the father is pressing the older son. He reminds him pointedly that this is "your brother!" Perhaps the Old Syriac and its Arabic children are closer to the intent of these final remarks than the more common "we should rejoice." Jeremias has written,

The Father is not speaking apologetically, "I had to make a feast," but reproachfully, "you ought to be glad and make merry, since it is *your* brother who has come home" (emphasis his; *Parables,* 131).

This is the second time the older son has been given specific information about what has happened. The first was the speech of the young boy in stanza 2. The boy opened with, "Your brother has come," emphasizing the action of the prodigal. That emphasis then disappeared as the boy reported that the father "recovered him with *shalom.*" In this latter phrase, the *father* is the actor and the result is reconciliation. The boy gave a good report. The father gives a better one. The details are as follows:

1. "To celebrate and rejoice was necessary." Again the father emphasizes the twofold aspect of what is happening. There is the external evidence of the *celebration*: the feast, the music, the dancing, the butchered calf, the crowd. But they as a family are also internally *rejoicing*. They are authentically joyful to see the prodigal restored.

Who is expected to rejoice is discussed above. If we side with Jeremias and the Old Syriac, then the father is not defending himself. Rather he is telling the older son,

> A party is the most natural thing in the world. I refuse to defend my actions. But you—are you going to join us? This is your brother and *you* also must rejoice!

On the other hand, if we opt for the more common Western interpretive addition and read, "It was necessary for *us* to rejoice," then the father *is* defending his actions. Perhaps the Greek original leaves the question open in order to stimulate the imagination in both directions. Thus brief reflection of the "we must rejoice" option is perhaps appropriate.

If the father is *defending* his *joy,* he is obliged to argue for that which should need no defense. Imagine the shepherd gathering his friends and then saying to them,

> Friends, please do not blame me. I know your feelings, but I am obliged to announce that I am actually happy that I found my lost sheep and managed to get it home. I know this is painful for you. Please try to understand.

Or does the reader/listener expect the woman to say to her assembled friends,

> I have found my lost coin after a long and difficult search. I know that for you this is a great sadness. But I don't feel that way. Actually I am very happy about it all. Even though this is hard for you, please do your best to understand my joy.

If the shepherd or the woman had made such a speech, the reader would wonder about the tragically twisted spirits of the assembled friends in each case. However, the father may be defending his joy. Perhaps by structuring the trilogy of stories in this order, Jesus is trying to help the Pharisaic audience (reflected in the older son) to see the utter unnaturalness of their stance in regard to his restoration of sinners.

2. "For this your bother was dead and has come to life." As many have noted, the older brother refers to the prodigal only as "this son of yours." The father has allowed many things in the older son's speech to pass without comment. This was too much. So the father does not scold or criticize but simply affirms that it is "your brother" who has been found.

As noted, "was dead" can best refer back to before the prodigal left the house. It was out of this relational death that he asked for his inheritance and left town. But after that death came resurrection. Here the verb is unambiguous with the simple *ezēsen*—he came to life. His coming to life happened at the edge of the town as he accepted to be found.

So again we must ask, "who found him?" The obvious answer is—the father. If the father had not paid the price to go out to find him, he would have been in the village and yet lost, regardless of where he lived or what he did. Vatican Coptic Arabic 10 turns this passive into an active and reads, "He was lost, and *we* found him." If Western versions from the King James to the New Revised Standard have taken the liberty to add "we" to the first line of this verse, do not these medieval Coptic-Arabic translators have the right to do so in the last line of the same verse? Their interpretive nuance is in any case clearly correct. The father *has* found the boy and without that finding he would have remained lost.

So now Jesus is face to face with his audience. This takes place on two levels. The audience is composed of Pharisees and scribes. Jesus is addressing them. In the parable, the older son represents authentically the feelings and attitudes of the audience and mirrors their complaint recorded in verse 2 that Jesus receives sinners and eats with them. So now in the parable the father, in humiliation in the courtyard of the home, represents Jesus himself. In the participation theater of the parable, the storyteller and the audience are on the stage and Jesus is saying to them,

You accuse me of welcoming sinners and eating with them. You are correct. This is precisely what I do. But I do not do it at night behind the door. Rather in broad daylight and before assembled guests, I search out sinners that I might by any means convince them to come in and eat with me. But my dear friends, do you not understand that this costly offer of love is made for outcasts *and* "incasts," for runaways and stay-at-homes, for prodigals *and* older sons, for the *'am ha-'arets and* the *haberim,* for the sinners *and* the Pharisees, for tax collectors and for scribes? In the parable, the actions of the father in the courtyard are my actions. You are the older son. Costly love was offered the prodigal. Even more costly love is offered to the older son. In spite of your hostility to me and my actions, I love you and urge you to sit and eat with me. When I sit and eat with sinners, we are not celebrating their sin but my costly love. That same costly love is now offered to you. My banquet table is spread. If you accept, then the banquet is an occasion of even greater joy. I seek not only them but also you! Come! Be reconciled to your brother! Accept the love I offer! I know that you are offended at my table fellowship with sinners. But *do you not understand,* my dear friends, that *if I do not sit and eat with sinners, then I cannot sit and eat with you!*

And so the parable abruptly stops. It does not end. It stops! A more dramatic scene can hardly be imagined. The musicians are silent and waiting eagerly to start up a new tune. The dancers are ready for their next routine. Guests, hushed and expectant, are waiting to resume the festivities. Servants, tense and motionless, await the chance to bring on the meal. The young boys in the courtyard and other onlookers are transfixed watching the unfolding drama. All are awaiting the older son's response. His response is not recorded. Why?

As indicated, Jesus has creatively placed himself and the audience on the stage. Now the audience must finish the play. What are the *haberim* (the Pharisees and scribes) going to do with Jesus? He has nothing more to say. His costly offer of love *to them* has been made. The outcasts accepted and are in fellowship with him. Will the "incasts" accept? Luke is respectful of the tradition he receives and does not tamper with it. Living after the events of Holy Week, it would have been very easy for Luke to have written a final passion scene. He does not do so. Thus the original dramatic tensions of the parable are preserved and continue to cry out for resolution to any perceptive reader in any age. In the hypothetical section added

189

to the text (in brackets) at the beginning of this chapter, I have tried to indicate my perceptions of how Jesus wants the drama to end. Some such final scene can alone complete expectations of the literary form and the dramatic tensions of the play. Would not something like the following bring about that literary and dramatic resolution?

---

8. ⌐And the older son embraced his father
   and entered the house
   and was reconciled to his brother          ????????????
   and to his father.                         ????????????
   And the father celebrated together with his *two* sons.⌐

---

Many of the same critical tensions that appear here also surface in Luke 7:36–50 in the story of the woman in the house of Simon. There also the "righteous" are upset with Jesus because he welcomes a sinner. Jesus' reply is that if he must avoid sinners then he will have to avoid Simon, because the woman whom Simon despises has just made up for his (Simon's) mistakes (Bailey, *Poet,* 1–21)! Many of the same issues also occur in the parable of the Pharisee and the tax collector in Luke 18:9–14 and in the story of Zacchaeus noted above (Luke 19:1–10).

Finally then, an attempt must be made to summarize what is being said theologically by this parable of the father and the two sons. At least the followng themes are bold and clear.

The response Jesus is trying to evoke from his original audience of Pharisees is something like the following:

We (the Pharisees) are the older son, and we too must repent and accept the love offered to us in/through God's unique representative—Jesus. Only then can we accept our brother.

The theological cluster of this parable is as follows:

1. *Sin.* The parable exhibits two types of sin. One is the sin of the law-breaker and the other the sin of the law-keeper. Each centers on a broken relationship. One breaks that relationship while

190

failing to fulfill the expectations of the family and society. The second breaks his relationship while fulfilling those same expectations.

2. *Freedom.* God grants ultimate freedom to humankind, which is the freedom to reject His love. Humankind is free to choose its own way even if that way causes infinite pain to the loving heart of God.

3. *Repentance.* Two views of repentance are dramatically illustrated. The first: earn your acceptance as a servant/craftsman. The second: accept the costly gift of being found as a son.

4. *Grace.* A freely offered love that seeks and suffers in order to save.

5. *Joy.* For the father, joy in finding. For the younger son, joy in being found and restored to community.

6. *Fatherhood.* The image of God as a compassionate father is given its finest definition in all of Scripture. That definition includes the offer of costly love to law-breakers and to law-keepers.

7. *Sonship.* Each son returns to the father either defining (the older son) or intending to define (the prodigal) his relationship to the father as that of a servant before a master. The father *will not* accept. The father offers costly love to each, out of his determinaton to have sons responding to love rather than servants obeying commands.

8. *Christology.* The father twice takes upon himself the form of a suffering servant who in each case offers a costly demonstration of unexpected love. The woman and the shepherd do some of the same on a lesser scale. There is a dramatic self-emptying in each case. The third parable embodies an implied one-to-one relationship between the actions of Jesus and the actions of the father in that each welcomes sinners into table fellowship. We would suggest that this unity of action also involves some form of a unity of person. The same theology is set in conceptual terms in John where Jesus first says in 5:17, "My Father is still working, and I also am working" (a unity of action). Then John 10:30 reads, "The Father and I are one" (a unity of persons). This parable clearly affirms the first, and the reader at least "overhears" the second.

9. *Family/community.* The father offers costly love to his sons in order to restore them to his fellowship in the context of a family/

community. Here and elsewhere in the NT, the family is a primary symbol of the nature of the church.

10. *Atonement.* The father's two acts of redeeming love are made
at great cost. Because of who he is and because of the costly
nature of the love offered, they generate incalculable atoning
power. Some of the deepest levels of the meaning of the cross
are clearly exposed.

11. *Eschatology.* The messianic banquet has begun. All who accept
the father's costly love are welcome as his guests. Table fellowship with Jesus is a proleptic celebration of the messianic banquet of the end times. The parable of the great banquet in Luke
14:15–24 precedes our parable. Luke (or his source) present
the reader with the former parable where to "eat bread in the
kingdom of God" finally means to accept table fellowship with
Jesus (Bailey, *Peasant,* 109–13). The same theme is woven into
this parable as well. It is a joyous banquet that prefigures Holy
Communion.

Some have suggested that the unifying theme of this great chapter is "the Gospel for the outcasts." Surely this is inadequate, for it
marginalizes the older brother. Is the Gospel not also for him?
Others have suggested "the joy of God at finding the lost." This also
falls short because there is no joy at the banquet over the older son
who has yet to enter the hall. Rather the central theme is "the offer
of costly love to *all.*" Insider and outsider, found or not-yet found,
at the edge of the town or the edge of the house—the love of God,
like the love of the father, comes in self-emptying humiliation to all
in the person of Jesus.

Amazingly, the great prayer for after Communion in the Church
of England liturgy, quoted above, is so carefully composed that it
can also be the prayer of any "older son" who *enters* the banquet
hall. Quoting one more sentence the prayer reads:

Father of all,
we give you thanks and praise,
that when we were still far off
you met us in your Son
and brought us home.
Dying and living,
he declared your love,

gave us grace,
and opened the gate of glory.


Indeed, the *Evangelium in Evangelio.*

# Notes

1. BT Berakoth tells of Rabbi Shila (third century A.D.), who administered "lashes to a man who had intercourse with an Egyptian/Gentile woman" (p. 58a). The man reported his beating to the government. R. Shila was then called in and asked, "Why did you flog that man? He replied: Because he had intercourse with a she-ass." The account ends with R. Shila killing the man (ibid.).
2. Marcion, the second-century heretic, rejected the OT and most of the NT. He admitted only Luke and the letters of Paul. But even Luke had to be edited to fit his anti-Old Testament views. The parable of the prodigal son was among those sections cut out of the Marcion version of Luke. The reason seems to be that the prodigal *starts* in the house of his father and then returns to the same house. For the story to fit Marcion's theology, the prodigal would need to have been adopted into a new house, because the God of the OT and the God of the NT were for Marcion different gods. For the story to fit the allegories of the fathers, a *Greek* pig-herder (rather than the prodigal) would have needed to return to the father and be accepted into the house as a son. The story is useless for either position. Marcion understood this. The early Christian allegorizers, it appears, did not.

## Chapter 5

# Luke 15 and Psalm 23
# A Vision Expanded

The shepherd psalm has been a favorite among many for centuries. This prominence is evidenced in tractate Pesahim of the Babylonian Talmud. In a discussion of the liturgy of the Passover celebration the following appears:

> Our Rabbis taught: At the fourth [cup] he concludes the *Hallel* and recites the great *Hallel:* this is the view of R. Tarfon. Others say, *'The Lord is my shepherd; I shall not want.'* What comprises the great *Hallel?* Rab Judah said: From *'O give thanks'* until *'the rivers of Babylon'* [i.e., Psalms 105–36]. While R. Johanan said: From *'A song of ascents'* until *'the rivers of Babylon'* [i.e., Psalms 120—36]. R. Aha b. Jacob said: From *'for the Lord hath chosen Jacob unto himself'* until *'the rivers of Babylon'* [i.e., Ps. 135:4–136:26] (BT Pes., 118a.).

Rabbi Tarphon was of the second generation of Tannaim (ca. A.D. 90–130, cf. Strack, *Introd.,* p. 105). Thus the discussion reflected in this text is early. Mark records that the last supper concluded with the singing of a hymn (Mark 14:26; Matt. 26:30). This hymn is commonly understood to be the second half of the *Hallel* (i.e., Psalms 105–136; cf. Taylor, 548; Cranfield, 428). The above Talmudic text would indicate that if Jesus and the apostles sang a part of the *Hallel,* it may have been considerably less than all of Psalms 105–36. But the striking part of this rabbinic discussion is the fact that for some rabbis the psalm sung on that sacred occasion was the shepherd psalm! Thus Psalm 23 could have been the hymn sung at the conclusion of the Last Supper (Mark 14:26).

In any case this Talmudic reference is clear evidence of the importance Psalm 23 had for the Jewish community in the early centuries. If it was an option for the conclusion of the Passover meal, it was already a much loved and honored psalm in those times.

At various points in the previous chapters we have noted some comparisons between Psalm 23 and Luke 15. My intention here is to present all the parallels we have observed between these two great texts and to reflect briefly on the theological significance of such parallels for a clearer understanding of Luke 15. Some repetition and summary has proved necessary in order to bring scattered ideas together and thus to allow this topic its own integrity. Initially, figure 9, shown in chapter 1, needs reexamining. It is as follows:

---

# Figure 9

| **Psalm 23** | **Luke 15** |
|---|---|
| The good shepherd and a lost sheep (vv. 1–4) | The good shepherd and a lost sheep (vv. 4–7) |
| | The good woman and a lost coin (vv. 8–10) |
| A noble host and a costly banquet (vv. 5–6) | A noble host and a costly banquet (vv. 11–32) |

---

Each text opens with a story about a good shepherd. Each ends with a noble host and a costly banquet. In Ps. 23:5a God prepares a banquet. Thus, in the psalm, God does the work of a woman, for women in the Middle East have traditionally prepared the meals. This theme is present yet muted in the psalm. Luke 15 records a full parable which positions the "good woman" in parallel with the "good shepherd" and the "good father."

Keeping this overall structure in mind, 13 points of comparison between the two texts can be noted. Summarized these are as follows:

# Figure 15
# Themes That Appear in Psalm 23 and in Luke 15

| Psalm 23 | Luke 15 |
|---|---|

### 1. The *Shepherd*

| | |
|---|---|
| The psalm *opens* with *shepherd* images. | The chapter *opens* with a *shepherd* parable. |

### 2. *Repentance*

| | |
|---|---|
| Repentance is discussed within a parable about a shepherd and his sheep. | Repentance is discussed within a parable about a shepherd and his sheep. |

### 3. A Sheep Is *Lost*

| | |
|---|---|
| In 23:3 the sheep is *presumed lost* for it is restored. "He restores my soul [*nephesh*]." | The sheep is *lost* as is the coin and as are the two sons. |

### 4. God *Restores* the Lost

| | |
|---|---|
| (With the lost sheep) "He [*returns/*]*restores* my soul [/life; *nephesh*]." | (With the lost son) *First* (self-restoration): "He returned to himself [*nephesh*]." *Second* (restored by the father): The *father finds* him and *restores* him to sonship. |

### 5. God and *Female Imagery*

| | |
|---|---|
| God does the work of a woman. God prepares a banquet. | A story about a good woman is parallel to a story of a good shepherd and to a story of a good father. The good father runs down the road like a mother. |

### 6. *Danger* and *Survival*

| | |
|---|---|
| The psalmist passes through a valley of *deep darkness/death* and *survives*. | The prodigal passes through a great *famine* and *survives*. |

196

### 7. *Protection* and *Comfort*

The psalmist is protected and comforted by the rod and staff of the shepherd. The banquet protects him from his enemies.

The prodigal is saved from the famine and protected from the hostility of his brother (and the village) by an embrace, a kiss, and a banquet.

### 8. *Holiness/Honor*

God acts "for his name's sake" (v. 3). God preserves his own (*holy*) *name*.

The *shepherd preserves* the *honor* of his name by finding the lost. The woman and the father do the same.

### 9. *Love*

The psalmist is followed by *mercy/love* (*hesed*).

The father has *compassion* when he sees the prodigal at a distance.

### 10. The Host Prepares a *Banquet* *before* the *Enemies* of the Guest

"You prepare a *table* before me in the *presence* of my *enemies*."

a. Jesus welcomes and *eats* with sinners in the *presence* of their *enemies* the Pharisees.

b. The father orders a *banquet* for the younger son to be held in the *presence* of his *enemies* (his brother and his brother's friends.)

### 11. The *Reversal* of *Roles*

God prepares a table before the psalmist. Ordinarily this is what the worshiper does for God.

The father gives his sons their inheritance well before his death. He shows costly love to each. They should host a banquet for him. He orders a table spread before them.

### 12. The *House*

The psalmist is brought back to *dwell permanently* in the *house* of God.

The sheep and the coin are returned to the *house*. The two sons are invited to *dwell permanently* in their father's *house*.

### 13. *Theology/Christology*

God the *shepherd*
  *restores* his sheep.
God *prepares*
  a banquet.
God *hosts*
  a costly banquet.

Jesus is the *shepherd* who finds
  and *restores* his sheep.
Jesus is the *woman* who *finds*
  her coin.
Jesus (on the road/in the
  courtyard) *invites* sons to a
  costly banquet.

---

Each of these 13 points merits reflection. They will be examined in turn.

---

### 1. The *Shepherd*

**Psalm 23**                    **Luke 15**

The psalm *opens* with *shepherd* images.

The chapter *opens* with a *shepherd* parable.

---

The popular mind of the church has always seen a good shepherd in Luke 15:4–7. As noted in chapter 1, the shepherd in Luke 15:4 is first criticized for losing his sheep but then becomes a model for a good shepherd through the rest of the story. Thus our traditional interpretation, although imprecise, is not mistaken. The first section of each text includes a picture of a good shepherd who cares for his sheep.

In Luke 15, the shepherd and the woman are blamed for losses sustained. The father is not. The fact that the father in the parable is a "good father" throughout the parable can also be traced to the psalm, where the central figure is blameless through the entire song.

198

## 2. *Repentance*

| Psalm 23 | Luke 15 |
|---|---|
| Repentance is discussed within a parable about a shepherd and his sheep. | Repentance is discussed within a parable about a shepherd and his sheep. |

In a number of cases, a theme assumed or noted briefly in Psalm 23 is expanded in Luke 15. This is a case in point. The theme of repentance is central to the text of Luke 15:4–7. The same theme appears in Ps. 23:3a in the phrase traditionally translated "he restores my soul." The Hebrew *naphshi yeshobeb* can be translated literally "he brings me back" or "he causes me to repent." The key word *yeshobeb* is an intensive form of the verb *shub* (to repent). Thus the theme of repentance is clear in the Hebrew text of Psalm 23 although lost in the English translations. Thus in each text a story about a shepherd and his sheep is the setting for a discussion of repentance. The Dominical comments on the parable of the lost sheep focus on the theme of repentance (Luke 15:7). In Sinai Arabic 84, Luke 15:4 reads, ". . . and go after the one which is lost, *hatta yarudduhu*" (until he brings him back). The traditional Arabic translation of Ps. 23:3a is "*yaruddu nafsi*" (he brings me back).

The same key verb appears in each. The translator of Sinai Arabic 84 thus creates a strong verbal connection between these two texts.

## 3. A Sheep Is *Lost*

| Psalm 23 | Luke 15 |
|---|---|
| In 23:3 the sheep is *presumed lost* for it is restored. "He restores my soul [*nephesh*]." | The sheep is *lost* as is the coin and as are the two sons. |

Here is a second example of expansion. The psalmist sings, "He brings me back." Only if the psalmist is in some sense lost, can he be brought back. If we translate "causes me to repent," the lostness of the singer is even more prominent. The next phrase affirms, "He leads me in paths of righteousness" (RSV). This phrase can be read as parallel to verse 2b, in which case the two following phrases would be seen to interpret one another:

*He leads me* beside still waters (v. 2b).
[and] *he leads me* in paths of righteousness (v. 3b).

In this case the second line would be a focus on the *integrity* of the *shepherd*. At the same time if verse 3b is seen with verse 3a, then the following two lines are brought together:

He brings me back (v. 3a).
He leads me in paths of righteousness (v. 3b).

Seen together, these lines focus on the *psalmist* who is *lost* and *wandering* in paths of unrighteousness and needs the shepherd who will "bring him back" and "lead him in paths of righteousness." In either case, taken together, verses 2–3 clearly assume a lost sheep in need of restoration to the fold.

In Luke 15 the lostness of the sheep is central to the tensions of the story. This theme in Luke 15 can also be seen as an expansion in story form of a clear but muted topic found in the psalm.

Another way to understand what is happening is to suggest that the author of the parables takes the *symbols* of the psalm and expands them by turning them into *stories*.

---

### 4. God *Restores* the Lost

| Psalm 23 | Luke 15 |
|---|---|
| (With the lost sheep) "He *[returns/]restores* my soul [/life; *nephesh*]." | (With the lost son) *First* (self-restoration): "He returned to himself [*nephesh*]." *Second* (restored by the father): The *father finds* him and *restores* him to sonship. |

---

200

In the psalm, God is the one who restores the *nefesh* of the psalmist to himself. The prodigal in the far country initially plans to return to *himself* (his *nefesh*). He remembers that the craftsmen who work in his father's house make good wages. He will do the same. He needs only to convince his father to trust him one more time and sponsor him for training as a craftsman. He will yet save himself. Thus the vision of the psalmist is perverted by the prodigal's speech in the far country.

But at the edge of the village that same vision is brilliantly demonstrated. The father in some sense represents God. That father empties himself by running down the road in public to welcome his son. Indeed the father's actions "cause [the prodigal] to repent." As the shepherd finds/restores the sheep, and as the woman finds her coin, so the father brings his son back to himself.

---

### 5. God and *Female Imagery*

| Psalm 23 | Luke 15 |
|---|---|
| God does the work of a woman. God prepares a banquet. | A story about a good woman is parallel to a story of a good shepherd and to a story of a good father. The good father runs down the road like a mother. |

---

Bold positive female images are set forth in each text.

The positive female imagery in the psalm is briefly yet clearly affirmed. God does the work of a woman by preparing a banquet for an occasion where heads are anointed and cups overflow. In verse 5 the psalmist writes, "You prepare a table before me." In the East (as in most of the West) women prepare banquets—not men.

Abraham meets his disguised heavenly guests, presses his hospitality on them, and then calls on Sarah to prepare some food (Gen. 18:6). The personified Wisdom of the book of Proverbs mixes her wine and sets her table and calls to the simple, "Come, eat of my bread and drink of the wine I have mixed" (Prov. 9:2–5). But in Psalm 23, as noted, God provides this service.

In the parable, this theme is given full exposure. A complete parable has a good woman as its main character. The story is particularly remarkable in the light of the decline in the place of women in the tradition. This decline can be traced from the OT through and beyond the NT period.

The positive female image in Psalm 23 is one of a number of such images that appear in the OT. Two such texts are examined in chapter 2 (Is. 42:13–14; 51:1–2). Indeed, the OT has many positive things to say about women (*IBD*, supplementary volume, "Women in the OT," Trible, 964–66). But in the intertestamental period, negative images seem to become more blatant and positive images less frequent. Ben Sirach's views on women, noted above, exhibit dark shadows and some lights. The lights should not be denied. But the shadows dominate (Bailey, *Women*). Gratefully, the stories of Esther and Judith provide a contrast.

From its earliest sources, rabbinic literature placed women in a secondary position. Tractate 'Aboth is a collection of the sayings of "the fathers." The document had its own independent existence but is often included with the Mishnah. The fathers quoted range from 300 B.C. to A.D. 200 (Danby, 446, n. 1). One of the sayings of one of the pre-Christian rabbis reads,

> Jose b. Johanan of Jerusalem said; . . . talk not much with womankind. They said this of a man's own wife; how much more of his fellow's wife! Hence the Sages have said; He that talks much with womankind brings evil upon himself and neglects the study of the Law and at the last will inherit Gehenna (M Ab. 1:5; Danby, 446).

Jose b. Johanan was one of the original five "pairs" of rabbis who comprise the earliest stage of the rabbinic sources (Strack, *Intro.*, 107–8).

Tractate Sotah of the Jerusalem Talmud admonishes, "Let the teachings of the Torah be burned, but let them not be handed over to women" (vol. 27, p. 95).

The Midrash Rabbah on Genesis (a fourth-century rabbinic commentary) reads, "Women are said to possess four traits: they are greedy, eavesdroppers, slothful and envious" (p. 383). The same volume also reads,

> Why does a man go out bareheaded while a woman goes out with her head covered? She is like one who has done wrong and is ashamed of people; therefore she goes out with her head covered.
>
> Why do (the women) walk in front of the corpse (at a funeral)? Because they brought death into the world. . . .
>
> Why was the precept of the Sabbath lights given to her? Because she extinguished the soul of Adam (p. 139).

In the Middle East, such views are not limited to the rabbis. Early church fathers can also be faulted, as can Islam. Yet the above references make clear that negative attitudes toward women were common in the religion and culture of Palestine before and after the time of Jesus. His vision of the worth of women is amazing in the light of the above texts. In Luke 15, between the story of the good shepherd and the good father, there appears the good woman.

In addition to this parable of the good woman, the father's welcome of the prodigal in 15:20 has clear overtones of acts expected of the mother or a sister. As noted, when the prodigal appears at the edge of the village, the father is expected to await him with stern aloofness in the house. Village society would allow for the mother to run down the road and shower her boy with kisses. The verb *kataphileō* means either to "kiss tenderly" or to "kiss again and again." In the Middle East males do kiss each other in greetings. The LXX uses this Greek word to describe Joseph kissing his brothers (Gen. 45:15). Yet the *kataphileō* is more easily applied to the mother than the father. Thus in 15:20 hints of female activity can again be discovered.

Thus a clear but muted theme of female activity appears in Psalm 23. In Luke 15 a woman is the heroine of a full parable. Further hints of female imagery appear in the father's initial greeting of the prodigal at the edge of the village.

## 6. *Danger* and *Survival*

| Psalm 23 | Luke 15 |
|---|---|
| The psalmist passes through a valley of *deep darkness/death* and *survives.* | The prodigal passes through a great *famine* and *survives.* |

Symbols of danger and death appear in each text. The psalmist passes through the valley. That valley is sufficiently dangerous that a leader (the shepherd) armed with a rod and staff is required. The psalm has a happy ending. The reader knows that the psalmist passes *through* the valley and emerges on the far side.

The prodigal is caught in a *great* famine in a *far* country. He affirms that he is starving to death and the story reports that no one gave him anything. He also survives.

## 7. *Protection* and *Comfort*

| Psalm 23 | Luke 15 |
|---|---|
| The psalmist is protected and comforted by the rod and staff of the shepherd. The banquet protects him from his enemies. | The prodigal is saved from the famine and protected from the hostility of his brother (and the village) by an embrace, a kiss, and a banquet. |

Two kinds of dangers face the psalmist. The first is the valley of the shadow of death/deep darkness. The shepherd's rod and staff protect and comfort him as he passes through that fearful valley. The second is the implied danger from the psalmist's enemies. With confidence the psalmist affirms that God is on his side, for God has spread a banquet before him in the presence of his enemies. This invokes a time-honored, unspoken pledge on the part of the host to support and protect him from those enemies.

The prodigal also faces two kinds of dangers. The first is the great famine in the far country. However understood, the parable pictures a prodigal who can only survive by returning to his father's house. But on return, the anger of his brother is a second danger. As seen above, this is not a story about three isolated individuals. Rather it is a story about three people *in a community.* There are people to buy the prodigal's inheritance, craftsmen, servants, guests, young boys, professional musicians/dancers, and the circle of friends claimed by the older brother. Taken together with the older brother, this community is a serious threat. By his public welcome, the father comforts the prodigal and assures him of protection from the anger of the brother, the brother's friends, and the community.

---

### 8. *Holiness/Honor*

| Psalm 23 | Luke 15 |
|---|---|
| God acts "for his name's sake" (v. 3). God preserves his own (*holy*) *name.* | The *shepherd preserves* the *honor* of his name by finding the lost. The woman and the father do the same. |

---

In earlier chapters this aspect of each text has been discussed at length. The motive of God in Psalm 23 is clear. He brings back/ causes to repent because of his own (holy/honorable) name. The same is easily understood to be the case for the shepherd, the woman, and the father.

After restoration of the lost (sheep, coin, son[s]), each in turn will be able to "hold his/her head high" like God in Ps. 23:3c. The shepherd and the woman will be respected by all because of the success of their search. The father will be congratulated by all at the banquet. Again Luke 15 clarifies and expands the psalm.

**9. *Love***

| Psalm 23 | Luke 15 |
|---|---|
| The psalmist is followed by *mercy/love* (*hesed*). | The father has *compassion* when he sees the prodigal at a distance. |

The mercy/love (*hesed*) of God for the psalmist is expressed in the text in verse 6. The motive of the shepherd and the woman must be deduced, but the father's compassion is affirmed by the storyteller (v. 20) and then expressed in words and actions by the father as he runs to "find" and restore the prodigal. Even greater love is shown to the older son as noted in the previous chapter.

**10. The Host Prepares a *Banquet* before the *Enemies* of the Guest**

| Psalm 23 | Luke 15 |
|---|---|
| "You prepare a *table* before me in the *presence* of my *enemies*." | a. Jesus welcomes and *eats* with sinners in the *presence* of their *enemies* the Pharisees. |
| | b. The father orders a *banquet* for the younger son to be held in the *presence* of his *enemies* (his brother and his brother's friends.) |

The psalm tells of a banquet. But it is not an ordinary banquet. This banquet is spread in the *presence* of the *guest's enemies*. It is a formal lavish banquet. The guest of honor is anointed, and the cup overflowing. But what is the significance of the reference to the *enemies*?

In modern Western terms, this means that anyone who gets into trouble with the top executive officers in the company for which he/she works suddenly becomes a leper in company circles. Few people stop by his/her desk for a chat and when he/she walks into the coffee room suddenly the room empties. The psalmist himself describes this very phenomenon in Psalm 31 where he writes,

> In you, O LORD, I seek refuge; . . .
> [for] you have taken heed of my adversities,
> and have not delivered me into the hand of the enemy; . . .
> I am the scorn of all my *adversaries,*
> a horror to my *neighbors,*
> an object of dread to my *acquaintances*;
> those who *see* me in the *street flee* from me (vv. 1, 7–8, 11).

So Ps. 23:5 reads, "You prepare a table before me in the *presence of my enemies.*" The psalmist has enemies. Anyone who stands with him will invoke on themselves the anger and opposition of those enemies. When opposed by formidable enemies, the psalmist's neighbors and acquaintances flee. But the writer is aware that God is willing not only to stand with him but to honor him by spreading a banquet before him. The banquet is not in secret, but is spread openly in the very presence of those enemies.

The winter of 1964/65, my family and I were living in Assiut, Egypt. The late President Nasser was then at the height of his power and popularity, and the anti-Americanism of the society was at an intense pitch. That winter four German students stopped at our front gate and asked if they could pitch a tent in our garden for the night. I granted permission but explained that I had to register them with the local police in order to comply with regulations. I filled out the required forms and sent them to the police. The students left the next morning. Four months later I suddenly found myself summoned to the court in Luxor (three hours away by train) to face felony charges. I was accused of having failed to register the four Germans properly. If found guilty, the penalty ranged from a stiff fine to eight years in prison. It was four months before the case was heard. In the meantime I experienced the psalmist's plight. I became a "horror to my neighbors, an object of dread to my acquaintances."

Literally some would cross the street to avoid me. Invitations to preach were canceled. Committees of which I was a member did not meet. The phone seldom rang. No one wanted to have their car seen parked in front of my house.

The trial was set for a Monday. As I prepared to travel to Luxor, I was suprised by joy when an elder in the Egyptian Presbyterian Church in Assiut bravely chose to go with me. We took the train on Saturday. On arrival the pastor of the Egyptian Presbyterian Church in Luxor invited me to preach for him the following morning. After the service those two men flanked me, locked their arms with mine, marched me down the center of the main street of Luxor, sat me down in a sidewalk cafe in full view of the town and *fed me a meal!* They prepared "a table before me in the presence of my enemies." They metaphorically anointed my head with oil and literally filled my cup to overflowing.

The next day, anxious to protect them, I urged them not to go with me to the court. With great intensity they answered, "You are our Christian brother, and we *must* go with you!" Later that morning justice was done. I was declared innocent and left the court a free man. In the process I discovered something of the meaning of the banquet spread at great cost referred to in Psalm 23.

Jesus understood more. In his parable the father orders a banquet to celebrate his restoration of the prodigal. But all are not pleased. The older brother and his circle of friends are *angry* at the banquet. The father is fully able to anticipate his older son's response to the banquet he orders. Indeed the prodigal can well say to his father,

> "Father, you have ordered a table spread before me in the presence of my enemies. My brother and his friends are outside. They are angry with me. When they discover what you have done for me, they will be angry also with you. They will then find a way to hurt you as deeply as they can."

On arrival, the older son decides to humiliate the father in the presence of his guests by staging a *public* drama of rejection in the courtyard of the ancestral home. Again a brief reference in Psalm 23 is expanded into a highlighted aspect of the parable in Luke 15.

## 11. The *Reversal* of *Roles*

| Psalm 23 | Luke 15 |
|---|---|
| God prepares a table before the psalmist. Ordinarily this is what the worshiper does for God. | The father gives his sons their inheritance well before his death. He shows costly love to each. They should host a banquet for him. He orders a table spread before them. |

In the OT, those who led in worship in the tabernacle "prepared a table" for God. The Hebrew verb *'araka* (to prepare) is used for both Moses and Aaron as they "prepare a table" for the Lord (Ex. 40:4; Lev. 24:8).

The *full* preparations for worship recorded in Exodus 40 are elaborate, but the preparation of the *table* appears to have been a minor affair. Aaron is instructed to place cakes and incense on the table, not more. By contrast, a grand occasion is sketched in Psalm 23. The table is spread, the cup is filled to overflowing, and the head of the guest is anointed with oil. All of these traditional acts took place at banquets. Thus when the worshipers "prepare a table" for God, it is a simple offering. But the psalmist records that when God prepares a table for *him,* an elaborate banquet is served. The reader of the psalm is amazed that God is doing this for the psalmist at all and is further suprised at the elaborate nature of the occasion.

The theme of the reversal of roles in the teachings of Jesus is presented to the reader of Luke before chapter 15. The parable of the waiting servants (Luke 12:35–38) tells a story of a master whose servants are waiting up at night for him to return home that they might serve him. Then suddenly the unheard of is promised. When the master does return, they will find that he will order *them* to recline while *he* takes the role of a *servant* and serves *them.*

This same theme is also possibly a part of the conclusion to Luke 15. The sons should prepare a banquet for their father after all he has done for each of them. He gave them his inheritance. He showed costly love to each. Rather *he* hosts a banquet where they are guests.

---

### 12. The *House*

| Psalm 23 | Luke 15 |
|---|---|
| The psalmist is brought back to *dwell permanently* in the *house* of God. | The sheep and the coin are returned to the *house*. The two sons are invited to *dwell permanently* in their father's *house*. |

---

The *house* as a center for refuge and restoration is a dominant part of each text.

The psalmist is brought back by God to God. God prepares a banquet for him [in the house]. The psalmist concludes with, "I shall dwell in *the house* of the LORD for the length of the days" (my translation).

The lost sheep is brought back by the good shepherd who returns to "the house" (Luke 15:6). At least from the Iron Age through the 19th century (A.D.), Palestinian villagers kept their animals at night in a part of the house. (The medium at Endor kills for Saul a "fatted calf *in the house*" [1 Sam. 28:24].) Thus in the parable not only is the shepherd returning to the house, but he brings the sheep back to that same house.

As regards the woman, the entire parable takes place in the house.

In the third parable, the prodigal leaves the *house/home*. The father waits at *home*. The concluding banquet is in the ancestral *home* as the older brother's story conclusively demonstrates. The older brother "approached the *house*" and refused to enter. The father's painful journey to the courtyard is to reconcile the older brother and bring him into the house where the banquet is in progress.

Thus each text concludes on the topic of life in the house.

The Christological question concludes the list.

---

### 13. *Theology/Christology*

| Psalm 23 | Luke 15 |
|---|---|
| God the *shepherd* *restores* his sheep. | Jesus is the *shepherd* who finds and *restores* his sheep. |
| God *prepares* a banquet. | Jesus is the *woman* who *finds* her coin. |
| God *hosts* a costly banquet. | Jesus (on the road/in the courtyard) *invites* sons to a costly banquet. |

---

As noted above, the Pharisees in Luke 15:2 complain, "This fellow welcomes *sinners* and *eats* with *them*." So Jesus then tells a story about a *father* who *welcomes* a *sinner* and *eats* with *him*. Who then is the father? Traditional interpretation is not in error. Early in the story this central figure is clearly a symbol for God the Father. But when the father twice in the same day leaves his home and offers costly love to his wayward sons and when he prepares a banquet for the prodigal, he becomes a symbol of the God who comes in humble form in order to redeem. The good shepherd, the good woman, *and* the good father—each pays a price to redeem. Each saves through costly love and each restores his/her own self-respect. Each celebrates a costly finding with a party.

If these two texts are interrelated in the manner I have suggested and if metaphorical theology can be seen as a serious form of theology, indeed the primary form of theology in Biblical literature, then the source of one of the the highest levels of Christology in the New Testament can be traced historically to this primitive trilogy of Jewish Palestinian parables and not simply attributed to the creative energies of a second generation of Greek Christians in the early church.

Thus, it is surely possible for a Christian to affirm in the new covenant,

The Lord is my shepherd. He is with me in the dark valley of the far country and the deeper darkness of the road and the courtyard. He brings me back. He restores me for my sake and for his name's sake. He spreads before me a costly banquet. My cup overflows, and I will dwell in the house of the Lord forever.

# Bibliography

| | |
|---|---|
| Arc. Gr.-Ar. | An archaic translation from Greek to Arabic of the four gospels (ninth century or before). Six copies of this translation have been identified. These are Berlin Staatsbibliothek Orientel Oct. 1108; Vaticana Borgiana Arabica 95; Sinai Arabic 54; 72; 74; 97. |
| Arndt | W. F. Arndt. *The Gospel According to St. Luke.* St. Louis: Concordia Publishing House, 1956. |
| Atiya *Arabic* | A. S. Atiya. *The Arabic Manuscripts of Mount Sinai.* Baltimore: Johns Hopkins Press, 1955. |
| Atiya *Catalogue* | A. S. Atiya. *Catalogue Raisonne of the Mount Sinai Arabic Manuscripts* (Arabic), two volumes. Alexandria: Galal Hazzi, 1970. |
| Bar-Hebraeus | Gregory 'Abul Faraj commonly called Bar-Hebraeus. *Commentary on the Gospels from the Horremum Mysteriorum,* vol. 2 (English translation). Ed. W. E. W. Carr. London: SPCK, 1925. |
| BT | Babylonian Talmud (Hebrew-English; New Edition). Ed. I. Epstein. London: The Soncino Press, 1967–90. (Cited by tractate.) |
| Bailey *'Assal* | K. E. Bailey. "Hibat 'Allah Ibn al-'Assal and His Arabic Thirteenth Century Critical Edition of the Gospels (with Special Attention to Luke 16:16 and 17:10)." *Theological Review* (Beirut), 1 (1978): 11–26. |
| Bailey *Cross* | K. E. Bailey. *The Cross and the Prodigal.* St. Louis: Concordia Publishing House, 1973. |
| Bailey *Eyes* | K. E. Bailey. *Through Peasant Eyes.* Grand Rapids: Eerdmans Publishing Company, 1980. |
| Bailey *Informal* | K. E. Bailey. "Informal Controlled Oral Tradition and the Synoptic Gospels." *Asia Journal of Theology,* 5 (April 1991): 34–54. |
| Bailey *Poet* | K. E. Bailey. *Poet and Peasant.* Grand Rapids: Eerdmans Publishing Company, 1976. |
| Bailey *Psalm* | K. E. Bailey. "Psalm 23 and Luke 15: A Vision Expanded." *Irish Biblical Studies,* 12 (April 1990): 54–71. |

Bailey          K. E. Bailey. "Women in Ben Sirach and in the New Tes-
  *Women*         tament." *For Me to Live: Essays in Honor of James Leon
                Kelso.* Ed. Robert A. Couchenour. Cleveland: Dillon/
                Liederbach Books, 1972, pp. 56–73.

BAGD            W. Bauer. *A Greek-English Lexicon of the New Testament
                and Other Early Christian Literature.* Trans. and ed. W.
                F. Arndt, F. W. Gingrich, and F. W. Danker. Chicago:
                University of Chicago Press, 1979.

Barr            A. Barr. *A Diagram of Synoptic Relationships.* Edinburgh:
                T. and T. Clark, 1966, © 1938.

Baumstark       A. Baumstark. "Das Problem eines vorislamischen christ-
                lichen-kirchlichen Schrifttums in Arabischer Sprache."
                *Islamica,* 4 (1929/30): 562–75.

Black           M. Black. *An Aramaic Approach to the Gospels and Acts.*
                Oxford: Clarendon Press, 1967.

Blass-          F. Blass and A. Debrunner. *A Greek Grammar of the New
  Debrunner      Testament and Other Early Christian Literature.* Chi-
                cago: University of Chicago Press, 1961.

Brown           R. E. Brown. *The Birth of the Messiah.* London: Geoffrey
                Chapman, 1978, © 1977.

Browne          L. E. Browne. *The Eclipse of Christianity in Asia.* New York:
                Howard Fertig, 1967, © 1933 Cambridge University
                Press.

Bultmann        R. Bultmann. *The History of the Synoptic Tradition.* New
                York: Harper and Row, 1968.

Burkitt         F. C. Burkitt, ed. *Evangelion Da-Mepharreshe,* vol. 1 (Syr-
                iac text). Cambridge: The University Press, 1904.

CBTEL           *Cyclopaedia of Biblical, Theological, and Ecclesiastical
                Literature,* vols. 1–10. John M'Clintock, James Strong,
                and others. New York: Harper and Brothers, 1878–82.

Corbo           V. Corbo. *The House of St. Peter at Capharnaum.* Trans-
                lated from Italian by S. Saller. Jerusalem: Franciscan
                Printing Press, 1972, © 1969.

Cranfield       C. E. B. Cranfield. *The Gospel According to St. Mark* (The
                Cambridge Greek Testament Commentary). Cam-
                bridge: The University Press, 1963.

Creed           J. M. Creed. *The Gospel According to St. Luke.* London:
                Macmillan, 1969, © 1930.

Crossan         J. D. Crossan. "Literary Criticism and Biblical Herme-
  *Literary*      nuetics." *Journal of Religion,* 57 (1977): 76–80.

Crossan         J. D. Crossan. *In Parables: The Challenge of the Historical
  *Parables*      Jesus.* New York: Harper and Row, 1973.

Dahdal    Nasir Dahdal. "The Berlin Arabic Gospels No. 1108 and Its Possible Pre-Islamic Origins." Unpublished manuscript, 25 pages.

Dalman    G. Dalman. *The Words of Jesus.* Edinburgh: T. and T. Clark, 1902.

Danby    H. Danby, trans. and ed. The Mishnah. Oxford: Oxford University Press, 1980, © 1933.

Dibelius    M. Dibelius. *From Tradition to Gospel.* London: James Clarke, 1971.

Dodd *More*    C. H. Dodd. *More New Testament Studies.* Grand Rapids: Eerdmans Publishing Company, 1968.

Dodd *Parables*    C. H. Dodd. *The Parables of the Kingdom.* London: Collins, 1969, © 1935.

Donahue    J. R. Donahue. *The Gospel in Parables.* Philadelphia: Fortress Press, 1988.

Eichrodt    W. Eichrodt. *Theology of the Old Testament,* vol. 1. Philadelphia: Westminster Press, 1961.

Ellis    E. E. Ellis. *The Gospel of Luke* (The Century Bible). London: Nelson, 1966.

Enc. Jud.    *Encyclopaedia Judaica,* 16 volumes. Jerusalem: Keter Publishing House, 1971–72.

Finegan    J. Finegan. *Light from the Ancient Past.* Princeton: The University Press, 1949.

Fitzmyer *Aspects*    J. A. Fitzmyer. *Luke the Theologian: Aspects of His Teaching.* London: Geoffrey Champman, 1989.

Fitzmyer *Luke*    J. A. Fitzmyer. *The Gospel According to Luke,* vols. 1–2. New York: Doubleday, 1981, 1985.

Flusser    D. Flusser. *Judaism and the Origins of Christianity.* Jerusalem: The Magnes Press, 1988.

Foakes-Jackson    F. J. Foakes-Jackson and Kirshopp Lake, eds. *The Beginnings of Christianity,* vols. 1–5. London: Macmillan, 1920–33.

Godet    F. L. Godet. *Commentary on Luke.* Grand Rapids: Kregel, 1981, © 1887.

Graf    Georg Graf. *Geschichte der christlichen arabischen Literatur,* five volumes. Citta del Vaticano 1944–53; vol. 1, 1944, Studi e Testi 113; vol. 2, 1947, Studi e Testi 133; vol. 3, 1949, Studi e Testi 146; vol. 4, 1951, Studi e Testi 147; vol. 5, 1953, Studi e Testi 172.

Guidi    I. Guidi. "Le traduzioni degle Evangelli in arabo e in ethopico." *Tipografia della Reale Accademia dei Lincei,* anno CCLXXV. Rome, 1888: 5–37.

H. and R.    E. Hatch and H. Redpath. *A Concordance to the Septuagint and the Other Greek Versions of the Old Testament,* two volumes. Graz, Austria: Akademische Druck- U. Verlagsanstalt, 1954, © 1897.

Hauptman    Judith Hauptman. "Images of Women in the Talmud." *Religion and Sexism.* Ed. R. R. Ruther. New York: Simon and Schuster, 1974, pp. 184–212.

Heinemann    J. H. Heinemann. "The Status of the Laborer in Jewish Law and Society in the Tannaitic Period." *Hebrew Union College Annual,* 25 (1954): 263–325.

Hengel    M. Hengel. *The Atonement: The Origins of the Doctrine in the New Testament.* Philadelphia: Fortress Press, 1981.

Ibn al-'Assal    *The Four Gospels in Arabic with Full Textual Apparatus.* Completed by Ibn al-'Assal in Egypt in 1252. The one extant copy with full notes is British Museum Oriental 3382. A copy in the Coptic Patriarchal Library in Cairo has perhaps one half of the notes. Other copies of the text with some notes are Oxford Bodleian Hunt 118 and Oxford Bodleian Arch Seld 68. Vatican Ar. 610 records the text without notes.

Ibn al-Salibi    Diyunisiyus Ya'qub Ibn al-Salibi. *Kitab al-Durr al-Farid fi Tafsir al-'Ahd al-Jadid, (The Book of Unique Pearls of Interpretation of the New Testament),* two volumes. Written in Syriac ca. 1150. Translated from Syriac into Arabic in the Syrian Orthodox Monastery of al-Za'faran in 1729. The Arabic was edited and corrected by 'Abd al-Masih al-Dawalani and published in Arabic in Cairo by the editor in 1914.

Ibn al-Tayyib    Ibn al-Tayyib. *Diatessaron de Tatien* (Arabic and French).
Dia.    Ed. and tr. A. S. Marmardji. Beyrouth: Imprimerie Catholique, 1935.

Ibn al-Tayyib    Ibn al-Tayyib. *Tafsir al-Mishriqi (al-Qiss 'Abu al-Faraj) lil-*
Tafsir    *'arba'ah 'Anajil (The Interpretation of the Four Gospels by [the Reverend 'Abu al-Faraj ('Abdallah Ibn al-Tayyib)] al-Mishriqi),* two volumes. Ed. and rev. Yusif Manqariyus. Cairo, 1908. Two manuscript copies of this work are found in Paris (Bibliothèque Nationale), Arabic 85 and 86.

IDB    *The Interpreter's Dictionary of the Bible.* Nashville: Abingdon, (vols. 1–4) 1962, (supplementary volume) 1976.

Jacob    E. Jacob. *Theology of the Old Testament.* London: Hoddor and Stoughton, 1958.

| | |
|---|---|
| Jastrow | M. Jastrow, comp. *A Dictionary of the Targumim, the Talmud Babli and Yerushalmi, and the Midrashic Literature,* two volumes. New York: Pardes Publishing House, 1950. |
| Jebb | John Jebb. *Sacred Literature.* London: n.p., 1820. |
| Jeremias *Jerusalem* | J. Jeremias. *Jerusalem in the Time of Jesus.* Philadelphia: Fortress Press, 1969. |
| Jeremias *Message* | J. Jeremias. *The Central Message of the New Testament.* London: SCM Press, 1965. |
| Jeremias *Parables* | J. Jeremias. *The Parables of Jesus.* Revised Edition. London: SCM Press, 1963. |
| Jeremias *Prayer* | J. Jeremias. *The Lord's Prayer.* Philadelphia: Fortress Press, 1964. |
| Jeremias *Promise* | J. Jeremias. *Jesus' Promise to the Nations.* London: SCM Press, 1958. |
| Jeremias *Theology* | J. Jeremias. *New Testament Theology.* New York: Charles Scribner's Sons, 1971. |
| Jewett | R. Jewett. *Dating Paul's Life.* London: SCM Press, 1979. |
| JPFC | S. Safrai and M. Stern, editors in cooperation with D. Flusser and W. C. van Unnik. *The Jewish People in the First Century,* vol. 2. Philadelphia: Fortress Press, 1976. |
| JT | *The Talmud of the Land of Israel.* Tran. Jacob Neusner. Chicago: The University of Chicago Press, 1982. (Commonly known as the Jerusalem Talmud.) |
| Kissinger | W. S. Kissinger. *The Parables of Jesus: A History of Interpretation and Bibliography.* Metuchen, NJ: The American Theological Library Association, 1979. |
| Kugel | J. L. Kugel. *The Idea of Biblical Poetry: Parallelism and Its History.* New Haven: Yale University Press, 1981. |
| Kummel | W. G. Kummel. *The New Testament: The History of the Investigation of Its Problems.* London: SCM Press, 1973. |
| Lachs | S. T. Lachs. *A Rabbinic Commentary on the New Testament (The Gospels of Matthew, Mark, and Luke).* Hoboken: KTAV Publishing House, 1987. |
| Lamsa | G. M. Lamsa. *The Holy Bible from Ancient Eastern Manuscripts (Containing the Old and New Testaments Translated from the Peshitta).* Philadelphia: A. J. Holman, 1957, © 1933. |
| Levin | B. Levin. *Die Griechischer-Arabische Evangelien-ubersetzung Vat. Borg. ar. 95 und Ber. orient. oct. 1108.* Uppsala: Almqvist and Widsells, 1938. |

Levison        N. Levison. *The Parables: Their Background and Local Setting.* Edinburgh: T. and T. Clark, 1926.

Lund        N. W. Lund. *Chiasmus in the New Testament.* Chapel Hill: University of North Carolina Press, 1942.

M        The Mishnah. Translated from the Hebrew with introduction and brief explanatory notes by Herbert Danby. Oxford: Oxford University Press, 1933, 1980. (Cited by tractate. The page number[s] of the Danby edition is also listed.)

Manson        T. W. Manson. *The Sayings of Jesus.* London: SCM Press, 1964, © 1937.

Marshall        I. H. Marshall. *The Gopsel of Luke.* Exeter: The Paternoster Press, 1978.

McFague        S. McFague. *Metaphorical Theology: Models of God in Religious Language.* Philadelphia: Fortress Press, 1982.

Metzger        B. M. Metzger. "Early Arabic Versions of the New Testament." *On Language, Culture, and Religion: In Honor of Eugene A. Nida.* Paris: Mouton, 1974, pp. 157–68.

Mid. Rab. Genesis        Midrash Rabbah, Genesis, two volumes. Tran. H. Freedman. London: The Soncino Press, 1983, © 1939.

Montefiore        C. G. Montefiore. *Rabbinic Literature and Gospel Teachings.* London: Macmillan, 1930.

Moore *Judaism*        G. F. Moore. *Judaism in the First Ceturies of the Christian Era,* vols. 1–2. New York; Schocken Books, 1971, © 1927, 1930.

Moore *People*        G. F. Moore. "The Am Ha-ares (the People of the Land) and the Haberim (Associates)." *The Beginnings of Christianity,* vol. 1. Ed. J. J. Foakes-Jackson and Kirshopp Lake. London: Macmillan, 1939, © 1920, pp. 439–45.

Neusner *Law*        J. Neusner. "Pharisaic Law in New Testament Times." *Union Seminary Quarterly Review,* 26 (1971): 331–40.

Neusner *Paul*        J. Neusner. "Review of Sanders' *Paul and the Jewish People.*" *The Jewish Quarterly Review,* LXXIV, no. 4 (April 1984): 416–23.

Newbigin        L. Newbigin. *The Light Has Come: An Exposition of the Fourth Gospel.* Grand Rapids: Eerdmans Publishing Company, 1982.

Nouwen        Henri J. M. Nouwen. *In the Name of Jesus: Reflections on Christian Leadership.* New York: Crossroad, 1990.

*NTS*        *New Testament Studies*

| | |
|---|---|
| Oesterley | W. O. E. Oesterley. *The Gospel Parables in the Light of Their Jewish Background.* London: SPCK, 1936. |
| Orwell | G. Orwell. "Politics and the English Language." *The Collected Essays, Journalism, and Letters of George Orwell,* vol. 4, *In Front of Your Nose, 1945–1950.* Ed. Sonia Orwell and Ian Angus. London: Secker and Warburg, 1968, pp. 127–33. |
| OTP | *The Old Testament Pseudepigrapha,* vols. 1–2. Ed. J. H. Charlesworth. New York: Doubleday, 1983, 1985. |
| Padwick | C. Padwick. "Al-Ghazali and the Arabic Versions of the Gospels: An Unsolved Problem." *The Muslim World,* XXIX (1939): 130–40. |
| Peters | C. Peters. "Problem sines bedeutsamen arabischen Evangelientextes." *Oriens Christianus,* 3te Serie, 11 (1936): 218–30. |
| Plummer | A. Plummer. *A Critical and Exegetical Commentary on the Gospel According to S. Luke* (The International Critical Commentary). Edinburgh: T. and T. Clark, 1922. |
| Rihbany | A. M. Rihbany. *The Syrian Christ.* New York: Houghton Mifflin, 1916. |
| Robertson | A. T. Robertson. *A Grammar of the Greek New Testament in the Light of Historical Research.* Nashville: Broadman Press, 1934. |
| Sa'id | I. Sa'id. *Sharh Bisharat Luqa (Commentary on the Gospel of Luke)* Beirut: Near East Council of Churches, 1970. |
| Scharlemann | M. L. Scharlemann. *Proclaiming the Parables.* St. Louis: Concordia Publishing House, 1963. |
| Scott | B. B. Scott. *Hear Then the Parable.* Philadelphia: Fortress Press, 1989. |
| Shahid *Arabs* | I. Shahid. *Byzantium and the Arabs in the Fourth Century.* Washington: Dumbarton Oaks Research Library and Collection, 1984. |
| Shahid *Martyrs* | I. Shahid. *The Martyrs of Najran: New Documents* (Subsidia Hagiographica, no. 49). Bruzelles: Societe Des Bollandistes, 1971. |
| Si. Gr.-Ar. | A translation of the four gospels from Greek to Arabic probably made in St. Catherine's Monastery at Mt. Sinai in the 10th to 11th centuries. This translation appears in Vaticana Borgiana Arabica 71; Sinai Ar. 69; 82; 84; 90; 91; 94; 95; 96; 103; 104; 106; 110. |
| B. T. D. Smith | B. T. D. Smith. *The Parables of the Synoptic Gospels.* Cambridge: The University Press, 1937. |

| J. P. Smith | J. P. Smith. *A Compendious Syriac Dictionary.* Oxford: Clarendon Press, 1967, © 1903. |
|---|---|
| Stendahl | K. Stendahl. *The School of St. Matthew and Its Use of the Old Testament.* Philadelphia: Fortress Press, 1968, © 1954. |
| Stewart | J. Stewart. *The Wind of the Spirit.* New York: Abingdon, 1968. |
| Strack<br>*Intro.* | H. L. Strack. "The More Important Teachers [in the Talmud]." *Introduction to the Talmud and Midrash.* New York: Atheneum, 1978, © 1931, pp. 105-34. |
| Str.-B. | H. Strack and P. Billerbeck. *Kommentar zum Neuen Testament aus Talmud und Midrasch,* six volumes. Munich: C. H. Beck, 1922–61. |
| Targum | *The Bible in Aramaic,* five volumes. Ed. A. Sperber. Leiden: E. J. Brill, 1959. |
| Taylor | V. Taylor. *The Gospel According to St. Mark.* New York: St. Martin's Press, 1966. |
| *TDNT* | G. Kittel and G. W. Bromiley, ed. *Theological Dictionary of the New Testament,* vols. 1–9. Grand Rapids: Eerdmans, 1964–74. (In each case the author of the essay is also noted.) |
| TeSelle | S. McFague TeSelle. *Speaking in Parables.* Philadelphia: Fortress Press, 1975. |
| Trimingham | J. S. Trimmingham. *Christianity Among the Arabs in Pre-Islamic Times.* London: Longmans, 1979. |
| Via | D. O. Via. *The Parables: Their Literary and Existential Dimension.* Philadelphia: Fortress Press, 1967. |
| Voobus<br>*Arabic* | A. Voobus. "The Arabic Versions." *Early Versions of the New Testament.* Stockholm: n.p., 1954, pp. 271–97. |
| Voobus<br>*Syriac* | A. Voobus. "Syriac Versions." *The Interpreter's Dictionary of the Bible,* supplementary volume. Nashville: Abingdon, 1976, pp. 851–54. |
| *ZNW* | *Zeitschrift für die neutestamentliche Wissenschaft* |

# Syriac and Arabic New Testament Versions

## *Unpublished Manuscripts*

| | |
|---|---|
| Syriac | Vatican Syriac 268 (Harclean) |
| Coptic-Arabic | Vatican Coptic 9; Vatican Coptic 10 |
| Syriac-Arabic | Vatican Syriac 269 |
| Arabic | Berlin: Staatsbibliothek Orientel Oct. 1108 |
| | British Museum: Oriental 3382 |

Mt. Sinai: Arabic 54; 68; 69; 70; 71; 72; 74; 76; 82; 84; 90; 91; 94; 95; 96; 97; 101; 103; 104; 106; 110; 112.

National Library, Paris: Oriental 85; Oriental 86

Oxford: Bodleian Arch Seld Arabic 68; Bodleian Hunt 118

Patriarchal Library, Cairo: Ibn al-'Assal gospels

Vatican Library: Vatican Arabic 13; Vatican Arabic 18; Vaticana Borgiana Arabica 71; Vaticana Borgiana Arabica 95; Vatican Arabic 610

## *Published Syriac and Arabic Translations Frequently Consulted*

Old Syriac:
*Evangelion Da-Mepharreshe,* two volumes. Ed. F. C. Burkitt. Cambridge: The University Press, 1904.

*The Old Syriac Gospels.* A. S. Lewis. London: Williams and Norgate, 1910.

Syriac Peshitta:
*The New Testament in Syriac.* London: British and Foreign Bible Society, 1905–20.

Arabic:
*Al-'Injil al-Muqaddas liRabbina Yasu' al-Masih (The Holy Gospel of Our Lord Jesus Christ).* Rome: In Typographia Medicea, 1590/91.

*Novum Testamentum Arabice.* Ed. Thomas Erpenius. Leiden: n.p., 1616.

*The Holy Bible, Containing the Old and New Testmaments, in the Arabic Language.* Newcastle-upon-Tyne: Printed by Sarah Hodgson, 1811. (The text of this edition is taken from the London Polyglot of 1657.)

# Index of Authors

Aristotle   144
Bailey, K.   10, 28, 39, 50, 52, 54, 55,
57, 58, 63, 64, 75, 94, 99, 110, 124,
128, 129, 131, 137, 144, 155, 162,
164, 167, 190, 202
Barr, A.   54
Baumstark, A.   38
Bietenhard, H.   79
Black, M.   64
Blass, F. and Debrunner, A.   42, 51
Bradshaw, P. F.   162
Browne, L. E.   34
Brown, R. E.   26, 51
Bultmann, R.   52, 161
Burkitt, F. C.   40, 66
Carlyle, T.   109
Champollion, J. F.   41
Charlesworth, J. H.   89
Cheng, N.   80, 92
Conzelmann, H.   55
Corbo, V.   101
Cragg, Kenneth   9, 175
Cranfield, C. E. B.   194
Creed, J. M.   52, 161
Dahdal, N.   51
Dalman, G.   51
Danby, H.   23, 24, 52, 59, 60, 72, 99,
107, 108, 110, 116–17, 124, 139,
140, 179, 202
Dibelius, M.   52
Dodd, C. H.   11, 86, 87
Donahue, J. R.   83, 118
Eichrodt, W.   78, 79
Ellis, E. E.   55
Epictetus   130
Finegan, J.   77
Fitzmyer, J. A.   41, 42, 51, 52, 54, 55,
56, 101, 112, 117, 161
Flusser, D.   31, 32
Foerster, W.   122
Frost, D. L.   161
Ginzburg, E.   80, 92
Godet, F. L.   118, 126, 127
Graf, G.   34, 40
Guidi, I.   35, 36, 38

Hauck, F.   161
Hauptman, J.   99, 106
Heinemann, J. H.   137
Hengel, M.   75
Jacob, E.   78
Jasper, R. C. D.   162
Jastrow, M.   82
Jebb, J.   52
Jeremias, J.   11, 61, 62, 65, 75, 80, 85,
99, 115, 118, 124, 128, 144, 150,
161, 174, 186, 187
Jerome   36
Jewett, R.   42
Julicher, A.   52, 161
Kissinger, W. S.   11, 121
Kittel, G.   42
Klijn, A. F. J.   89
Kugel, J. L.   45, 48
Kummel, W. G.   39
Lachs, S. T.   59, 113, 137, 141
Levin, B.   38
Levison, N.   114
Lohse, E.   50
Lund, N. W.   51, 162
Luther, M.   36
Manson, T. W.   11, 112
Marshall, I. H.   42, 51, 112, 117, 150,
159, 161
McFague, S. (TeSelle)   18, 162
Montefiore, C. G.   86, 87, 88, 136
Moore, G. F.   25, 31, 32, 87
Neusner, J.   30, 31, 32, 59
Newbigin, L.   12
Nouwen, H. J. M.   154
Oesterley, W. O. E.   100, 112
Orwell, G.   19
Padwick, C.   39
Peters, C.   38
Plummer, A.   43, 58, 91, 112, 168, 173,
178, 184, 185–86
von Rad, G.   168, 169
Ratushinskaya, E.   80, 92
Rengstorf, K. H.   61
Rihbany, A.   19, 20, 21, 29, 147
Robertson, A. T.   42, 51, 52, 159

Safrai, S.  43
Sanders, E. P.  89
Sanders, J. T.  161
Scharlemann, M. L.  21
Scott, B. B.  11, 118
Shahak, I.  61
Shahid, I.  34
Shakespeare, W.  112
Simon, R.  38
Smith, B. T. D.  112
Smith, J. P.  82, 134
Solzhenitsyn, A.  80, 92
Stendahl, K.  42, 43, 52

Stewart, J.  109
Strack, H.  194, 202
Strack, H. and Billerbeck, P.  131
Strathmann, H.  126
Taylor, V.  194
Teselle, S. (McFague)  18, 162
Thomas Aquinas  16
Thompson, F.  88
Trible, P.  96, 202
Trimingham, S.  34
Via, D. O.  17
Voobus, A.  27, 35, 38

# Index of Biblical References

## Old Testament

Genesis
  18:6   201
  18:7   156
  25:5–6   113
  26:6   168
  32:24–32   146
  37:14   168
  43:27–28   168, 169
  45:14–15   147
  45:15   203
Exodus
  4:18   168
  10:16   133
  18:1   59
  40:4   209
Leviticus
  11:7   127
  11:44   68
  24:8   209
Deuteronomy
  14:8   127
  21:17   120
  21:18–21   179
  32:6   114
  32:18   96
1 Samuel
  3:10   140
  12:1–6   94
  28:24   210
  28:24–25   156
1 Kings
  8:46   88
  21:1–16   119
  25:6   168
2 Kings
  14:8   168
Nehemiah
  13:23–27   179
Psalms
  2:7   11
  23   11, 30, 65, 68, 69, 70, 71, 77, 80, 84, 92, 172, 195–212
  23:3   68, 69, 77, 78, 79, 80, 85, 105, 131, 199
  23:5   94
  23:5a   195
  31:1, 7–8, 11   207
  89:26   114
  105:36   94
  120:36   94
  131:1–3   96
  131:2   68
  134:4–136:26   194
Proverbs
  9:2–5   201–2
  19:2   146
  31:11   108
  31:16   107
  31:18   107
  31:20   107
  31:24   107
Ecclesiastes
  7:20   89
Isaiah
  5:1–6   84
  5:1–7   17, 94
  5:14   68
  40–55   79, 86, 94
  40:11   77
  41:14   78
  42:13–14   95, 202
  43:1–7   78
  43:3   78
  43:3–4   80
  43:14   78
  46:2   68
  46:3–4   96
  47:1–3   144
  47:4   78
  49:5   68, 86
  49:7   78
  49:22   77
  51:1–2   94, 95, 202
  53:6   88, 89, 91

53:7–8a  17, 18
55:8–9  17
57:19  151
63:16  114, 157
64:8  114, 157
66:10–14  157, 158
Jeremiah
    3:4–19  114
    3:12  77
    4:19–22  77
    8:18–22  77
    13:17  77
    14:17  77
    23:1–4  92
    23:1–8  68, 69
    23:8  69
    30:19  69
    31:9  114
    31:20  77
    50:19  69
Ezekiel
    16:4  29
    34  65
    34:1–16  84

34:1–24  69, 70
34:11–15  70
34:11–16  92
34:15–16  84
34:16  70
34:17–19  70
34:24  70
34:30–31  70
36:22–23  78, 105
36:23  79
36:32–36  78
39:27  68
Daniel
    10:19  168
Hosea
    1:10  140
    11:1–4  77, 143
Amos
    6:1–4  156
Habakkuk
    3:2  177
Malachi
    1:6  114
    2:10  114

# New Testament

Matthew
    5:14  107
    5:14–15  96
    6:9  80, 157
    7:1  177
    18:10–14  92
    18:12  65
    18:12–14  76
    22:1–14  92
    26:30  194
    28:8  144
Mark
    2:27  53
    5:6  144
    6:3  23
    6:55  144
    9:15  144
    10:17  144
    14:26  194
    15:36  144
Luke
    1:1  56

1:1–4  52
1:1–9:50  54
1:2  42, 43, 52, 56
1:3  44
1:5–20  97
1:26–38  97
1:46–55  97
1:68–79  97
2:7  29
2:25–38  97
2:40–52  26, 27
4:1  27
4:24–27  97
5:36–39  97
7:11–17  97
7:36–50  33, 97, 190
7:46  30
8:1–3  94, 97, 107
8:14  119
8:43–48  98
8:49–56  97
9:51  54, 55

9:51–19:48   9, 54, 56
10:25   56
10:33   143
10:36   178
10:38–39   55
10:38–42   94
10:41–42   98
11:1–13   55
11:5–8   98
11:9–10   46, 47
11:29–32   98
12:35–38   209
12:45–46   98
12:51–53   98
13:1–15:32   58
13:10–16   98
13:16   98
13:18–21   98
13:22   55
13:31   55
13:34   106
13:34–35   56
14:1–6   98
14:12–15:13   57
14:15–24   92, 192
14:26–27   98
15   71, 80, 84, 195–212
15:1   82
15:1–3   57
15:1–7   54–92, 83
15:1–10   92
15:1–32   92
15:2   63, 148, 211
15:4   66, 67, 94, 101, 199
15:4–7   63–92, 64, 68, 70, 76, 77,
        80, 83, 87, 89, 90, 111,
        198, 199
15:4–10   98
15:4–32   90
15:6   66, 82
15:7   89, 105, 122, 176
15:8   66
15:8–10   93–108, 94, 100
15:9   52, 66
15:10   105
15:10–11   112
15:11–12   111
15:11–24   109–162, 110, 175
15:11–32   49, 63, 141
15:12   152, 157

15:13   143, 178
15:13–14   121
15:15–16   125
15:17   129, 131
15:18–20   133
15:19   134–35
15:20   142, 143, 203
15:20–24   62, 63
15:21   135
15:21–22   151
15:24   155, 160
15:25   90, 120
15:25–26   165
15:25–32   163–93
15:27   123, 138, 168
15:27–28   167
15:28   173
15:28–30   90
15:29–30   175
15:30   124
15:31   183
15:32   159, 160, 185
16:5–7   56
16:13   48
17:7–10   141
17:34   98
17:35   98
17:11   55
18:1–8   98
18:1–14   55
18:4   130
18:9   90
18:9–14   33, 97, 176, 190
18:18   56, 144
18:22   98
18:35–42   98
19:1   55
19:1–10   82, 83, 98, 190
19:9   98
19:41–44   56
20:1–24:53   54
20:27–36   99
21:1–4   99
21:23–24   46
23:26   99
23:27   99
23:49   99
23:50–56   99
24:1–49   99
24:12   144

227

John
 3:5 16
 5:17 191
 10:1–18 77
 10:3 102
 10:11 76
 10:12 72, 102
 10:13 77
 10:30 191
 12:1–8 107
 18:28 177
 20:2 144
Acts
 1:21–22 43
 2:39 150
 12:11 130
 18:3 24
 21:1 42
 21:1–15 42
 27:1 42
Romans
 1:16 92
 1:24 118
 1:26 118
 1:28 118
 5:8 150

 7:9 159
 7:17 134
 8:15 137
 14:9 159
1 Corinthians
 11:23 52
 13:6 179–80
 15:3 52
2 Corinthians
 5:19 151
Galatians
 1:6 73
 3:1 73
Ephesians
 2:5 160
 2:13 150
 3:18–19 7
Titus
 2:13 51
1 John
 4:7 16
 5:1 16
Revelation
 1:17 51
 20:5 159

228

# Index of Old Testament
# Apocrypha and Pseudepigrapha

2 Baruch
   9:1   89
Prayer of Manasseh
   v. 8   89
Testaments of the Three Patriarchs:
   Testament of Abraham
   9:3   89
   10:14   89

Wisdom of Ben Sirach
   8:5   89
   19:30   144
   22:3   106
   25:22   107
   26:5   121, 140
   33:19   23
   33:23   114
   42:6–7   103
   42:13–14   99

# Index of Rabbinic References

*Targum Onkelos*
  I, 75   169

*Mishnah*
'Aboth (Pirke 'Aboth)
  1:1   52
  1:5   202
  1:6   50
  2:2   23
  4:5   24
Baba Bathra
  8:5   120
  8:7   116–7
  9:7   107
Baba Metsi'a
  7:8–9   72
Demai
  2:3   60
'Erubin
  7:4   139
Hagiga
  2:7   60
Kelim
  12:7   107
Ketuboth
  7:10   65
Kiddushin
  4:14   65
Megilla
  1:1–3   140
Pe'a
  8:7   124
Sanhedrin
  7:4   179
Shabbath
  11:2   139
Sota
  3:4   99
Toharoth
  7:4   6
  8:3   108

*Mekhilta*  59

*Babylonian Talmud*
Baba Kamma
  75b   114
  91b   145
Bekoroth
  30b   25
Berakoth
  9b   146
  31b   96
  43b   60, 125, 171
  58a   193
  82b   128
Kiddushin
  36a   141
  82a   65
Mo'ed Katan
  9a   81
Pesahim
  26a   24
  49a   26, 33
  65b   145
  118a   155, 194
Sanhedrin
  25b   65
  99a   89
Shabbath
  10a   141
  13a   60
  21b   139
  31a   175
  98b   145
  107a   145
  113a   145
  147a   145
  152a   155
  155a   128
Soferim
  41a2   65
Sukka
  52b   65
Ta'anith
  23b   145

# INDEX OF RABBINIC REFERENCES

*Jerusalem Talmud*
Ketuboth
    2:10   121
Kiddushin
    1:5   121
Mo'ed Katan
    2:10   121
Sota
    vol. 27, p. 95   202

*Midrash Rabbah*
Genesis
    p. 139   96, 202–3
    p. 383   202–3

Leviticus
    7:2   88
Deuteronomy
    2:24   136
Ruth
    7:11   121
Song of Songs (Shir-ha-Shirim)
    i, I, 79b   100
Lamentations
    1:7   138

# Index of Middle Eastern Christian Sources

## Syriac Versions of the New Testament

Old Syriac  36, 37, 66, 103, 123–24, 134, 146, 186, 187
Peshitta  36, 37, 40, 66, 103, 124, 134– 35, 146, 186
Harclean  36, 37, 66, 146, 186

## Arabic Unpublished Manuscripts of the New Testament

Arabic Diatessaron (ed. A. S. Mardji)  37, 39, 40, 170, 176, 186
Archaic Greek-Arabic gospels (cited as Arc. Gr.-Ar.) (Berlin 1108; Vaticana Borgiana Arabica 95; Sinai Arabic 54; 72; 74; 97)  37, 38, 51, 66, 103, 119, 146, 161, 170, 175–76, 186
Ibn al-'Assal critical edition of the four gospels (cited as Ibn al-'Assal) (British Museum Oriental 3382; Oxford Bodleian Hunt 118; Oxford Bodleian Arch Seld 68; Coptic Patriarchal Library, Cairo, Ibn al-'Assal gospels; Vatican Ar. 610)  37, 38, 39, 59, 119, 132, 135, 146, 154–55, 166, 174, 176, 186

Mt. Sinai Greek-to-Arabic gospels (cited as Si. Gr.-Ar.) (Vaticana Borgiana Arabica 71; Sinai Ar. 69; 82; 84; 90; 91; 94; 95; 96; 103; 104; 106; 110)  37, 38, 68, 146, 173, 183, 186
Sinai Arabic 68  132, 146, 186
Sinai Arabic 84  199
Sinai Arabic 101  132
Sinai Arabic 112  132
Ibn al-Tayyib gospels (Paris Arabic 86)  146
Vatican Arabic 13  59, 107
Vatican Arabic 18  82
Vatican Coptic 9  135, 147
Vatican Coptic 10  59, 119, 146, 147, 188

## Early Printed Arabic Versions

Rome 1590/91  133, 186
Leiden 1616  133, 186
London Polyglot  133

## Eastern Christian Authors

Ephraem the Syrian (d. ca. A.D. 378)  33, 40, 41
Ibn al-Tayyib ('Abdallah al-Mashriqi) (d. A.D. 1043)  40, 41, 61, 66, 74, 85, 126, 127, 113–14, 133–34, 137, 147, 150, 152, 155, 195, 161, 166, 171–72, 173, 174, 176, 180

Ibn al-Salibi (d. A.D. 1171)  40, 41, 113, 114, 147, 153, 184–85
Bar-Hebraeus (Gregory 'Abul Faraj) (d. A.D. 1286)  123
Ibrahim Sa'id (d. ca. A.D. 1974)  113–14